A Gift From

Richie Richardson

In Memory of

Shirley Hill

CRIMSON SNOW

CRIMSON SNOW
Britain's First Disaster in Afghanistan

Jules Stewart

SUTTON PUBLISHING

First published in the United Kingdom in 2008 by
Sutton Publishing, an imprint of The History Press
Cirencester Road · Chalford · Stroud · Gloucestershire · GL6 8PE

British Library Cataloguing in Publication Data
A catalogue record for this book is available from the British Library.

Hardback ISBN 978-0-7509-4825-8

Typeset in Photina.
Typesetting and origination by
The History Press.
Printed and bound in the United Kingdom.

Contents

To the memory of my mother and father

LIST OF ILLUSTRATIONS

'It's coming to a crash in Central Asia.
I daresay it'll be staved off for the present,
but it must come to something hereafter,
to be decided whether England or Russia should
reign there, both pushing from different sides.'
Prime Minister Viscount Melbourne to
Queen Victoria, 7 April 1839

FOREWORD

General Sir David Richards KCB CBE DSO

Entertaining, easy to read, yet accurate and authoritative, I wish this excellent book had been published before I deployed to Afghanistan in May 2006 to command NATO's International Security and Assistance Force. While Jules Stewart vividly recounts a sorry tale in British military and diplomatic history that took place 165 years ago, the lessons for the international community's effort in Afghanistan today are pertinent and timeless.

I have read other descriptions of Great Britain's failed attempt to impose its will on Afghanistan in 1841–2 but none capture what happened, or the enduring personalities and atmospherics of the country, as well as Stewart does. Despite being separated by so many years from Macnaghten and Elphinstone, repeatedly I found myself chuckling in recognition of an event, tactic or person and thinking 'nothing's changed'! Even knowing the country as well as I now do, the book sheds fresh and authoritative light on what makes Afghanistan and its people tick. Repeatedly my forerunners in that beautiful but blighted country misjudged its leaders, underestimating a fierce resolve to run their own lives. Too rarely did they seek properly to understand the ruthless nature of their opponents or the tribal loyalties and customs that determine responses to unfolding events. While certainly trying to do much better in 2008, in the event today's diplomats and soldiers too frequently make the same errors.

Should the history of the First Afghan War stand as a lesson for today? In many respects the answer must be yes. The confused aims, the petty squabbling between vain people, the inability to act with a sense of urgency and in a manner that accords with the psyche of the people they seek to help, all these remain common threads today. As is the disconnection between military and political activity, well brought out by Stewart when he quotes George Lawrence's letter to *The Times* on the prospects for the Second Afghan War: '. . . a new generation has arisen which, instead of profiting by the solemn lessons of the past, is willing and eager to embroil us in the affairs of that turbulent and unhappy country. . . . Although military disasters might be avoided, an advance now, however successful in a military point of view, would not fail to turn out politically as useless.' Resolving this conundrum remains the biggest issue for today's policy makers, one aggravated by the inherently disunited nature of a multinational campaign. While military gains are made daily, in the absence of well-resourced, coherent and timely political and economic measures, they may count for nothing.

In other respects, though, I believe today's war is different from those that preceded it, and here I appear to disagree with Stewart. This war is not a British-only affair. It is fought at the behest of the Afghan government, UN mandated and actively supported by over fifty of the world's richest nations. After a hesitant start, lessons have been learnt. A greater sense of urgency and better coordination is now evident in the application of both military and non-military measures. Huge amounts of money are entering the country and beginning to have real effect. Importantly, reliable polling in late 2007 tells us that well over 80 per cent of the Afghan population still wants its democratically elected government and the international community to succeed. The Taliban are supported by less than 10 per cent of the population. It is for this reason that I quote again from Jules Stewart's thought-provoking final chapter. He says: 'The Afghans will always win', inferring that they and the foreigner are always on opposite sides. While the lessons of history tell us that we do not have forever, in this Afghan war the Afghan people and the foreigner are for now on the same side. The trick will be to ensure that we remain so through a visionary and generous strategy that reflects the reality and needs of Afghan culture. *In'sh'Allah*!

ACKNOWLEDGEMENTS

I am indebted to many friends who offered their timely suggestions and corrections during the preparation of this book. I would especially like to thank Mark Baillie, Helen Crisp, Humayun Khan, Duncan McAra, the editorial team at Sutton Publishing and the research staff at the Royal Geographical Society, the Royal Archives and the Royal Society for Asian Affairs.

PLAN OF
BRITISH CANTONMENT AT KABUL
AND ENVIRONS

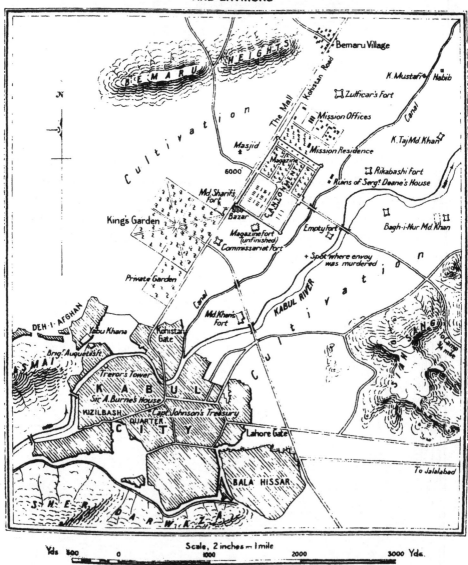

Plan of the British cantonment at Kabul.

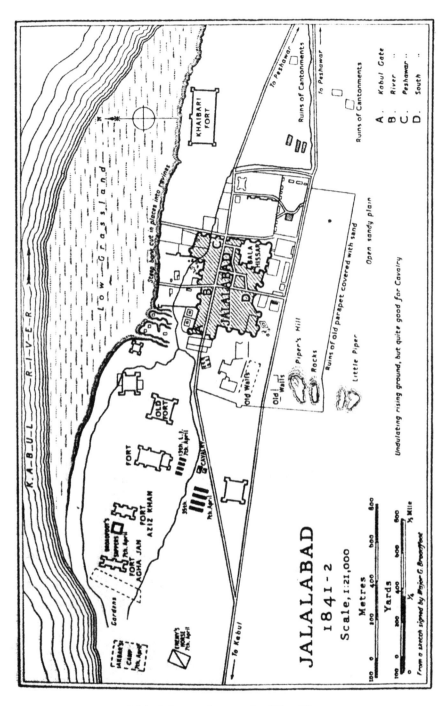

Jalalabad during the siege by Akbar Khan.

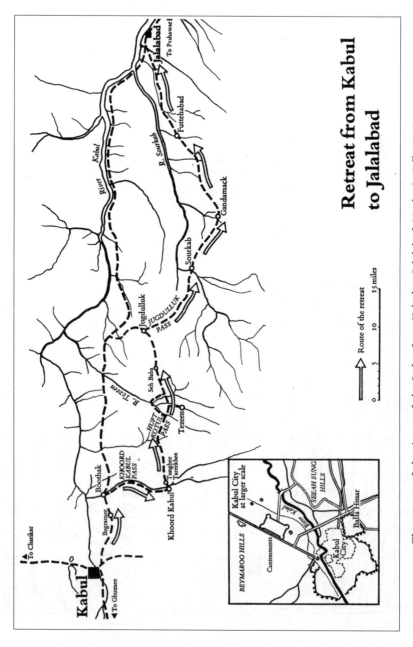

The retreat of the Army of the Indus from Kabul to Jalalabad (*Author's Collection*)

Chapter 1

NORTH-WESTWARD, HO!

O n a summer evening in 1839, a young Cossack officer by the name of Captain Yan Vikevitch wearily climbed the steps to his St Petersburg hotel room. Vikevitch lit the coal fire in his room, ignoring the muggy heat that rose from the River Neva below his window. The gallant young officer then reflected on what he would say to his friends in the farewell letter he was about to write. Once the logs in the grate were burning brightly, Vikevitch gathered his expedition reports and diaries, and one by one, consigned them to the flames. He then took pen in hand and filled several sheets of coarse Russian notepaper with declarations of remorse over the failure of his mission to Afghanistan, as agent of Tsar Nicholas I, and the humiliation he had suffered only hours before at the hands of the Russian foreign minister, Count Karl Nesselrode. When he finished, the 30-year-old Lithuanian-born aristocrat laid down his pen, pulled his service revolver from its leather holster and blew his brains out.

One would not have considered the death of a relatively obscure tsarist army officer, no matter how tragic the circumstances, the sort of incident to visit disaster on a great empire. Yet Vikevitch's suicide figured in the train of occurrences of that fateful year, which were swiftly to sweep the Raj to the brink of catastrophe and trigger the greatest single military debacle the British ever suffered in India.

Nearly a decade before Vikevitch's untimely demise, the Government of India in Calcutta had turned its gaze north-westward to the Indus, the great river that flows from the high Tibetan plateau on a southerly course to debouch 2,000 miles downstream in the Arabian Sea. Beyond the Indus lay the legendary trading posts of Central Asia – Bokhara, Samarkand, Tashkent, Khiva – tempting morsels for an empire bent on aggressive expansion. The Indus offered swifter access than the Ganges, the traditional waterway and overland route to these markets. The advent of steam navigation meant that cotton goods and other merchandise could be easily shipped upstream to these great bazaars, thus it was now imperative to secure the Indus as a commercial waterway for British commerce.

The Government of India was confronted with a number of obstacles to realising its commercial ambition, and these were hardly of a trivial nature. For starters, the land west of the Indus stretching to the rugged hill country that borders Afghanistan was the domain of the powerful and warlike Sikhs, while further south lay the deserts of Sind, whose amirs were capable of massing considerable forces against foreign trespassers. Between the Indus and Afghanistan the ferocious Pathan hill tribes had to be reckoned with, the fearsome warriors who always stood ready to swoop on an intruder. The British knew almost nothing about these fanatical tribesmen, and even twenty years later when the North-West Frontier was annexed to the Indian empire, the Government did its best to keep the Pathans at arm's length. But beyond the Sikh kingdom and the territories of the Amir of Kabul, there lurked an even greater threat to Britain's commercial interests in Central Asia. The Tsar's armies were on the march, like a bubbling lava flow spreading across the steppes, drawing ever nearer to the borders of British India. Here lay the playing fields of the Great Game, the scene of intrigue and confrontation between two great powers vying for supremacy in Central Asia, a conflict immortalised by Rudyard Kipling in *Kim*, his masterpiece of not-so-fictional espionage.

With the Duke of Wellington in power at home and Britain's military policy in the hands of Secretary at War Lord Palmerston, a name that became synonymous with 'gunboat diplomacy', there was never any question of government passivity towards Russian expansionism. St Petersburg's advance in Turkestan and the defeat of the Persians by imperial Russian troops had set alarm bells ringing in London, giving urgency to the task of securing the lands beyond the Indus for British trade, while not overlooking strategic military considerations. British India needed to prepare for a military showdown, for those in power in London knew full well that the Russian offensive would not be halted by bolts of Harris tweed and other goods that Britain was anxious to place in Asian markets.

Russia's race to the River Oxus and her defeat of the Shah of Persia's forces brought the Tsar's imperial armies to the northern and western frontiers of Afghanistan, and in the 1830s all eyes were on the porous borders of this 'country', a territory as politically fragmented in the nineteenth century as today. The stakes in the Great Game had been ratcheted up. No longer could this confrontation be played out as a race to capture markets of Central Asia, though the British continued to cloak their ambitions cautiously under the guise of commercial policies. For Britain, the spectre of Cossack cavalry patrols along the banks of the Oxus was the stuff of nightmares. The truth is that the threat was more apparent than real, for this line of advance would take an invader over the forbidding peaks of the Hindu Kush, an invasion route only slightly less formidable than the great Himalaya range itself. Far more worrisome was the presence of Russian troops in Persia and their proximity to Herat. This fortified city in western Afghanistan was an easy march from the Russian garrisons, and from there it was a straightforward trek along the 500-mile direct road to Kabul. Were Russia able to count on the allegiance, or at least the acquiescence, of the Amir of Afghanistan, there would be nothing to stop the Tsar's armies from pouring across the Khyber Pass into India. The Government quite rightly regarded Herat, as manifested in its official records, 'the Gate of India, from its being the main route of invading armies, it possesses more strategical importance than, perhaps, any other point in Asia'.[1]

For more than fifty years, the supremacy of the Honourable East India Company's political, but not its commercial, functions in British India had been effectively subordinated to the Crown. The process of winding down 'John Company's' power was dramatically brought to a close after the 1857 Sepoy Mutiny, when the Company lost its administrative functions and India became a formal Crown colony.

But in 1830 the East India Company was still a powerful and influential force, whose Board of Control campaigned vigorously to expand British trade beyond the Indus. In this ambition the Company found a willing ally in Lord Ellenborough, the man who held the Cabinet post of President of the Board of Control at the East India Company, effectively equivalent to Secretary of State for India. Ellenborough, who as one of Wellington's closest confidants had the Iron Duke's ear at all times, was a zealous Russophobe who took a prominent part in shaping the Government's Indian policy. He was also a man given to volatile passions. In the same year that Ellenborough laid the foundations for the great push across the Indus, he divorced his wife for adultery with the German Prince Karl Phillip von Schwartzenberg, with whom he fought a duel and collected £25,000 in damages. Ellenborough looked on with horror as one by one, the tsarist troops gobbled up the Khanates of Central Asia. His diaries are filled with agitated notes on the Russian opening of the route to Baghdad, the presence in St Petersburg of Afghan and Sikh ambassadors and the inevitability, sooner or later, of a clash of arms between the two great empires on the banks of the Indus. Ellenborough warned Wellington of his conviction that Russia's ultimate aim was to secure Persia as a road to the Indus.

The job of putting the Government's hawkish plan into action fell to a 54-year-old seasoned India hand named William Cavendish-Bentinck, or Lord Bentinck, the second son of the Duke of Portland, who twice served as Prime Minister. Bentinck had been appointed Governor of Madras while still under 30. He later served as Envoy to Sicily and commanded a division in Spain during the Peninsula War. Having distinguished himself as a soldier, politician and administrator, in 1827 his father's close friend, Prime Minister George Canning, recalled William from Rome, where for ten years he had been languishing in agreeable idleness, to serve as Governor General of India.

Bentinck's primary objectives were to put the Government's financial house in order, following the ruinous Burmese War, and do everything in his power to advance the judicial and administrative systems, all of which he accomplished with a considerable degree of success. He was not concerned with achieving great military victories or annexing new territories to Britain's Indian empire, but the home Government entertained other priorities. One of Bentinck's first charges was to despatch a mission up the Indus to the Punjab, to deliver five massive English dray horses as a gift from King William IV to the Sikh ruler Maharaja Ranjit Singh, a diminutive, mouse-like figure who had lost an eye to smallpox. This was ostensibly in return for the Kashmir shawls that the previous Governor General, Lord Amherst, had delivered to the King of England as a gift from the Sikh chieftain. In reality, the embassy to Ranjit was little more than a camouflage for conducting a survey of the river, the aim being to assess its navigability as a trade route to Central Asia.

It was now time for one of the leading players in the First Afghan War drama to step onto centre stage. Bentinck's choice for envoy to the court of Ranjit Singh was a 25-year-old Scottish adventurer and accomplished linguist who was languishing in the rather mundane position of assistant to the resident in Cutch, a remote district of Gujarat in western India. For Lieutenant Alexander Burnes, Bentinck's marching orders, which were despatched via the Governor of the Bombay Presidency, Sir John Malcolm, came as a wish fulfilment. Burnes had set off in early 1830 to carry out just such a survey of the Indus valley, but he was recalled at an early stage for fears that his voyage might provoke the amirs of Sind, whose country he would have to cross. Bentinck had by now warmed to the project, all the more so when Burnes returned a glowing report of the opportunity of extending the blessings of British civilisation to the peoples of Central Asia. Burnes's boss, the Political Agent Sir Henry Pottinger, had meanwhile embarked on his own mission to cajole the amirs of Sind into opening the Indus to British trading interests. Burnes became the first European since Alexander the Great to navigate the course of the Indus, and with Pottinger the two men scored successes beyond the Government's most optimistic expectations by securing separate treaties from the amirs and Ranjit Singh, thus granting British vessels transit rights on the river. The wily Ranjit was not unduly troubled by the prospect of British shipping moving through his dominions. As Sir Penderel Moon accurately points out, the Government's enthusiasm for steam navigation on the Indus was something of a chimera, for the Maharaja knew 'more than Bentinck or Burnes about its [the Indus's] shallow, sand-banked waters'.[2]

5

Burnes's star was clearly in the ascendant. By now he had completed his perilous journey through the wilds of Central Asia, that was to earn him the dashing sobriquet of 'Bokhara Burnes'. It was in that fabled city that Burnes narrowly escaped the clutches of the murderous Amir Nasrullah Bahadur Khan, who was later to have two British officers, Lieutenant-Colonel Charles Stoddart and Captain Arthur Conolly, cast into a vermin-filled pit and publicly beheaded. On this journey, Burnes was also conceded an audience with the Afghan ruler Dost Mohammed Khan, a meeting that set the scene for his later official embassy to Kabul. On this occasion, commerce and politics were not on Burnes's agenda, though he obviously made a favourable impression on the Amir, who offered him the command of the Afghan army. When Burnes graciously declined, the Dost asked if he could recommend a friend.

On a visit to England in 1834, the young explorer was given a hero's welcome by London's literary glitterati, who celebrated the publication of his book on travels to the remotest parts of Central Asia, a best-seller which earned the author £800, a small fortune in those days. Burnes became the most sought-after dinner party guest in fashionable Mayfair salons. He was showered with honours: the Royal Geographical Society awarded him their Gold Medal, he received the French Geographical Society's Silver Medal, the Royal Asiatic Society elected him a member, as did the Athenaeum Club, and he was everywhere fêted by statesmen and fellow explorers, including the legendary explorer Baron Alexander von Humboldt.

Burnes the intrepid Scots traveller arrived back in India at the height of the anti-Russian hysteria, with Bentinck's successor, the Earl of Auckland, casting about for a trustworthy agent to lead a delegation to Afghanistan. Auckland was a lifelong bachelor, exquisitely educated at Eton and Christ Church, Oxford, who travelled about India with his two adoring sisters, who acted as his hostesses. After performing some splendid humanitarian work to relieve the famine of 1838, Auckland's thoughts began to turn to British India's North-West Frontier, which bulked large in the Empire's foreign policy. Sadly, he was singularly ill-suited to challenge the spread of Russian influence in Afghanistan. One of his biographers describes him as a man 'prey to Russophobia . . . he acted precipitately, induced a crisis which probably need not have occurred, and did not show any great talent in dealing with it'.[3] This is getting ahead of the story, but it is worthwhile bearing in mind that from the Burnes mission forward, Britain's Afghan policy rested in the hands of a diffident, vacillating administrator who was almost totally ignorant of Asia.

The purpose of the mission to Kabul, on the face of it, was to persuade Dost Mohammed to open his country to East India Company traders. Persuading the Dost to shut the door on Russian interference in his country's affairs was all but written into the brief. Burnes was the obvious choice to lead the expedition to Kabul and it was in that city that he eventually met his end, the first high-profile victim of Britain's Afghan folly.

The Afghan ruler whom Burnes was charged with winning over to the British cause required little persuasion, for Dost Mohammed went to great lengths to profess himself a steadfast friend of the Raj. No sooner had Lord Auckland taken possession of the sprawling mansion of Government House in Calcutta, the Amir fired off a flamboyant letter of welcome expressing his 'extreme gratification of your Lordship's arrival, enlightening with your presence the seat of government, and diffusing over Hindoostan the brightness of your countenance'. Auckland's coming, in the eyes of the enraptured Dost, figured as nothing less than 'the envy of the garden of Paradise'. The king went so far as to invite Auckland to 'consider me and my country as your own'.[4] He would have cause to regret that remark.

Auckland had inherited his predecessor's determination to secure new markets for British manufacturing, as well as the home Government's fears of Russia's designs on India. The Governor General assured Dost Mohammed of his wish that Afghanistan, despite historical realities to the contrary, then as now, should be a 'flourishing and united nation', benefiting from 'a more extended commerce'. So that the Dost would better comprehend exactly what the Government of India had in mind, Auckland would, 'ere long, depute some Gentleman to your Court, to discuss with you certain commercial topics, with a view to our mutual advantage'. Auckland reminded the Dost of Bentinck's grand scheme to open the Indus to navigation and he gave assurances that the new British ruler of India would second this 'philanthropic purpose'. One could already detect the insinuation that the Amir ruled his country at the British Government's pleasure, though two more years were to pass before Auckland despatched an army into Afghanistan to oust the man for whom he now declared to hold in 'unfeigned regard and esteem'. The letter went on to assure the Dost of Britain's peaceful intentions towards Afghanistan. 'My friend, you are aware that it is not the practice of the British Government to interfere in the affairs of other independent states, and indeed it does not *immediately* [author's italics] occur to me how the interference of my Government could be exercised for your benefit.'[5] True enough, though Auckland soon found reasons aplenty to remove the Amir from power for British India's benefit. In light of what followed, one is at pains to suppress a wince at the Governor General's hypocrisy.

Auckland handed Burnes his plan of action in September 1836. He was instructed to conduct a commercial mission to the countries bordering the Indus, proceeding first to the Court of the amirs of Sind, to remind the potentates of their obligations under a recently concluded treaty giving permission for British survey work and navigation along the river. Burnes was instructed to lay down buoys and erect navigation landmarks, and to ensure the shipping lanes were open for British vessels between the river and the sea. Once Burnes had obtained undertakings from the tribal chieftains of Sind, he was to continue upriver to Attok, a city under Sikh dominion, to secure Ranjit Singh's permission for British shipping to go through his territory, since this was not covered in the general treaty. Lastly, Burnes was to journey onwards to Kabul, with instructions to brief Dost Mohammed on the Government's commercial objectives. Burnes was to take with him gifts for the Sind chiefs and the Afghan ruler. These were 'not to be of a costly nature, but should be chosen particularly with a view to exhibit the superiority of British manufactures'. Burnes was furthermore under instruction to have 'strict regard to economy in all your arrangements, which you will easily be able to do, as parade would be unsuitable to the character of a commercial mission'.[6] These orders came to Burnes via Auckland's Chief Secretary William Macnaghten, another leading protagonist in the Afghan drama. Here one detects the first portent of disaster, for it was Macnaghten's parsimony, albeit under orders from the Supreme Government, that ignited the powder keg in Kabul. For his troubles, Macnaghten shared Burnes's fate of being hacked to pieces by an Afghan mob. Four months before Burnes's arrival in Kabul on 20 September, Auckland wrote to the Dost apprising him of his old acquaintance's forthcoming visit to discuss ways of facilitating trade between Afghanistan and India.

When Burnes rode into Kabul, the Dost, another of the main characters in the spectacle on which the curtain was about to lift, had been on the throne for a decade. The Amir was 43 years old and at the pinnacle of his power, a position he had reached through the time-honoured Afghan expedient of stepping over the bodies of his opponents. The Dost was a Barakzai, one of the two rival clans that belonged to the ruling Afghan Durrani dynasty, the other being the Saddozai family. The decades of tribal feuding that preceded the Dost's accession to the throne marked a period of almost impenetrable intrigue in Afghan politics. But it is worth noting the highlights to better understand the roles of the two major factions in their later dealings with the British invaders. It would certainly have served the British well to ponder the machinations of Afghan duplicity and ruthlessness before marching an army into that country.

The death in 1773 of Ahmed Shah, founder of the Durrani Empire that once extended as far as Delhi, plunged the Afghan clans into twenty years of internecine strife that has been likened to England's Wars of the Roses, with Lancaster and York the counterparts of the Afghan Barakzai and Saddozai tribes. When Ahmed Shah's grandson, Zeman Shah, took over with the support of the Barakzais, he set out to conquer the Punjab and restore Afghanistan to its former glory. His ambitions were soon undermined by plots to overthrow him, so the Amir rounded up as many enemy tribal leaders he could lay his hands on, and let loose an orgy of decapitations. One of the plotters, Futteh Khan, managed to escape the executioner's axe and fled to Persia where he linked forces with Mahmud, Zeman's disloyal brother, who happened to be one of the chief plotters. Together, the two conspirators were able to defeat and imprison Zeman. It is strictly forbidden for an Afghan pretender, no matter how princely, to sit on the throne of Kabul if he is sightless. So taking a belt-and-braces approach to affairs, Mahmud had his brother's eyes pierced by a lancet. Mahmud's rule was a tumultuous one, fatally weakened by threats of Persian invasions and tribal discontent. Very soon another of Zeman's brothers, Shah Shuja ul Mulk, rose up to topple Mahmud, who was locked away in the bowels of the Kabul dungeon. Shuja was reputed to be a disreputable character, once a wanderer on the edge of starvation, a peddler and a bandit who raised money by plundering caravans. It was as a mere creature of circumstance that he reached the throne, though he was never able to enforce his writ beyond Kabul and Peshawar, as Mahmud's brother Firuz held Herat, and Futteh reigned as the warlord of Kandahar. In 1809 Mahmud escaped from his cell and with Futteh defeated Shuja near Gandamak, the place where thirty-three years later the last remnants of the British Army were to be annihilated.

Shuja escaped to the Punjab, where he had his first encounter in Lahore with Ranjit Singh. Apart from Shuja's frustrated attempt to enlist Sikh support to regain his kingdom, little is known of what transpired in this meeting. In fact, the deposed Afghan king found himself virtually Ranjit's prisoner – it was only through Shuja's wife's pleading, and the promise to hand over the fabled Koh-i-Noor diamond to Ranjit, that Shuja's freedom was secured. This massive 105-carat gem, once the largest diamond in the world, was in the early nineteenth century part of the Afghan Amir's royal treasures. Legend has it that it was discovered 5,000 years ago in India, and had been held by various Indian and Persian princes who fought bitterly over it for centuries. It was finally seized by the British as a spoil of war, and became part of the Crown Jewels when Victoria was proclaimed Empress of India in 1877. Rather than being given leave to depart, Shuja was allowed to escape. This he effected by digging a tunnel with his staff to the city's main drain, where transport had been arranged. Travelling by night, Shuja fled first to Simla, and finally to Ludhiana, where he and his 600 wives took up residence at vast expense to the British exchequer.

The Government of India would soon have great things in store for the deposed Saddozai pretender, who was meanwhile invited to bide his time as a British pensioner in Ludhiana in the company of his pathetic brother Zeman. Mahmud did honour to the Afghan tradition of brutality, repaying Futteh Khan's services by having him blinded and murdered in 1818. This proved to be a deadly error, for his treachery so enraged the Barakzai clan that it sparked a bloody fratricidal war, as a result of which, Mahmud was deprived of all his territories but Herat. His remaining possessions were divided among Futteh Khan's brothers. Of these, Dost Mohammad received Ghazni, to which in 1826 he added Kabul, the jewel of the Afghan trophies.

In 1833 Shah Shuja, in collusion with his British hosts and the Maharaja Ranjit Singh, came out of his retirement to mount one final, inglorious campaign to regain the throne of Kabul. Shuja laid the groundwork for his advance on Afghanistan in late 1831 by offering to leave Ranjit's supremacy in Kashmir and Peshawar unchallenged. For his part, should the Sikh leader agree to acknowledge Shuja as Amir, 'the Maharaja's name will become famous throughout the world'. When this propitious moment came to pass, Shuja pledged Ranjit his unconditional allegiance and vowed to respect the territories under the Sikh's dominion. Ranjit replied with an offer of a detailed treaty, setting out among other things, the gifts that were to be exchanged between the two sovereigns, prohibiting the slaughter of cows and, more to the point, demanding that the Sikhs relinquished all claims to the lands held by Shuja. Following eastern tradition, the Saddozai pretender sat down to negotiate some parts of the treaty, taking issue, for instance, with the prohibition on slaughtering cattle, but in the end both parties agreed to treat the enemies of either as a common foe.

Before starting on his expedition, Shah Shuja understandably sought to put his family's financial affairs in order. To this end he wrote to the Governor General, explaining that on arrival in Ludhiana he had three children and a pension of 4,000 rupees a month. Now that his brood had swollen to twenty-nine children, the hard-pressed Shuja was obliged to sell his jewels and other possessions to support his extended family. Could the Governor General, he implored, see his way clear to extending a reasonable advance before Shuja set out to invade his homeland? Bentinck assured him that his family would not be abandoned to destitution, to which Shuja despatched another note requesting six months of his stipend in advance. Bentinck sent him the money and on 28 January 1833, Shuja was on the march, crossing the Indus six months later to set up camp in Shikarpore, with Kandahar in his sights. The amirs of Sind took umbrage at Shuja crossing their territory and sent an army against him, which was routed with severe losses on both sides. Exhilarated by the scent of victory, on 9 February 1834 Shah Shuja ordered his tents to be pitched in the direction of Kandahar. The city was taken in May, roughly coinciding with Ranjit Singh's triumphant march into Peshawar. Dost Mohammed was rumoured to have taken poison, while other reports had him fleeing the capital with the taxes he had levied to prosecute the war with Shuja. Both stories turned out to be false: Ranjit himself informed the Government that the Dost was in fact marching fast to Kandahar at the head of 30,000 cavalry and infantry, only to then turn his host around and return to Kabul in despair on learning of Ranjit's entry into Peshawar. After several months' sulking in his palace, the Dost took his courage in both hands and again sallied forth to meet the hated Saddozai at Kandahar. The Amir's Kandahar brethren rallied their battered forces to join hands with the Dost, and together on 2 July they inflicted a crushing defeat on Shuja, in a battle that left 5,000 dead along the Kabul road. Shuja fled to Ludhiana to take up his former life as a British pensioner, but this was only for another year, after which he was brought out of retirement to once again lay claim to his throne, this time with the backing of the two most powerful armies in India.

Burnes entered Kabul with great pomp and splendour in the autumn of 1837, where he was received at the Jalalabad Gate by a body of Afghan cavalry led by the Amir's favourite son, the duplicitous Akbar Khan who five years later was to mastermind the massacre of the Kabul garrison. Akbar was on that day at his most solicitous, offering Burnes a ride into the city on his own elephant, to conduct him to his sumptuous quarters in a garden adjacent to the palace.

Hardly had Burnes been a fortnight in Kabul, when it became apparent that he had interpreted the Government's brief as something far more extensive than the simple negotiation of a commercial treaty. This may have been cockiness on the part of a highly ambitious young celebrity, though there is no ruling out Auckland's connivance in investing the mission with a hidden agenda. The official papers make no reference to any political role, yet by 4 October Burnes was briefing Macnaghten on such matters as the Persian influence in Kabul, and the extent to which the powerful Persian community of that city could bring pressure to bear on Afghan politics. Burnes had some uncomfortable news to report to the Governor General. The Kizilbash, or Persian Shi'a warriors who were close to the Dost, had taken an extremely hostile view of the British agent's arrival in Kabul. The Amir, Burnes informed Macnaghten, was seeking an alliance with Persia, and this in turn fuelled the Government's fears of a Persian attack on Herat. The city was in the hands of the Saddozai chieftain Kamran Shah, Shah Shuja's nephew, who ruled as the puppet of his villainous *vizier* (chief minister) Yar Mohammed, who was for Burnes 'the wickedest man in Central Asia'. John Kaye's description leaves little doubt to the *vizier*'s utter repulsiveness: '. . . a stout, square-built man, of middle height, with a heavy, stern countenance, thick Negro-like lips, bad straggling teeth, an overhanging brow, and an abruptly receding forehead'.[7] The Kizilbash knew that the Government of India would react with alarm to any form of alliance between the Dost and the Shah of Persia, hence Burnes's efforts to draw Afghanistan into the British camp came as an unwelcome development.

The letter was despatched to Fort William, the Governor General's official residence in Calcutta, and the following day Burnes fired off another report, this one dealing with his first formal meeting with Dost Mohammed, which had taken place on 24 September. On that day Burnes had strolled from his residence to the throne room of the Bala Hissar, Kabul's massive hilltop fortress, where he was greeted by the Dost, with nobody else from his courtly entourage in attendance, apart from his son Akbar Khan. Burnes had always held the Amir in high esteem, and his admiration was in no way diminished by the unhappy circumstances of Burnes's final departure from Kabul in the spring of 1838. 'Power frequently spoils men,' Burnes wrote in his account of the mission to Afghanistan, 'but with Dost Mohammed neither the increase of it, nor his new title of Amir, seems to have done him any harm.'[8]

The meeting began shortly before lunch and carried on, with a break for supper, until midnight. Burnes wasted no time in spelling out the Government's plans for the Indus and the countries bordering the river. The Dost listened, nodding politely as Burnes expounded at length on the benefits Afghanistan would derive from the flow of British goods to Kabul and the markets beyond the Hindu Kush. All the while, Burnes knew what was at the back of the Amir's mind, and this had little to do with commercial treaties. When at last Burnes fell silent, the Dost began putting forth his own case, a debate that would have the Amir and Auckland locked in a thorny, time-consuming political wrangle, and one that inevitably doomed the British mission to failure.

Dost Mohammed lived with an obsessive desire to reassert his sovereignty over Peshawar, the summer capital of the Afghan Court, a city lying in a pleasant valley some 200 miles east of Kabul in present-day Pakistan's North-West Frontier Province. Peshawar had always been regarded as the jewel in the Afghan crown and its loss to Ranjit Singh was a source of perennial vexation to the Amir. The strategically important valley was conquered by the Sikh armies in 1823, though at that time Ranjit hesitated to annex the territory outright to his Punjab dominions. The Vale of Peshawar, as it is known, was contested by Afghan and Sikh forces for years thereafter, until in 1834 Ranjit felt himself powerful enough to call Peshawar his possession alone. Dost Mohammed made two futile attempts to wrest control of the city: in 1835, when the Amir withdrew rather than risk battle with a superior force, and again in 1837, when Akbar Khan was forced to retire from the battlefield at Jamrud, at the mouth of the Khyber Pass, despite having won a pyrrhic victory over the Sikhs. Peshawar remained a Sikh possession until 1849, when the Punjab and with it, the North-West Frontier territory, were annexed by the British. Dost Mohammed could never reconcile himself to the loss of Peshawar and he employed this as his opening gambit with the British Envoy, who was now seated cross-legged before him on a pile of embroidered cushions.

'But,' replied the wily Amir to Burnes's entreaties to open up Afghanistan to British goods, 'I am involved in difficulties which are very prejudicial to commerce. My hostilities with the Sikhs narrow my resources, compel me to take up money from merchants, and even to increase the duties to support the expenses of war.'[9] The meaning behind the Amir's remarks, though laced with Oriental ambiguity, was quite clear to Burnes: the price for free access to Afghan markets and trade routes was an undertaking by the British Government to help restore Peshawar to Afghan suzerainty.

Burnes had foreseen the Dost's reaction and was 'not unprepared for his irritation', smarting as the Amir understandably was from the recent loss of his prized possession. The British Envoy quietly reminded his host that as history had shown, it was all but hopeless for the fragmented Afghan forces to challenge the hated foe Ranjit Singh on the battlefield. What Burnes left unsaid, and of this the Dost was all too painfully aware, was that the British Government and Ranjit Singh were bound by a treaty of friendship. Any move by Britain in favour of the Afghan cause would constitute a violation of that treaty and bring the risk of open confrontation with the powerful Sikh maharaja. This was a risk the Government was not prepared to take – at least not yet.

Dost Mohammed did not immediately give up hope of British intervention to help him wrest Peshawar from the Sikhs. A few weeks after his interview with Burnes, the Amir addressed his Kandahar kinsmen in a letter brimming with optimism, to the effect that a settlement over Peshawar might yet be achieved with the aid of British diplomacy. This amounted to an eleventh-hour attempt to dissuade the Kandahar chiefs from sending one of their sons as emissary to the Court of the Shah of Persia, who was at that moment massing an army against Herat, a piece of intelligence the Dost had obtained by intercepting Burnes's correspondence with Calcutta. It was the sinister Yar Mohammed who had persuaded his master Kamran Shah to seek Persian help to resist the Dost's efforts to bring Afghanistan's second city under Kabul's hegemony. The *vizier* was also conniving with the Amir's brothers in Kandahar, despite the clan rivalry, to forge an alliance with Herat. Dost Mohammed countered by urging the sirdars (chieftains) to ally themselves not with the Persians, but with the British, who are 'near to us, and famous for preserving their word'. The Dost would soon have ample cause to dismiss Auckland's assurance, that 'it is not the practice of the British Government to interfere in the affairs of other independent states', as a remark dripping with deception.

The British Raj employed a cadre of agents beyond India's borders, usually at diplomatic posts in various rough spots throughout Central Asia. These men were known as 'newswriters', a euphemism for informant. On 22 October, one of these anonymous newswriters delivered to Burnes a report confirming his worst suspicions, namely that the Kandahar sirdars had resolved to send a legation to Persia. The chief sirdar's son, Mohammed Omar Khan, had departed Kandahar with a retinue of 150 soldiers and servants, bearing as gifts an elephant for the Shah and four Kashmir shawls for the Russian Ambassador to Tehran. He took with him a letter from his elders, in which the sirdars all but prostrated themselves before the 'King of Kings'. In it, the chief sirdar put himself entirely at the Shah's disposal, 'particularly with reference to the capture of Herat'. The Kandahar envoy offered the Shah his 'entire submission, and my solicitude for the service of your Majesty'.[10] The Kandahar chiefs had elected to strengthen ties with Persia, Burnes was told, on the one hand for fear their brother Dost Mohammed would exploit his friendship with the British to their exclusion, but more immediately to pacify the Shah, whose advance eastward posed a threat to their independence. Far more worrying for the Dost as well as for Burnes, intelligence had leaked regarding Persia's promises of an alliance with Kandahar, the result of which would be, once Herat had fallen to the Shah's Russian-backed army, the cessation of that city to the Kandahar sirdars. Under such a scenario, Dost Mohammed would certainly be dispossessed of his throne by the combined Persian–Kandahar forces, though little did he realise at the time who were to be his real usurpers.

With the Persians and their Russian allies massing under the gates of Herat, and Dost Mohammed pleading for British support in his feud with Auckland's ally Ranjit Singh, commercial relations had now become a secondary issue in Burnes's mission to Kabul. The Dost was caught in the jaws of a vice, and to his tormented mind, only the British could extract him from his predicament.

Unfortunately, this was not how Auckland saw it – or how

he was persuaded to see it by his all-powerful chief secretary, the Russophobe Macnaghten, and other influential voices in the Governor General's entourage. One of the more intriguing of these characters, who could have been cast in a supporting role in the drama now beginning to unfold, was James Lewis, alias Charles Masson, archaeologist, numismatist, army deserter and spy, who in 1834 pitched up in Kabul as newswriter to the Government of India. For reasons unknown, Masson had deserted from his regiment, the Bengal Artillery, at Agra in 1827, and made his way on foot beyond British jurisdiction to the Indus, wandering across those badlands in native dress. Masson must have been moving under an incredibly lucky star, for his flaming red beard and green skullcap would hardly have rendered him inconspicuous to the inquisitive native eye. All the more pity that no known portrait of Masson has survived. When he reached Bushire, a town on Iran's south-west coast, Masson concocted a tale for the British resident, bizarrely claiming to be an American from Kentucky who had been engaged in archaeological research for the past ten years in his travels across Europe and Asia. That Masson was an archaeologist of note there is no doubt, for the former clerk of a London insurance company happened to be the discoverer of an immense lost city north of Kabul, that had been founded by Alexander the Great. Masson's collection of Buddhist relics are held by the great museums of England, including the British Museum (6,200 coins), the Ashmolean, the Fitzwilliam in Cambridge and the Victoria and Albert in London.

In late 1832, Karmat Ali, the newswriter in Kabul, alerted the Government to the presence of a shabbily dressed Englishman in Kabul who, despite his deplorable demeanour, had a fluent command of Persian and appeared to be engaged in some sort of surveying work, judging by the astrolabe and sextant he carried with him. Captain (later Lieutenant-Colonel) Claude Wade, Political Agent at Ludhiana, got on the case and in two years' time he had gathered enough evidence to reveal Masson's true identity. Wade reported his findings to Calcutta and shortly thereafter, in exchange for services as Government agent, Lord Ellenborough at the Board of Control wrote a secret despatch, on the Governor General's recommendation, conferring on Masson a royal pardon for having deserted the ranks. A few weeks later, Masson was on the Government's payroll as resident intelligence agent in Kabul, directly answerable to Captain Wade. Masson's only interest in Afghanistan was to explore its ancient ruins and dig up coins: he had no wish to take on the role of informer and only reluctantly did he become a player in the Great Game. One can safely assume that his appointment amounted to a matter of thinly disguised blackmail – take the job or face a court martial and the hangman's noose.

Once Masson was installed in Kabul he began forwarding regular despatches to Ludhiana, and Wade in turn struck up a lively correspondence with Macnaghten, to whom he regularly fed doses of Masson's observations on Afghan royalty. Masson's prejudices lay firmly in the Saddozai camp, that is, with Shah Shuja. Of the defeated pretender, Masson argued that Afghanistan would have benefited from a victory over Dost Mohammed in Shuja's recent attempt to unseat his Barakzai rival. 'The wishes of all classes turn to his [Shuja's] restoration,' he writes in a despatch to Wade, in which he later states, 'It occurs to me that less violence would be done to the prejudices of the people, and to the safety and well-being of our relations with other powers, by facilitating the restoration of Shah Shuja than by forcing the Afghans to submit to the sovereignty of the Amir.' Of the Barakzai clan in general, Masson held a very gloomy view: 'They are indeed their own enemies, but their eternal and unholy dissensions and enmities have brought them to be considered as pests to the country, and the likelihood is that affairs will become worse, not better.' Masson's pro-Saddozai sympathies were reinforced by reports from Sir John McNeill, the British Government resident in Tehran, who assured Wade that the Saddozai family had 'a strong hold on the prejudices, if not on the affections, of a large portion of the Durranis [Afghans]'.[11] Thanks to Wade's correspondence with Macnaghten, these two high-ranking informants effectively helped to poison the mind of the chief secretary and through him, the Governor General, against the Dost and his Barakzai clan.

The Government tragically failed to take on board what amounted to Masson's worthiest piece of advice, that no British army should be employed in restoring Shuja to the throne of Kabul. Masson stepped off stage in early 1838 when he was recalled to Peshawar, where he resigned from government service. In keeping with his turbulent career, on his way home Masson was caught in the siege of Kalat, in Baluchistan, as the British forces were advancing on Afghanistan. When Masson was sent to convey the defenders' demands to the British Political Agent at Quetta, he was imprisoned as a traitor and spy. He was released several months later and made his way back to England, where he married an 18-year-old farmer's daughter from Watford and lived the last nine years of his life on a small East India Company pension, quietly writing and working on his coin collection.

Burnes, who had met Masson and eventually succumbed to his case for the Saddozai camp, soldiered on in Kabul as honest broker between the ever more obstinate entreaties of the Amir and Auckland's refusal to yield an inch. Burnes's diplomatic predicament took on a greater urgency two months after his arrival at the Amir's court, when in November 1837 a large Persian army, backed by Russian advisers, advanced into Afghanistan fielding 10,000 infantry, 2,000 cavalry and 30 guns. The dreaded, though not unexpected, siege of Herat was under way. Mohammed Shah's designs on Herat had been in the forefront of the Government's thinking for at least a year. Macnaghten let the cat out of the bag in November 1836, in a policy statement despatched to McNeill in Tehran. Auckland's omnipotent chief secretary told the British representative in Persia that he must consider British India's commercial interests in the region subordinate to political concerns. Above all, Macnaghten stressed, Afghanistan needed to be protected against foreign aggression 'from the west', meaning Persia and far more worryingly, Russia. Macnaghten was convinced that the Persians' contemplated advance on Herat was a plot hatched by the Russian Ambassador to Tehran. 'Under these circumstances, it seems impossible for the British Government, either in England or in India, to view with indifference the gradual encroachments of Persia in the direction of our India dominions.'[12] McNeill was instructed to depute a British officer to Herat to mediate in the feud between Mohammed Shah and the city's ruler, Kamran Shah. This was the cue for one of the most colourful characters in the cast of players to make his appearance. The man waiting in the wings was Eldred Pottinger, a 27-year-old Irishman serving in the Indian

Army, who in a year's time was to successfully organise the defence of the besieged city.

The bitter feud between the Shah of Persia and the ruler of Herat to which Macnaghten alluded, and which served as the pretext for the Persian invasion, was Kamran Shah's unsavoury practice of rounding up members of the city's Shi'a population and selling them into slavery. Persia was then, as Iran is today, a majority Shi'a Muslim country, in contrast to the Afghans who are predominately Sunni. Burnes himself saw this 'outrageous conduct' as justification for sending an army against the city. Macnaghten was equally repulsed by the slave trade, which Britain had outlawed in 1807, but it was the second part of a report from Burnes that sent his antennae flailing about. Burnes doubted Persia's ability to bring Herat to its knees single-handed. 'If she succeeds in humbling Kamran without the co-operation of the Afghan chiefs [that is, the Kandahar sirdars],' he wrote, 'it must be through the influence of Russia, by whose counsels there can be very little doubt she is directed to Herat.'[13]

On the face of it, there was every good reason for alarm at the prospect of a Russian-backed army massing at the gates of an Afghan city. Herat and its surrounding territory is where all the great roads leading to India converge. Kaye, who was a Great Game contemporary, asserts that it would be possible for a light force to forge a passage across the Hindu Kush, 'but it is only by the Herat route that that a really formidable well-equipped army could make its way upon the Indian frontier from the regions of the north-west. Both the nature and the resources of the country are such as to *favour the success of the invader* [author's italics]'.[14] Chilling stuff, but it is useful to note that with regard to Russian designs on India, the Government had nothing whatsoever to go on but circumstantial evidence.

Kamran Shah and his *vizier* Yar Mohammed marched back to Herat on 17 September at the head of the army, having spent the previous weeks campaigning in Seistan in eastern Persia, where they laid waste to the fortress of Jowayan, a victory the Afghans achieved at vast military and political cost, as was soon to become evident. The effect of the siege was to leave Kamran's military forces badly crippled, and inflame the Shah of Persia's determination to crush his Afghan enemy. Kamran returned to find the city's bazaars buzzing with rumours of an impending advance by the Persian army. On 23 November, these fears materialised into reality when the advance Persian guard took up its position on the plain outside Herat's north-west gate, to commence a bombardment that was to continue almost unbroken for a year.

Mingling in the crowd that stood in the marketplace to witness Kamran Shah's victorious return from the Seistan campaign was Lieutenant Pottinger, the nephew of Burnes's former chief Henry Pottinger. The young Bengal Artillery officer had spent several months travelling across Afghanistan disguised as a horse trader, the identity he assumed for an intelligence-gathering mission on orders of his uncle. On reaching Kabul, Pottinger adopted the cover of a Muslim *syud*, a descendant of Mohammed. Both these subterfuges were carried off with sufficient aplomb to see Pottinger safely across hundreds of miles of bandit-ridden, cut-throat country, from which he had arrived safely at Herat in early September 1937. He took up residence in one of the city's caravanserais, passing unrecognised as a European among the assembled merchants from the distant reaches of Central Asia.

Pottinger revealed his identity in a letter he sent to Yar Mohammed, in which he enquired whether his services might be of use in organising the city's defences. The *vizier* would doubtless have taken much delight in contemplating this infidel's head spiked on the city ramparts. At the same time, the crafty chief minister reasoned that in this hour of Herat's plight Britain, the mightiest foreign power in that part of the world, was not to be antagonised. So why not bring Pottinger into the fold and see whether this English officer, and perhaps his government, could offer some assistance in seeing off their Persian foe? Yar Mohammed received him fresh out of his bath in his dressing room, and a few days later Pottinger was taken to an audience with Kamran Shah himself. Pottinger was only too willing to impart his military expertise to the Herati forces, for he as well as his superiors perceived a Persian victory as a direct threat to Indian security.

The following months saw a sequence of barbarous tit-for-tat atrocities carried out on both sides of the city walls. The Afghans upheld their reputation for savagery on the battlefield, graphically exemplified after every sortie by the custom of paying a bounty to soldiers who brought in a Persian head or two. Pottinger found the habit of collecting these bloody trophies revolting as well as counter-productive, for the skirmishers would spend more time in severing the heads of their fallen enemies than in destroying the Persian trenches. This became such a popular sport that on one occasion, after an unsuccessful sortie, an Afghan soldier brought in a pair of ears, for which he was paid a small bounty of a couple of ducats. Half an hour later another man came back from the battlefield with a muddied head under his arm, but which under examination proved to be that of an Afghan comrade who had been killed in action, and whose ears were strangely missing. The soldier was pursued and thrashed to within an inch of his life, but the bearer of the ears disappeared without a trace, most probably having deserted to the Persian camp.

The siege had been raging for more than five months, when the Government of India decided to take matters in hand. On 6 April 1838, the British Envoy McNeill arrived at Herat to attempt to negotiate a cessation of hostilities. He was invited into the royal tent a week later to find the Shah seated on an impromptu throne placed atop a raised platform covered with fine carpets. What McNeill had to say brought the Shah down a peg, for he informed the Persian ruler that in the opinion of Her Majesty's Government, the hostilities constituted a direct violation of the friendship treaty that existed between Persia and Britain. The interview ended two hours later with a sobering warning from McNeill: the British Government would consider the taking of Herat as an act of war. Never mind that the ninth article of the treaty precluded Britain from interfering in wars between the Afghans and Persia – the Government now read this clause as being invalidated by the first article, which stipulated that the pact had been ratified between two independent powers. With Persia perceived to have fallen under Russian influence and control, this was no longer deemed valid.

If the Shah felt any distress at the prospect of taking on the British Army, he certainly kept it well concealed. On the other hand, his actions on the following days may have been a ploy for the benefit of the gallery to demonstrate that he had concluded a peace on his own terms. On 18 April the Persian batteries opened up with their deadliest bombardment of the entire campaign. The cannon fire was so heavy that it sent parts of the wall crumbling to the ground, the Afghans responding by exploding mines that were laid in the path of the advancing Persian troops. Yar Mohammed and Pottinger stood on the battlements observing the spirited defence of their men, and at night when Pottinger was settling into bed for some well-earned sleep, a messenger rushed in to announce McNeill, who had courageously ventured into the city to negotiate a truce. The Envoy was wasting his time, for on 21 April another British officer was despatched from the Persian camp with a discouraging message from the Shah, who resolutely refused to accept British arbitration. There ensued a further two months of futile attrition, in which the desperate garrison began pulling down houses for fuel, butchering cavalry horses for food and expelling non-combatants from the city to reduce the number of mouths to feed. Then in the early hours of 24 June, the Persians launched a massive artillery barrage on all four sides of the city. Writing within living memory of the conflict, Kaye reports that the bombardment was followed by 'a perfect lull, more ominous than the uproar that preceded it. The signs of the coming assault were plain and intelligible.'[15] The deployment of the Persian force and storming of the walls that followed was carried out with deadly precision. Pottinger observed that the siege was being pushed forward with an energy that had not marked the earlier part of the campaign. It therefore came as no surprise when on the following morning, the Afghans discovered on the body of a slain Persian official a packet of letters revealing that the battle plan had been drawn up by Russian officers in the Persian camp. This was gold dust for the Russophobes in Calcutta and London, which naturally reinforced the predictable reaction.

On this day Pottinger earned his reputation as the hero of Herat. Much to the alarm of the Afghan defenders, the Persians attacked with such ferocity that the advance guard managed to force a breach in the *fausse-braie*, the city's fortified inner walls and last line of defence, which were thought to be impregnable. On hearing the din outside his quarters, Pottinger rushed to the wall where he found the garrison in full retreat and the *vizier* crouched under the ramparts in a miserable state of despair. Pottinger struggled to rally Yar Mohammed to action, but each time he begged the *vizier* to lead his men forward, he collapsed in despair, until the Englishman had no choice but to risk his neck by dragging him forcefully to the breach. Yar Mohammed wavered, then as if seized by a mad impulse he grabbed a large staff and fell upon the retreating Afghan soldiers, who turned like whipped dogs and charged down the narrow passageway to drive the startled Persians from the walls. 'Had Yar Mohammed not been roused out of the paralysis that had descended upon him, Herat would have been carried by assault,' writes Kaye. 'But the indomitable courage of Eldred Pottinger saved the beleaguered city. The Persians, seized with a panic, abandoned their position and fled. The crisis was over, and Herat was saved.'[16]

Herat lies nearly 2,000 miles from Calcutta, hence Auckland had no way of keeping up with the day-to-day progress of the siege, and this was the cause of a fatal flaw in the Government's military and political strategy in Afghanistan. The Governor General relied at best on monthly despatches from the field, and the reports that were delivered to Fort William filled him with anxiety. It emerged that Count Ivan Simonich, the Russian envoy, had turned up at the Shah's camp outside Herat, hard on the heels of McNeill's embassy. What Auckland did not know, and he remained ignorant of this development until it was too late, was that despite providing the Shah with money to wage his campaign and Russian military expertise, Simonich had in the interim been abruptly recalled from Persia by the Tsar. An unexpected occurrence had triggered a sudden U-turn in Russian imperial policy towards Persia.

Auckland was at the end of his patience with Russian interference in Persia's affairs. It was to be gunboat diplomacy in a style that was certain to gladden the heart of Lord Palmerston, who was serving his second term of office as Foreign Secretary. The Bombay Presidency was instructed to despatch two warships with all haste to the Persian Gulf, where they were to be held in readiness for action against the Shah, should he fail to get the message that his presence was not wanted at Herat. On 4 June a squadron of five warships, led by the steamers *Sermiramis* and *Hugh Lindsay* with detachments from three regiments and the Marine battalion, set sail for the island of Karrack, the modern Kharg, a few miles off the Persian coast. No sooner had the first British sailor set foot on the island, the startled governor tendered his unconditional submission. From that day, news of the British landing began to snowball. By the time it reached the Persian camp, the British were said to have destroyed the Persian Gulf ports, landed a large force at Bushire, and were now advancing on Shiraz.

Palmerston took great delight in this show of British might. Whatever encouragement the Foreign Secretary might need to fear Russia's expansionist ambitions, this was supplied in large doses by McNeill's inflammatory reports to London. On 25 June, McNeill wrote to Palmerston: 'If Persia should succeed in taking Herat . . . I conceive that it would be hopeless for us to attempt to preserve a footing in Afghanistan or in Persia: both these countries, in short Central Asia, would be lost to us.' And further on, 'I can assure your Lordship that there is no impediment . . . to the march of a large army, I would say of even a hundred thousand men, from the frontiers of Georgia to Kandahar or, as I believe, to the Indus.'[17]

McNeill was *persona non grata* in the Persian camp and he therefore sent his military secretary Lieutenant-Colonel Charles Stoddart to note the ease with which Britain had invaded his country, and to take this as good reason to withdraw his forces from Herat. Stoddart, a 32-year-old rising star in the ranks, went beyond his instructions and told the Shah that failure to lift the siege would mean war. A few months later, McNeill sent Stoddart on another mission: this time to conclude a treaty of friendship with the Amir of Bokhara, a dreadful, bloodthirsty tyrant by the name of Nasrullah Khan. Stoddart's self-confidence proved to be of little avail on this expedition, for Nasrullah threw him and his companion Captain Arthur Conolly into the 'pit of plagues', where they languished until he decided to have them pulled out and beheaded.

Stoddart's threats were not wasted on Mohammed Shah. In early September, the Persians began to break up camp and on the 9th, the Shah mounted his horse and commenced the long march back to Tehran. If the Government could rejoice over its success in thwarting the Russians at 'the Gate of India', there was little joy to be derived from the rapidly deteriorating political situation in Kabul.

It took at least a month for news to travel from Afghanistan to India, either Calcutta or the Government's summer retreat at Simla. Thus Auckland could be forgiven for failing to know that the siege of Herat had been lifted. What was inexcusable was Auckland's obstinate refusal, once he had learnt of the Shah's retreat, to reverse his decision to launch the invasion of Afghanistan on the pretext of checking a hypothetical Russian advance on India. This was one of the causes of the coming disaster – the other was the sabotaging of Burnes's mission to Kabul. To understand how the Government betrayed Burnes, we must return to late 1837 and the Persian offensive on Herat.

When Mohammed Shah was setting out to lay siege to Herat, Major Sir Henry Rawlinson, a subaltern who later served as Political Agent at Kandahar in the Afghan war, was riding across a remote part of Persia to join the Shah as McNeill's advance agent. Rawlinson had covered 700 miles on horseback in one week and for a moment, as he crossed a broken plain, he was tempted to disbelieve his tired and dust-caked eyes, when in the distance he spied a party of horsemen in Cossack dress. When Rawlinson nervously drew up to the heavily armed group of Russians, he discovered one of them to be Captain Yan Vikevitch, en route to Kabul. In his saddlebag, Vikevitch carried a 3ft-long letter to Dost Mohammed, powdered with gold leaf, introducing himself as the emissary of Tsar Nicholas I.

Vikevitch had first come to the Russian Government's attention as a young student of outspoken views, to the extent that after taking part in a demonstration in favour of Polish independence the Government saw fit to pack him off to an honourable exile in the military colony of Orenburgh. Vikevitch's sharp intelligence and linguistic abilities were soon spotted and, as a result, he obtained a virtual release on condition that he agreed to carry out surveying work in Central Asia. The Russian Government at that time began mooting the idea of sending an agent to Kabul to neutralise British influence and as Kaye observes, 'there seemed to be no likelier man than Vikevitch to perform, with advantage to the state, the dubious service required of him'.[18] In September 1837, Vikevitch was despatched to Tehran where he received his final instructions from Count Simonich.

Burnes was making no headway in his endeavours to negotiate a workable entente between Dost Mohammed and Auckland. The Amir continued every step of the way to profess himself a loyal friend of British India. There was no reason to doubt his sincerity, albeit spawned by self-interest, for the Dost stood to gain by befriending the English, the only power that would stand between his throne and the encroaching Persian army. But there was the eastern border to consider as well, with the mercurial Ranjit Singh and his mighty Sikh forces in control of the west bank of the Indus. In exchange for throwing in his lot with the Government of India, the Dost sought on the one hand, a guarantee of British protection against a hostile Persia, and secondly – and this was the real bone of contention – Auckland's assistance in negotiating some form of Afghan sovereignty over Peshawar, now firmly in Sikh hands. The Governor General's response was largely dictated by his hawkish chief secretary, Macnaghten. Britain would offer Afghanistan its friendship and aid as befits the generosity of a great power towards a lesser neighbour – nothing else. 'In regard to Peshawar,' Auckland wrote, 'truth compels me to urge strongly on you to relinquish the idea of obtaining the government of that territory. It becomes you to think earnestly on the mode in which you may effect a reconciliation with that power prince [Ranjit Singh], to whom my nation is united by the direct bonds of friendship, and to abandon hopes which cannot be realised.'[19] Burnes must have cringed with horror when he read the Governor General's final comments: 'Should you seek connection with any other powers without my approbation, Captain Burnes . . . will retire from Kabul, where his further stay cannot be advantageous. I am persuaded that you will recognise the friendly feeling which has led me to state the truth to you, as you can guide your actions as you may consider most proper for yourself.'[20]

Burnes could only humbly beg the Dost's patience and comprehension, both of which were fast running short. A weak ruler he might be, but a proud Afghan nevertheless, and not one to suffer bullying and gratuitous insults. It was in these circumstances that the negotiations became deadlocked, until a new twist was added to the plot.

On Christmas Eve, Burnes was sitting down in his residence to ponder the latest despatches from Calcutta, when his servant came in to announce a visitor. Here was an unexpected occasion, and more so when Burnes was told that the man in uniform waiting outside was a *feringhee*, a foreigner. Captain Yan Vikevitch, who had arrived in Kabul the previous day, had come to pay his respects to his English counterpart.

From the morning on which Vikevitch entered the city gates, brandishing his rambling letter of introduction from the Russian Emperor (a document that was never authenticated to anybody's satisfaction), the Cossack officer's mission bore the air of a nonstarter. The Dost, who still held out hope for an arrangement by which he might persuade the Government of India to intercede on his behalf with Ranjit Singh, gave Vikevitch the cold shoulder. The Amir refused to receive the Russian visitor and a few days later, he even asked Burnes whether he thought Vikevitch should be expelled. Burnes demurred, but when he at last suggested that this would be the best course of action, it was too late. All of this escaped the attention of Auckland and his entourage of Russophobes, who only saw in Vikevitch's presence the realisation of their worst fears for Russian designs on India.

Vikevitch had turned up in Kabul in the midst of the festival of Eid, marking the end of Ramadan, the month-long Muslim period of fasting. His arrival, according to Burnes, produced a considerable sensation at Kabul. 'On his entering the city [Vikevitch] paid me a visit,' writes Burnes, who invited him to dinner. 'He was a gentlemanly and agreeable man, of abut 30 years of age, and spoke French, Turkish and Persian fluently, and wore the uniform of an officer of Cossacks, which was a novelty in Kabul. I found him intelligent and well informed on the subject of Northern Asia.' That was the first and last time that Burnes laid eyes on his Russian rival. The British Envoy confessed his inclination to befriend Vikevitch, but he also felt compelled to restrain this feeling, 'as the public service required the strictest watch, lest the relative positions of our nations should be misunderstood in this part of Asia'.[21] As indeed they were.

By early 1838, the Dost's patience had drawn to an end. Nothing was to be expected from Auckland, therefore the Amir felt he had no choice but to shift his allegiances to the Russians who, through their agent in Kabul were, if necessary, prepared to promise the moon. The Dost informed Burnes that he had set the vernal equinox, the first day of the Afghan calendar which falls around 20 March, as the final date he was prepared to wait for Calcutta to show a change of heart. Burnes communicated this melancholy news to Macnaghten in a despatch that showed the British agent had undergone a change of heart of his own. Burnes had begun to sense which way the wind was blowing. The letter reveals incipient signs of a shift of allegiance, from champion of Dost Mohammed's cause to supporter of Auckland's determination to be shot of the troublesome Amir. Burnes was starting to tell the Governor General what he wanted to hear. Firstly, Burnes let it be known that Vikevitch had convinced Dost Mohammed of the superiority of Russia's autocratic system over a slow-moving, procrastinating British democracy, 'which showed to him [the Amir] the advantage of allying himself to Russia, where no such inconveniences existed'.[22] By early March, Burnes realised that nothing was to be lost by putting the Government's wishes to the Dost in the most naked terms. If the only possible outcome was Burnes's explusion from Kabul, much better to ensure his own good standing with the Government hard-liners by laying down the law with the Amir. 'You must never receive agents from other powers, or have aught to do with them, without our sanction,' he told a disheartened Dost. 'You must dismiss Captain Vikevitch with courtesy and you must surrender all claim to Peshawar on your account, as that chiefship belongs to Maharaja Ranjit Singh.'[23] In return, Burnes could pledge the Government's good offices to bring about a reconciliation between the Amir and Ranjit. In other words, the Government of India was proposing that the Dost serve up his country as a puppet state, in return for British goodwill. Burnes's despatches make no mention of Dost Mohammed's reaction to this offer: it is not known whether he tore his splendid white beard in despair or roared with hilarity. However, it would have been a source of great solace to the Amir to know that after three more years of ignominious abuse by his former allies, he was to have the last laugh.

Things now began to spiral towards their inevitable conclusion. On 21 April the Dost had Vikevitch paraded through the streets of Kabul in regal fashion. Small wonder, for it was understood that the Russian had written to Ranjit, urging him to quit Peshawar. Burnes's last meeting with the Amir took place at the Bala Hissar on 25 April, when Dost Mohammed notified him that he had finished treating with the British Government. After an emotional farewell and pledges of enduring friendship, the following morning Burnes mounted his horse and rode out of Kabul. Burnes's mission had failed miserably, but this was the only possible outcome. As Kaye observes, 'He [Burnes] talked about the friendship of the British Government. Dost Mohammed asked for some proof of it, and no proof was forthcoming. The wonder is, not that the Amir at last listened to the overture of others, but that he did not seek other assistance before.'[24]

What fate now awaited the 30-year-old Cossack captain whose presence in Kabul had struck terror in the hearts of British statesmen from Calcutta to London?

Vikevitch departed Kabul a happy man, even as Burnes was making his way towards Peshawar. Vikevitch rode to Herat, having successfully discredited the British embassy and having promised everything that Dost Mohammed wanted, including money to wage war on Ranjit Singh. Mission accomplished, Vikevitch reflected with a glow of satisfaction. His Russian masters thought otherwise.

After the debacle at Herat, the Tsar and his ministers had no wish to provoke a military showdown with Britain. The Russian empire had spread to the borders of Afghanistan. Russian caravans were journeying across the steppes carrying goods to the great bazaars of Central Asia. Most of the region's commerce was in Russian hands, and this was good enough. There was no need to risk an open confrontation with British India, as long as Russia was in control of the trade routes that had been the original objective of the Burnes expedition.

Count Nesselrode, the Russian foreign minister, told Lord Durham, the British Ambassador in St Petersburg, that Russia had more to fear from Britain's expansionist policies than Britain from Russia's support for the Shah of Persia, which had in any case been withdrawn. Furthermore, Nesselrode assured the British Envoy that Count Simonich as well as Vikevitch had exceeded their authority, the former for goading the Persians into attacking Herat, and the latter for going beyond his remit which, like Burnes's, had been strictly of a 'commercial nature'. Simonich was recalled to St Petersburg and though his fate is unknown, it is reasonable to assume that he survived in some capacity on the imperial diplomatic payroll. Vikevitch returned to Russia expecting a hero's welcome. Instead, he was disowned by Nesselrode, who not only refused to receive him, but professed to have no knowledge of 'some adventurer' who was reported to have been engaged in unauthorised intrigues at Kabul. Vikevitch, discredited and broken in spirit, trudged down the marble steps of the foreign ministry to return to his hotel room.

So there it was, the summer of 1838 and Auckland had finally succeeded in undermining the good faith of Dost Mohammed who now stretched his hand westward, more in desperation than by design, to seek protection from his enemies. The Dost could no longer be counted as an ally, and whatever stories the Russians might concoct about peaceful intentions and commercial interests, there stood the tsarist troops on the banks of the Oxus. The Government of India had a duty to protect its empire from foreign encroachment and the buffer against those hostile intentions was Afghanistan. Measures were now required to secure that country's allegiance, but it was clear that this could not be achieved with Dost Mohammed on the throne of Kabul. So the bizarre reasoning went, and it could not have been more deeply flawed. Kaye's authoritative view of British policy towards Afghanistan and Russia is at radical variance with the official line advanced by Calcutta. 'The dangers which threatened the security of our Anglo-Indian empire, in 1837–8,' he writes, 'were seen through the magnifying medium of ignorance, and greatly exaggerated in the recital.'[25]

Sir Henry Marion Durand, whose rough manner had earned him the reputation of an *enfant terrible* among British Army officers, held the Government's Afghan policies in total contempt. Durand was an eyewitness to the successes and setbacks that preceded the terrible catastrophe of 1842, for he had accompanied General Sir John Keane's column on the march to Kabul in 1839. He was no armchair critic: when the column reached the crucial fortress of Ghazni, Durand, under fire, blew open the gate and enabled the garrison's capture. As a result of a bitter falling out with Burnes and Macnaghten over how best to protect the occupying forces in Kabul, Durand returned to India and thus saved his own life. He spent most of 1840 at the hill station of Mussorrie, where he prepared maps of the campaign and wrote damning reports of the Government's Persian and Afghan policies. He wrote:

> The exaggerated fears of Russian power and intrigue entertained by Ellis, McNeill, Burnes and Wade, the flame of which was communicated by them to the British and Indian Governments, invested Herat with a fictitious importance wholly incommensurate with the strength of the place and its position in regard to Kandahar and the Indus. To speak of the integrity of the place as of vital importance to British India, was a hyperbole so insulting to common sense as scarcely to need refutation.[26]

The Government's Afghan policy fares no better, in Durand's opinion, particularly in the choice of envoy sent to win Dost Mohammed's allegiance. 'The conduct of the mission, official and private, had sunk it into contempt, and the irascible vanity of Burnes . . . impelled him to a line of conduct hasty and injudicious, and which, wanting in truth, composure and dignity, exasperated the Amir,' he says. 'Thus terminated a mission which, entrusted to wiser and better men, might have had very different results.'[27] Had the Governor General and his advisers heeded Durand's warnings, tragedy might have been averted. But Durand, the man whom *The Times* recognised in its obituary as 'the ablest of [India's] statesmen', never had Auckland's ear. Macnaghten and company saw to that, and the reason was clear: 'His independence of character and bluntness of speech alienated more than one Governor General from this perilously able subordinate.'[28]

Auckland, Macnaghten and Wade, along with the politicians in London, now had the Dost in their sights. The Amir had proven himself to be the enemy of Britain, spurning the hand of friend-ship and wooing the Russians into his camp. The security of British India demanded his removal from power. The stage was set for the next act, which precipitated Britain into a military disaster of a magnitude not equalled until the fall of Singapore a hundred years later.

Chapter 2

'An Aggression Destitute Even of Pretext'

Auckland had some explaining to do. The Secret Committee of the Court of Directors of the East India Company, taking Burnes's mission at face value, namely that he had been sent solely to negotiate a trade agreement with Dost Mohammed, wished to know the reason for the Envoy having returned empty-handed. The Honourable Company's Board of Control in London, whose members included privy councillors and ministers of the Crown, directed orders to the Company's servants in India through this powerful Secret Committee. Auckland's version of the mission's failure was contrived to whip up fears of Russian involvement in Afghanistan. In May 1838, with the fall of Herat a foregone conclusion in the Government's thinking, Auckland explained to the Committee that the spread of Russian and Persian influence in Afghanistan had induced Dost Mohammed to press his claims on Peshawar and to reject British friendship. On these grounds it was decided to withdraw Burnes from Kabul. This was a blatant distortion of the facts, though whether Auckland was privy to political realities was always an open question. His inner circle of advisers saw to that. Giving it even more urgent 'spin', Auckland dramatically announced to the Committee members that the crisis had reached such a critical point that he might be forced to take urgent action using his executive powers. 'The emergency of affairs may compel me,' he stated, 'to act without awaiting any intimation of your views upon the events which have recently occurred in Persia and Afghanistan.'[1] Auckland had embarked seven months before on a splendid progress, travelling across northern India by barge, carriage, horse and elephant, with 12,000 camp followers and 1,000 camels in tow, finally settling in Simla, where he was to languish for the better part of two years. During this crucial time, the Governor General was out of touch with Calcutta, which left him totally at the mercy of Macnaghten, Henry Torrens and John Colvin, three of Auckland's closest advisers, and all of whom suffered from acute Russophobia.

The saddest fact is that nobody seems to have a good word about Auckland, at whose feet most would lay the blame for launching Britain into a totally avoidable, unnecessary and ruinous war. Yet he was as much the tool of more determined men's machinations as Shah Shuja was to be Britain's poodle in its war on Afghanistan. On this point the chroniclers, then as now, voice unanimity. Durand's disdain for the Governor General's character has already been noted. To this may be added the opinion of Patrick Macrory: 'This worthy mediocrity was not the man to stand up against the ambitious designs of Lord Palmerston, backed as they were by the Governor General's own immediate staff, who were soon to show themselves too clever by half.'[2] Michael Edwardes takes the view that, 'Auckland's worst quality was that he was no judge of men, of their character and worth. This was compounded when he cut himself off from the main centre of the Government of India, at Calcutta, from his own Council and a wide range of experience, at just the time when he needed the peace of a settled establishment and all the expert opinion he could find.'[3]

Apart from reiterating the need to stop Russia, that 'formidable element of disorder and intrigue', Auckland spoke to the Secret Committee in the vaguest terms of how the Government intended to counter the tsarist threat. For now, there might not be cause to take hostile action against Dost Mohammed, who was regarded as a man of 'equivocal feelings', but one would have to keep a watchful eye on him. To Auckland's mind, the key to the matter was Herat: if the city fell, the Government would have to move swiftly to safeguard India's integrity. The Governor General threw the ball into the Secret Committee's lap – he appealed for guidance from the home Government, while behind the scenes Macnaghten and the others were setting out their agenda for Afghanistan. A cold and cautious individual Auckland might be, but one who was notoriously infirm of purpose and, Durand writes, 'it was by gradual steps that he unfortunately suffered the alarms, real or pretended, of others, and their importunities, ultimately to prevail over his own judgement'.[4]

Auckland gave evidence to the Secret Committee in May, at which time he suggested the Government had no desire to become embroiled in an Asian war that could ultimately bring on a confrontation with Russia. Three months later, he was singing a more belligerent tune. 'Of the justice of the course about to be pursued, there cannot exist a reasonable doubt,' the Governor General ominously declared to the Committee members on 13 August. 'We owe it to our own safety to assist the lawful sovereign of Afghanistan in the recovery of his throne. The operations which we are about to undertake, will doubtless be attended with much expense. But this consideration must, I feel assured, be held comparatively light, when contrasted with the magnitude of the object to be gained, which is no less than to raise up a barrier to all encroachments from the westward.'[5] In other words, British India was going to war. The 'lawful sovereign' Auckland referred to was, of course, the deposed Amir and British pensioner Shah Shuja, though precisely why the Saddozai claim to the throne should have carried any more legitimacy than that of the Barakzai clan was never satisfactorily explained. Auckland went on to assure what must have been a rather startled Committee that Dost Mohammed was an unpopular ruler, who was seeking to forge an alliance with British India's enemies the Persians, and plotting to secure foreign (i.e. Russian) aid to wage war on Britain's ally Ranjit Singh. By the time this doctrine was discredited as nonsense, British India had suffered the most horrific consequences in lost lives and battered prestige. This book's purpose is not to draw moral conclusions for what is happening in today's world; however, the parallels with the doctrine of Weapons of Mass Destruction, used to justify the use of military force in a nearby theatre of war, cannot escape notice.

What had transpired between May and August to bring about this extraordinary shift in policy? In June, Shah Shuja was taken by carriage from his gilded retirement in Ludhiana to the Sikh capital of Lahore for a meeting with his old acquaintance Ranjit Singh. Macnaghten, acting in his capacity as agent of the Government of India, had achieved his objective: the Afghan and Sikh potentates had agreed to work together to drive Dost Mohammed out of

Afghanistan. Auckland, in fact, had already made plans to receive the Amir in India, where he would take Shuja's place as a British pensioner in Ludhiana.

The Governor General also informed the Secret Committee of an initiative to revive a treaty between Shuja and Ranjit, ratified in 1833, only this time it would be a tripartite agreement to include Britain. The significance was that Auckland was not only going to despatch his Afghan protégé, with Ranjit's complicity, across the border to reclaim his throne, but also that the British Government was to assume an active role in this enterprise.

The beauty of the treaty was that it enabled Auckland to kill two birds with one stone: Shuja was persuaded to relinquish his claim to Sikh-held territory on both banks of the Indus, namely Kashmir *and* the Vale of Peshawar. Macnaghten's skilful manoeuvrings were the work of extreme political cunning: 'These countries and places are considered to be the property, and to form the estate of the Maharaja, and the Shah neither has, nor will have, any concern with them,' the text stated. 'They belong to the Maharaja and his posterity, from generation to generation.'[6] It was, on the face of it, a win-win situation. Shuja was almost effortlessly thrust from oblivion back into the seat of power in his native land. Ranjit was over the moon at the prospect of doing a deal with British backing that would consolidate his dominions. When asked by Macnaghten whether he would like to renew his old treaty with Shuja and ally himself with the British Government, or take care of Dost Mohammed's claim to Peshawar on his own, Ranjit unhesitatingly chose the former alternative. It was, he exclaimed, 'adding sugar to milk'.[7] The only weak spot in the plan, which all parties chose to ignore, was how and by whom Shuja was to be kept on his throne. Never mind, the strategic minutiae could wait, for now it was full speed ahead to Kabul.

Once Shuja was duly reinstated and had established his authority in Kabul, it was agreed he would send Ranjit an annual tribute, out of gratitude for lending him the support of the Sikh army. The gift list included 55 high-bred horses 'of approved colour and pleasant paces', 11 Persian scimitars, 7 Persian poniards, 25 good mules, fruits of various kinds, musk melons 'of a sweet and delicate flavour', pieces of satin and 101 Persian carpets. Ranjit

Singh obviously had a rather exalted opinion of his own worth, but a rather lowly one of his Afghan ally, who was to receive in return a mere 55 shawls, 25 pieces of muslin, 5 scarves, 5 turbans and 55 loads of rice. It was further agreed that whatever booty they succeeded in looting from the Barakzai family would be equally divided between the two contracting partners. The clause that brought most comfort to Auckland bound Shuja, on the one hand, to refrain from entering into any form of negotiations with a third party without the knowledge and consent of the British Government and their Sikh allies and secondly, to resist by force of arms any encroachment on his territory by a foreign power.

By now, the Government had succeeded in putting across its message, to the extent that most people accepted as fact the existence of an imminent Russian–Persian threat to Britain's Indian empire. The sceptics had been reduced to a minority, though some of the voices of protest, as typified by Durand, continued to bellow loudly in the wilderness. Lord Salisbury, Victoria's future prime minister, put his finger on it when he said, 'You must either disbelieve altogether in the existence of the Russians, or you must believe that they will be at Kandahar next year. Public opinion recognises no middle holding ground.'[8]

Auckland and Macnaghten spent the next few weeks conferring on how to justify to the world at large the Government's decision to send an army, with no provocation whatsoever, into a neighbouring country to oust its ruler. This took the form of the Simla Manifesto, a rambling and turgid document which *The Times* reproduced in full on its leader page, appraising it to be one of 'the highest political importance'.[9]

On 10 September Auckland had given orders for mobilisation of a force destined for operations in Afghanistan. In short order, the number of men under arms in India had swollen from 190,000 to 203,000 troops. On 1 October he issued the Manifesto explaining his reasons for going to war, namely to put Shah Shuja back on a throne from which he had been evicted nearly thirty years before. The Governor General pointed to the Dost's attack on

Britain's ally Ranjit Singh in the Khyber, an act which Auckland alleged added a political dimension to Burnes's commercial mission to Kabul. Far from accepting the Government's proposals for a peaceful settlement of differences with the Sikhs, the Amir and his Kandahar brothers had made common cause with the Persians. Hence the collapse of Burnes's mission and his withdrawal from Kabul, which necessitated a more vigorous policy towards Afghanistan.

The Dost, Auckland claims, 'avowed schemes of aggrandisement and ambition injurious to the security and peace of the frontiers of India, and he openly threatened, in furtherance of these schemes, to call in every foreign aid which he could command'. Later on, Auckland tells us of a 'pressing necessity' to espouse the cause of Shah Shuja, 'whose popularity throughout Afghanistan had been proved to his Lordship by the strong and unanimous testimony of the best authorities'.[10] In the first place, it should be recalled that the Dost's 'schemes of aggrandisement' were confined almost exclusively to the recovery of Peshawar. There is no evidence to suggest he ever entertained any fantasies about enlisting Russian bayonets to bring this about, and the notion that the Tsar would be prepared to risk war over this cause is utter nonsense. Secondly, one wonders who in the Governor General's Simla entourage qualified as a 'best authority' on Afghan public opinion. Burnes was the only one ever to have served there, and there is no mention in his despatches of the populace clamouring for Shah Shuja's return. Shuja's face had only been seen once in Afghanistan in the past three decades, and that was when he was routed at Kandahar. His entry into Kabul the following year was greeted with outstanding indifference by the few sullen citizens who turned out to observe the conquering army. But this was not simply a case of false pretexts: the Simla Manifesto lied in its execution as well as its premises. Lest an anxious public worry about the Army getting bogged down in a prolonged and messy occupation, Auckland ended his declaration with a pledge to withdraw the force once Shah Shuja was secured in power and the integrity of Afghanistan established. Tragically, that was not the way things were destined to turn out.

A breath of fresh air, from a familiar quarter, emerged to denounce this Manifesto for what it was: a disgraceful sham. This came as usual from the resolute voice of Sir Henry Durand. 'In this proclamation, the words *justice* and *necessity*, and the terms *frontier* and *security of the possessions of the British Crown*, and *national defence*,' he wrote, 'were applied in a manner for which there is fortunately no precedent in the English language.' No precedent to the Simla Manifesto, perhaps, though it is arguable that this document set a precedent of its own, serving almost as a template for statements issued by world powers 165 years later in extraordinarily similar circumstances. 'All scruples at first entertained by the Government had now been swept away,' Durand concluded. As for the invasion itself Durand, who was a career officer, had nothing but scorn. 'Never before, during the history of the British power in India, had so wild, ill-considered, and adventurous a scheme of far-distant aggression been entertained.'[11] This was not the wild clamour of some disaffected crank. Men of higher station than Durand, such as Auckland's predecessor Lord Bentinck, dismissed the invasion plan as an act of incredible folly. Mountstuart Elphinstone, the statesman who had led a mission to Kabul thirty years previous and was regarded as the leading Afghan authority of his day, considered it hopeless to attempt to maintain Shah Shuja on the throne of that turbulent land. No lesser a voice than that of the Duke of Wellington, a man who had never set foot in Afghanistan but who knew a thing or two about military strategy, condemned the Manifesto's contents as an act of obsession. He prophesied, and how right the Iron Duke was, that crossing the Indus to set up a puppet government in Afghanistan would precipitate a perennial march into that country.

The Simla Manifesto, which should be noted bore the signature of Macnaghten 'with the Governor General', was torn to shreds by the British and Indian press. 'There was not a sentence in it that was not dissected with an unsparing hand,' Kaye tells us. 'If it were not pronounced to be a collection of absolute falsehoods, it was described as a most disingenuous distortion of the truth.' Kaye himself spotted the blatant contradiction in the Manifesto, in that Auckland deliberately linked the siege of Herat to the failure of the Kabul mission. 'But with all his own and his secretary's ingenuity, his Lordship could not contrive . . . to make the two events hang together by any other than the slenderest thread.'[12] Kaye reasoned that there was no justification for taking Mohammed Shah's attack on Herat as a justification to wage war on Dost Mohammed. 'It [the war] was commenced in defiance of every consideration of political and military expediency,' Kaye writes, 'and there were those who, arguing the matter on higher grounds than those of mere expediency, pronounced the certainty of its failure, because there was a canker of injustice at the core.'[13] Kaye's contemporary Archibald Forbes also pronounced Auckland's line of thought as devoid of logic. 'If Shah Shuja had a powerful following in Afghanistan, he could regain his throne without our assistance,' he writes. 'If he had no holding there, it was for us a truly discreditable enterprise to foist him on a recalcitrant people at the point of the bayonet.'[14] As for the East India Company, the Court of Directors stood firmly opposed to a war which in their view, could only damage British India's commercial interests west of the Indus. The Company did no more than discharge their duty of signing the papers put before them by the Governor General's staff. It was Sir Penderel Moon who delivered the *coup de grace* to Auckland's allegation that Dost Mohammed was openly conspiring with Russia and Persia. 'This was a travesty of the facts and a deliberate misrepresentation of Dost Mohammed's views and intentions,' he writes. 'It was also glaringly inconsistent with much that Burnes had reported from Kabul.'[15] Burnes's final memos before quitting Kabul still spoke favourably of the Dost as a friend of England and a reasonable man who was willing to reach a compromise solution in his quarrel with Ranjit Singh.

The Government was in no mood for killjoys. Almost everything in Burnes's reports that cast doubt on the wisdom of Auckland's policies was ruthlessly deleted from a Government Blue Book on Afghanistan. Having seen his last-ditch attempt at a negotiated settlement crushed underfoot Burnes, a born survivor who aspired to higher things, quickly fell into line behind his superiors. Burnes's acquiescence did not go unrewarded. It was only natural for Macnaghten, the driving spirit behind the whole scheme, to be given the job of Envoy and Minister to Kabul. Burnes, for his part, was appointed Envoy to the Chief of Khelat and ordered to go ahead of the advancing troops to establish good relations with the amirs of Sind and the Khan of Khelat. This was an important though

decidedly less illustrious office, but Burnes's disappointment
vanished, when after a moment of angry frustration, he retrieved
Auckland's letter of congratulations from the waste-paper basket.
Captain Burnes saw with great delight that the envelope had been
addressed to 'Lieutenant-Colonel Sir Alexander Burnes, Kt.'.

Preparations now got under way for the first war of Queen Victoria's
reign. On the morning of 20 October 1838, Auckland and the
Commander-in-Chief in India, General Sir Henry Fane, emerged
from a meeting to announce that a name had been chosen for the
expeditionary force. It was to be christened with great splendour
the 'Army of the Indus'. The various corps were ordered to rendezvous at Karnal, a town 80 miles north of Delhi on the Grand Trunk
Road, by the end of October. With the onset of winter at hand,
Auckland had chosen the worst season of the year for campaigning. Auckland was a practitioner in half-measures and, as such, he
opposed the formation of a grand force to march on Afghanistan.
British India's highest-ranking military figure doubted the wisdom
of despatching an army across the Indus. Fane could boast an
outstanding military record. He had been promoted to Brigadier
General at age 30, in 1808, the youngest man in the British Army
to attain that rank, and he had fought under Wellington against
the French and in Spain. He won the reputation of being, next
to General Sir Willoughby Cotton, the best commander of cavalry
in the army. In the end, Auckland's and Fane's misgivings were
overridden by political exigencies. What Auckland had originally
envisaged was a token British force in support of two armies
under the command of Shah Shuja and Ranjit Singh. Auckland's
intermediary Macnaghten told Ranjit that he wished the Sikhs to
undertake the expedition entirely on their own. The Maharaja was
not impressed. Ranjit received Macnaghten in Lahore, seated regally
in a golden chair, dressed in simple white, wearing the Koh-i-Noor
diamond on his arm. He told Macnaghten that he was happy to
cooperate with the English to rid Afghanistan of Dost Mohammed,
but that he would not allow his troops to bear the brunt of the
offensive alone. The Government quickly realised that to ensure

success, this would have to be a combined Anglo-Sikh undertaking. The Sikhs had no trouble in fielding a proper army – Ranjit had 31 regiments of infantry, 9 of cavalry and 288 pieces of artillery – but while Shuja's soldiery was raised in his name, the Government's troops were collected in the Company's territories and under the command of Company officers. The strength of the Army of the Indus raised for service in Afghanistan consisted of one brigade of artillery, a cavalry brigade and five brigades of infantry. In all, the two Company presidencies of Bengal and Bombay sent 15,000 men, while another 6,000 levies were raised to serve under Shah Shuja. The deposed Saddozai monarch could scarcely believe his luck. Not only were his British patrons going to oust the despised Barakzai chieftain Dost Mohammed, but the East India Company was going to raise an army on Shuja's behalf to re-establish his authority in Kabul.

This was to be a massive undertaking, not only in the number of troops involved, but also taking into account the train of back-up personnel and baggage animals that trailed in the distance. The two British contingents marched with some 80,000 camp followers and a similar number of camels, as well as hundreds of bullocks to haul the guns and carts. The field commanders had issued orders against carrying excessive baggage, but these were largely ignored. There are records of an officer of the 16th Lancers being attended by forty personal servants – one General Officer travelled with forty-three baggage camels of his own, some of which carried loads of more than half a ton.

As this great mobilisation was taking place, nearly 2,000 miles away something occurred which, in the words of one contemporary observer, 'rendered the invasion of Afghanistan an aggression destitute even of pretext'.[16.] The Persians had raised the siege of Herat, fully three weeks before Auckland issued the Simla Manifesto. Granted, news travelled slowly in those days and it would have been almost impossible for this intelligence to have reached Simla before the Manifesto's proclamation on 1 October. Yet there can be no denying that with the removal of the threat to Herat, the whole *raison d'être* for the invasion dissipated into thin air. Stoddart sent a letter to Macnaghten on 10 September, informing him of the withdrawal of the Shah's forces. 'His Majesty [the Shah] proceeds without delay . . . to Tehran,' wrote the ill-starred Stoddart. 'This is in fulfilment of His Majesty's compliance with the demands of the British Government.'[17] The Shah's submission took place on 14 August. This was a different matter than the actual lifting of the siege, for the ensuing six weeks provided sufficient time for the news of the capitulation to have been received at Simla. Even during the turbulent days of the British occupation of Kabul, letters took no more than a month to travel from that city to Calcutta. It seems curious that Auckland, though unaware that the Shah's army had abandoned the field, could claim no knowledge of what was afoot. Macnaghten, for one, was in no way fazed by this development. He and Auckland's other advisers had decided on war, and war they were to have. The chief secretary, speaking at his most belligerent on Auckland's behalf, explained that while the Governor General regarded the end of the threat to Herat a just cause of congratulation to the Government of British India and its allies, 'he will continue to prosecute with vigour the measures which have been announced, with a view to the substitution of a friendly for a hostile power in the eastern provinces of Afghanistan, and to the establishment of a permanent barrier against schemes of aggression upon our North-West Frontier'.[18]

Auckland was not about to dismantle the huge military apparatus the Government had put into place to confront the Persian threat. But he was prepared to offer a gesture of appeasement to his numerous doubters and critics. Shah Shuja's 6,000-strong force marched from Ludhiana in mid-November, and the Governor General contemplated concentrating a British army of about 27,000 men on the banks of the Sutlej by the end of that month. What brought about a change of plans came from within the army itself, and at the very highest level. General Fane found it difficult to accept the logic of mobilising a huge fighting force to march on an enemy that no longer existed. This 'altered state of affairs', which was Auckland's euphemism for the Shah of Persia's capitulation, coupled with the Government's obstinacy in pursuing the war, left Fane with no option but to ask to be relieved of his command. Some would argue that Fane stepped down on grounds of poor health rather than disenchantment with Auckland's official policy. Fane was sixty and a very ill man, with less than two years of life left in him. He died at sea on his way home to England on board the *Malabar* in March 1840, as the Indiaman was sailing past the Azores. The fact remains that Fane stepped down first as commander of the Army of the Indus, on learning that Herat no longer needed to be relieved. This was the general's real grievance, which preceded his resignation as Commander-in-Chief, a decision that may well have been ultimately motivated by his weakened physical state.

Auckland's token gesture was to cut the number of British troops by 5,500 to bring the expeditionary force down to 21,500 men, one would have thought quite a hefty number of trained troops to reduce a country like Afghanistan – or so it would have seemed. Of the invasion's almost numberless strategic failings, one of the most witless was to equip the soldiers with the Brown Bess musket, a weapon that had remained unmodified since Waterloo. 'Effective at no more than 150 yards, it was not, as was soon to be discovered, a match for the long Afghan *jezail* which had four times its range.'[19] The troops marching through the narrow passes would have occasion to curse the weapons they held in their hands, as well as the officers who placed them there.

Fane handed over the Army of the Indus to General Sir John Keane, who led the Bombay contingent, in January 1839. Another Major-General, Sir Jasper Nicolls, was appointed Fane's successor as Commander-in-Chief of India. Nicolls played a largely passive role throughout the Afghan war. He had always harboured serious reservations about Auckland's invasion policy, and in particular the haphazard manner in which it was put into execution. Nicolls' single most important recommendation throughout the campaign, which could have saved the British Army, was to pull the doddering, gout-stricken commander of the Kabul force, Major-General William Elphinstone, a cousin of the illustrious Mountstuart, out of that city and to replace him with General Sir William Nott, a classic tough-as-boot-leather soldier. Nicolls' proposal fell on deaf ears in Simla. For all his professional excellence, Nott was a maverick, disliked in higher quarters for the notorious chip he carried on his shoulder. He found himself in regular conflict with the politicals, but more pertinently, with his superior officers. The fatal falling out took place before the storming of Khelat, when Keane ordered

Nott to place himself under the command of Major-General Sir Thomas Willshire. Nott replied that he could not take orders from an officer whom he considered his junior, a remark that reached Auckland's ears. The infuriated Governor General compelled Nott to submit, and rubbing salt in the wound, he ordered him to refund 9,000 rupees that he had drawn as temporary commander of the 1st Division. This led to a violent verbal clash with Keane, who swore he would never forgive Nott's conduct, to which Nott bid him a good evening and turned on his heel. As he had predicted, the appointment of Commander-in-Chief in Afghanistan went to a Queen's officer, Elphinstone, a man whose incompetence Nott delighted in proclaiming to all and sundry.

The corps that had been mustered for the occupation of Afghanistan assembled at the end of November at Ferozepore, a town about 50 miles south of Amritsar near the present India–Pakistan border. The Government had committed some of British India's most outstanding military figures to the enterprise. Keane was appointed commander of the Bombay Division and the officer who was to take charge of the entire Army. The Bengal troops in five brigades were under the command of General Cotton. The gathering of the British and Sikh forces at the Sutlej has been aptly described as the 'Ferozepore Circus', with an array of Gilbert and Sullivan-style excesses epitomised by Cotton himself, who travelled in his own buggy and had appropriated 260 camels for his and his servants' gear. Yet it was a colourless occasion compared with the gathering that took place less than four years later at the same spot, to welcome home the Army that was sent in to redeem British battle honours.

On 27 November, Auckland rode into camp under a pre-arranged plan by which the Governor General and Ranjit Singh would ceremoniously cross the Indus together. Two days later the Maharaja made his appearance at Ferozepore in great splendour, perched on his elephant's *howdah*, amid the roar of artillery and a military band. Auckland, dressed in an equally sumptuous blue uniform and riding an elephant of his own, came forth to greet his ally. It was the first and last meeting between the two men. Ranjit was by now a decrepit man of 59, whose life of debauchery was shortly to bring on a swift decline and the stroke that carried him off six months later.

There was a crush of elephants at the Durbar tent as British officials clambered down from their mounts to escort the diminutive Ranjit into the inner chamber to be handed, among other gifts, a portrait of Queen Victoria rendered by Auckland's sister Emily Eden. The Sikhs, not to be outdone, the following day received Auckland in glittering steel helmets and chain armour, in their tents of crimson and gold, where the British delegation was regaled with a display of near-naked dancing girls. The only hitch was that amid all this magnificence, Auckland was on that day informed that the siege of Herat had been lifted and the Shah was on his way home.

On 1 December Shah Shuja, at the head of two regiments of cavalry, four regiments of infantry and a troop of horse artillery, under the command of Major-General John Simpson, pitched up after a two-week march from Ludhiana. Shuja had missed out on the Oriental festivities, but no matter, his destiny lay across the frontier, which he now commenced to cross with the Bengal Division following hard on his heels a few days later. The party was over, the invasion of Afghanistan had begun.

The columns of men that marched ahead of the long train of braying, roaring baggage animals could be seen from the surrounding hills, stretching to the horizon amid clouds of ochre dust. Cotton crouched comfortably in his horse-drawn carriage, leading the Bengal Division on a line of march south-westerly along the left bank of the Sutlej into Sind, thence to follow the Indus to a crossing point at Bukkur, a picturesque Moghul fort located midstream in the river, which was reached on 29 January. From there, the Bengal troops moved 26 miles to Shikarpore, a town that commanded the trade route through the notorious Bolan Pass. The most direct road to Kabul led through Lahore and Peshawar, and from there across the Khyber Pass into Afghanistan. This was the route to be followed by the Sikh forces. There was a snag, in that the Punjab was an independent state under Sikh rule. The British might be Ranjit's beloved comrades-in-arms, but there was no question of allowing an East India Company army to march across his land, lest Auckland found some pretext for garrisoning foreign troops in the Maharaja's territory.

The Sikhs, however, were at the time preoccupied with the rapidly deteriorating health of their ruler Ranjit. Auckland's last meeting with the Maharaja took place towards the end of 1838 at the Lahore Durbar, where the two leaders agreed their joint plan of action against Dost Mohammed. It was an affair on a gigantic scale in which the rations provided for the Governor General's party alone amounted to 4,000 chickens and 15,000 eggs per day. Ranjit was at his bacchanalian best, with half a dozen sets of nautch-girls dancing and screaming in front of the dignitaries' table, the crash of bands and firing of cannons, fireworks blazing and goblets overflowing with an exotic concoction of emeralds, grapes and oranges. Ranjit had already suffered a stroke the previous year, which left him semi-paralysed. Now, after several days of debauched entertaining for his British guests, the Maharaja was taken violently ill with another seizure. By June, Ranjit was losing his grip on life, and to prepare himself for the end, he ordered vast treasures to be given away to charity. These included 11 cows with gilded horns, 25 satin dresses, 10 gold and silver images, 5 golden deer, 1 elephant, 2 diamond rings and 2,000 rupees in cash plus five times his weight in grain to be given to the Brahmins. The end came on 27 June, when the Maharaja was laid on the floor to die in the lap of Mother Earth, and his heirs were left to squabble among themselves for supremacy of an empire that a decade later was blown to pieces by the guns of their erstwhile British allies.

The Bengal contingent of the Army was met in Shikarpore with scenes of gaiety accompanied by martial music, for Keane's Bombay troops that had landed at Karachi in early December were already encamped to greet them. A mood of exhilaration prevailed in the British tents, officers and other ranks all heady with excitement over what promised to be a grand military promenade, with victory assured at the end of the campaign. The cracks in the Army's ill-conceived strategy began to appear on 23 February, when the columns moved out in driblets from Shikarpore into the wastes of the Kachi desert, and from there to the mouth of the Bolan Pass.

The plan was to advance from Quetta to Kandahar, 'a strangely devious route', as Kaye points out, for the Army was about to traverse two sides of a triangle, instead of shaping its course along the third. The British at once ran into trouble with the amirs of Sind. The treaty concluded with these potentates two years previous provided for British survey work and navigation to be carried out along the Indus, but it was expressly stipulated that no troops or military stores were to be transported on the river. Auckland saw fit to ignore this clause and adopt instead a system of intimidation and coercion, for which the Army was to pay dearly. If the amirs refused to cooperate or offered any resistance to the troops, they were to be fined 250,000 rupees and deprived of their possessions. Moreover, the amirs were forced to supply the troops with provisions and baggage animals on their passage through Sind. Henry Pottinger and Alexander Burnes were deputed to deliver terms to the rulers of Lower Sind and Baluchistan, respectively. Both envoys were received coldly, making it plain to imagine what sort of reception awaited the advancing columns. Under these circumstances, the amirs were not unnaturally loath to provide the troops with the stores and baggage animals that were demanded of them. Lacking proper supplies, trekking across a hostile and desolate land, attrition quickly set in: there were mass desertions by officers' servants and camel drivers, herds of cattle fell sick and died of starvation and dysentery by the wayside, food and supplies grew scarce, so that the tens of thousands of camp followers who straggled behind were put on half-rations, and those of the fighting men were also later reduced. The suffering of the troops was intense, as was vividly described by James Atkinson, who served as Superintending Surgeon of the Army. 'The prospect was gloomy and threatening enough,' he writes, 'but the measure of limiting the allowance to the smallest possible amount no doubt averted from the troops a more awful and tremendous visitation, that of actual starvation.' The prospect was not only threatening, it was a hardship the men had to bear for weeks on end. 'The quantum of allowance thus reduced was not, however, of short duration, for it was nearly three months before the commissariat was enabled to supply full rations.'[20] By the time the Army reached Quetta, grain for the animals had given out altogether and only a kind of rough local groats, known as *khasil*, was to be found for fodder. The several units were on the march for eleven days before they reached Quetta, where two battalions under General Nott were left behind to garrison the town, while a brigade was sent ahead to secure the treacherous Bolan Pass. It took Cotton eight days to lead his column through the 60-mile-long defile, a punishing march on which hundreds of camels and bullocks were killed during a storm. The troops had to endure one march of 28 miles without water, all the while fighting off attacks by bandits who swarmed down from the heights above the pass. The heat was so intense, with temperatures soaring above 110°F, that men dropped on the road. One report speaks of a Lieutenant Corrie of Her Majesty's 17th and ten of his men, who died of heat exhaustion, after stopping under a tree where they imprudently refreshed themselves by drinking brandy.

The Army's plight was dire in the extreme. Kaye describes the men surviving on 'famine allowances', suffering the present and dreading the prospect of venturing into a hostile land in their state of exhaustion. 'Their hearts died within them at the thought that a day was coming when even the little that was now doled out to them might be wholly denied,' he writes.[21] The Army was saved from starvation, even before entering Afghanistan, by Burnes, who rushed to Khelat to persuade the powerful Khan, in effect the ruler of Baluchistan, to release stores of grain and provide sheep for the troops. Burnes was only half-listening when the Khan, with prophetic truth, pointed out that though the British might restore Shah Shuja, they would not carry the Afghans with them and that the invasion would end in calamity. But having been offered an annual subsidy of 150,000 rupees, the Khan cheerfully affixed his seal on a treaty that also bound him to accept the supremacy of Shah Shuja, a remarkable feat considering the desperate nature of Burnes's mission.

After a week's halt, the soldiers and camp followers of the Army of the Indus were sufficiently restored to health to continue their slow advance 100 miles east, to cross the Khojak Pass into Afghanistan, which was accomplished without incident. Kandahar was reached unopposed on 25 April by Shah Shuja, who made a grand entry, unfortunately without the attendance of the city's dignitaries, the Governor and his brothers having fled

80 miles west to Girishk, on the road to Herat, without striking a blow. This fortified town later entered the annals for the few successful acts of gallantry in the war. It was near this spot that a small garrison of sepoys under a native officer withstood a siege of nine months by an overwhelming force, a finer deed than 5,000 fighting men in Kabul were able to achieve against an Afghan mob. Macnaghten was filled with jubilation over the enthusiastic reception given Shah Shuja by the people of Kandahar, many of whom strewed flowers and loaves of bread before the royal cortège as it passed through the streets. The Envoy conveyed to Auckland this happy news, while assuring the Governor General that the populace had greeted the British officers as liberators from their Barakzai oppressors, and that all were overjoyed at the prospect of having a Saddozai monarch back on the throne. Within a fortnight, Macnaghten was forced to rethink the situation, when at a grand investiture ceremony for Shuja, the returning king was received with disdain by his subjects, whose initial curiosity had faded into sullen indifference. This was particularly true of the Ghilzais, one of the two largest groups of Pathans, along with the Durranis, who occupy the north of Kandahar and extend eastwards towards the Suleiman range. This nomadic warrior tribe was to wreak utter havoc on the British troops during the coming campaign. Shuja chose to turn a blind eye to the fact that he had been foisted on Afghanistan by an army of *feringhees*. The official report put it in the bluntest of terms: 'The Afghans regarded the intrusion of the British with hatred, and stragglers [of the advancing columns] were assassinated.'[22] The citizens of Kandahar, and later those of Kabul, looked on Shuja as an invader clinging to British coat-tails, and this was to be his undoing.

By late June, the 'politicals', as they were called, had raised sufficient funds to purchase supplies and transport animals from the local chieftains. Keane was determined not to lose momentum by lingering at Kandahar, so he took a calculated risk. A small flying column of a thousand men had been despatched to Girishk, where they easily routed Dost Mohammed's followers and imposed

Shah Shuja's authority. The western sector could be pronounced secured. Now Keane trained his sights on the main prize: Kabul. The Commander-in-Chief assembled a striking force of 8,000 regular troops, supported by 4,000 of Shuja's levies and an even vaster host of 50,000 camp followers. The force began its trek from Kandahar on 27 June, but owing to the length of the baggage columns it had to march out in four contingents on successive days, the slow-moving transport covering at best 10½ miles per day. The Army's obstinate insistence on travelling with a vast array of servants and camel drivers proved to be an encumbrance every stage of the way on the march to Kabul – on the retreat it was the cause of disaster. Even under these circumstances, Keane took extreme measures to speed up the advance. He had collected enough supplies to march his men on half rations for a month, and decided to chance it. He also gave orders to reduce the amount of equipment carried by leaving behind twelve guns, including the only four 18-pounders that had reached Kandahar. Keane's decision was based on intelligence provided by the politicals, who assured the military commanders the big guns would not be needed in the assault on Ghazni's fortifications, which were described through hearsay as 'despicable'. Nobody had bothered to send scouts to reconnoitre this citadel, lying as it did directly in the Army's route to Kabul, and which Dost Mohammed held to be the pièce de résistance of his defence network.

Leaving aside the logistical mistakes, the military side of the British campaign had up to then been favoured with incredible luck. The disunion of the Barakzais, after the Kandahar sirdars sent an envoy to the Shah of Persia, threw the family alliance into disarray. The city was left in a weakened state, so that the Army was able to march in without firing a shot. Dost Mohammed showed little surprise at the fall of Kandahar, and one wonders if he actually rejoiced at the humiliation its capture heaped on his disloyal brothers. Had the clan united to declare jihad against the invaders, encouraging as well the Khan of Khelat to join the holy war, the famine-starved Army of the Indus might have been trapped in a fatal pincer.

It was no less a stroke of luck that Keane managed to pull off his daring march to Kabul, despite committing a 'grievous military error', in the words of Durand, who rode with the column. Keane had no right to leave behind the only guns that were capable of blowing in the fortress walls of Ghazni. 'But, as if in mockery of human prudence and foresight,' Durand writes, 'war occasionally affords instances in which a mistake becomes, under the inscrutable will of Providence, the immediate cause of brilliant and startling success: and such this error ultimately proved.'[23] On 21 July, Keane and his men appeared before the gates of Ghazni. It was an admirable achievement, considering the recent debilitated state of the men, the widespread illness among the troops and baggage animals, and above all the fact that forty-two years later, with improved communications and transport, General Sir Donald Stewart took only two days less to cover the same distance in the Second Afghan War.

Dost Mohammed staked his hopes on breaking the British offensive under the massive crenellated walls of Ghazni. The Amir had plenty to occupy his attention in other quarters. With the Sikhs pressing on his eastern border – although their role never went beyond a show of force – and the British troops pressing from Kandahar, the Dost sent his son, Akbar Khan, to confront Ranjit Singh, mainly by inciting the Afridi tribesmen of the Khyber Pass to harass the Sikh column. The 10,000 troops of the combined northern force were under the military, as well as the political, control of Wade, the representative of British India at the Sikh court. Two other sons, Haidar Khan and Afzal Khan, were given the unenviable task of holding Ghazni and the surrounding countryside. Meanwhile, the Dost's Afghan dominions were crumbling before his eyes. Many of his subjects were in flight, had offered their submission to the British conquerors, or were rising up in revolt against the new amir. Kohistan is in the hill country north of Kabul, between the capital and the Hindu Kush. It has always been a turbulent region, its people's rebellious nature perhaps a manifestation of their homeland, lying where the Eurasian landplate and Indian subcontinent meet and collide. The Dost had to confront an open rebellion by the Kohistanis, as well as the Kizilbash, who made up the Persian community living chiefly in Kabul, and who also happened to be of the minority Shi'a sect. There had never been a more appropriate moment to exploit a weakened and vulnerable Amir.

Keane had brought up a strong column of foot artillery and European cavalry and infantry, more than sufficient to ensure victory over undisciplined levies. The danger was having to tackle the Afghans in their speciality as guerrilla fighters, or take on fortified posts like the one the troops now saw before them. Friction between the Army and the politicals, which dogged the entire campaign, was exacerbated by Macnaghten. He had come up from Kandahar and, wittingly or not, divulged to people in his camp the battle plans received from Keane. The attack depended on an element of surprise and could have been compromised by this leaked information, which found its way into the fortress and caused the defenders to maintain a dropping fire from the ramparts all night. Nevertheless, the general communicated to Auckland the troops' enthusiasm for a fight, while not underestimating the Afghan force of around 6,000 horsemen and foot soldiers waiting at the fort. 'We are told that the town and citadel is to be resolutely defended by the infantry, and that large bodies of cavalry are to attack us outside,' Keane wrote on the eve of battle. 'It will be put to the proof tomorrow.' Keane laboured under no illusions, knowing that Ghazni represented the most formidable obstacle on the road to Kabul. 'It is not only that the Afghan nation and, I understand, Asia generally, have looked upon it as impregnable, but it is in reality a place of great strength . . . far more so than I had reason to suppose from any description that I had received of it.'[24] The latter comment speaks volumes about a lack of proper intelligence, yet another source of dissension between the military and the politicals.

Late on 22 July, a deserter from the Barakzai clan made his way to Keane's tent on the Ghazni plain. This was Abdul Rashid Khan, a nephew of Dost Mohammed, who provided the general with a valuable piece of information. Keane, in the company of Cotton and the Army engineers, had reconnoitred the fort at daybreak, searching in vain for weak chinks in the armoured walls. Shah Shuja, who was with the party, by now considered it a lost cause. He advised giving Ghazni a wide berth and carrying straight on to Kabul. But Rashid Khan had some useful intelligence to report: the walls could not be broken by the guns the Army had brought along, but one of the entrances to the citadel, the Kabul Gate, was not properly fortified. It could, with the firepower at Keane's disposal, be blown in. That was the news Keane had been awaiting. He immediately gave orders for the assault to begin the following morning before dawn.

Another incident on that same day gives some clue as to why Shah Shuja's return to Afghanistan failed to excite any enthusiasm among his countrymen. A party of Ghazi horsemen had poured down on Shuja's tents in an attempt to do away with the man they despised as a betrayer of Islam, the traitor who had allied himself with the British infidels. The Ghazis were much-feared warriors who marched behind the standard of radical Islam. A counter-charge led by two British officers scattered the attackers, of whom some fifty were captured and brought into Shuja's camp. The Ghazis stood defiantly before Shuja, hurling insults at the pretender, when suddenly one of the prisoners drew a knife and stabbed a royal attendant. Shuja then calmly gave orders for all of them to be beheaded. The Ghazis were methodically hacked to death in the royal presence, a slaughter that occupied the better part of the afternoon. The blood-thirsty ruthlessness of Shah Shuja on that day marked quite a contrast with the praise that Auckland and Macnaghten had heaped upon his character in their reports.

That night, under a blustery sky that threatened rain, the batteries of artillery were gradually put into position at about 400yd from the ramparts. The moon had set at half-past ten, while Brigadier William Dennie was taking a storming party of four companies and a main column of British soldiers into position near the gate. A wing of native infantry was stealthily advancing towards the eastern wall, where they were to feign an attack to draw the enemy's attention once the explosives at the gate were detonated. The officer in charge of the whole storming party was General Robert ('Fighting Bob') Sale, who set a record among officers for collecting wounds in the Afghan campaign. On that day Sale took a scimitar wound in the face, which did not prevent him from continuing to direct the advance of his column. This was typical of Sale's fame as a fearless general who led from the front. He was revered by his men for riding about 2 miles ahead of his troops and fighting like a private. The day he was wounded, Sale was found by a British officer rolling on the ground, locked in hand-to-hand combat with the Afghan who delivered the scimitar blow to his face. Sale looked up at the startled captain of infantry and politely asked him to pass his sword through the infidel's body, which he obligingly did. The general, it might be added, was at the time nearly 60 years old.

Durand took the demolition party to within 150yd of the battlements when a shot rang out, followed by a shout from the wall that touched off a volley of musketry. The walls were instantly illuminated by blue flares, exposing the crouching figures below that were desperately edging along the ramparts for cover. The Afghans fired volley after volley, but failed to bring down a single man. Durand seized the moment to rush forward and lay a bag of powder, with a fuse, at the gate. The others came up quickly behind to drop their powder, 300lb in all, just as the native infantry launched their diversion attack and Keane's guns opened up from the plain: the assault on Ghazni had begun. Durand crept forward to uncoil the fuse, and was spotted by the Afghan defenders who jumped up on top of their parapets to pour fire at the foot of the wall, along with stones and any other missiles they could lay their hands on. One of the sappers tried to ignite the fuse, but his match failed. When he finally got it to light, working under fire, the fuse went out. Maddened with frustration, the engineer drew his pistol and fired at the fuse in a desperate attempt to set it alight. At the third attempt, the fuse gave off a steady blaze and the sapper dived for cover.

The gate was down, all was smoke and confusion inside the fort, and Dennie and Sale waited with their troops for the signal to attack. This never came, for the bugler had been shot through the head. Durand rushed up to the nearest party of infantry and after several agonising minutes of negotiating up the chain of command, a bugler was found: Dennie charged the gate with his four companies, Sale following behind with the main column. The debris-ridden gateway quickly became the scene of fierce hand-to-hand combat, sword against bayonet. Durand, who found himself in the thick of the fighting, reports that 'a few brave men' swept the gate clear of Afghan swordsmen to allow Sale's column to advance: 'The loud hurrahs of our men and the storm of musketry told Keane that Ghazni had been won.'[25] By sunrise, the Afghans had fled in panic, and a good thing too, for a drawn-out defence would have cost Keane well in excess of the 200 men he lost on the day. The Afghans took much heavier casualties, with nearly 2,000 killed or wounded. To add to the jubilation, the citadel was found to be well stocked, so that the troops were able to relieve the hunger and exhaustion they had been forced to endure since arriving at Kandahar.

It was by any measure a brilliant military operation, carried out with extreme gallantry and heroism, and one wonders why the storming of Ghazni is not assigned a more exalted station in the annals of British military victories. Keane's guns opened up at 3 a.m. and two hours later the British colours were planted on the citadel, less than forty-eight hours after the column had come before their objective. The general, in his report to Auckland, could hardly contain his euphoria, which reflected the general spirit of elation in the ranks. 'I have the satisfaction to acquaint your Lordship that the army under my command have succeeded in performing one of the most brilliant acts it has ever been my lot to witness during my service of 45 years in the four quarters of the globe,' Keane writes, 'in the capture, by storm, of the strong and important fortress and citadel of Ghazni.'[26] Keane was, for his service, elevated to the peerage as Baron Keane of Ghazni.

It is tempting to give Auckland the benefit of the doubt and assume that his tongue was tucked deep into his cheek, when in his reply he lauded 'the happy effects produced by the perfect cordiality and unanimity obtained between the political and military authorities' in the Afghan campaign.[27] Yet one fears that his memo was written in all sincerity, a reflection of the great wall that Macnaghten and his collaborators had erected around the Governor General.

There was more good news to report from the Afghan theatre of operations, this time on the eastern front where on the very day that Keane was celebrating his victory at Ghazni, Wade and the Sikh troops had won a strategic action in the celebrated and fiercely defended Khyber Pass. In this engagement a column under Wade and Shahzada Timur, Shuja's eldest son, captured the fort of Ali Musjid, a small outpost that had always held the Sikhs in check and which still commands a strategic position high in the pass.

The fall of Ghazni sent shock waves across Afghanistan. It was the unthinkable: messengers galloped in relays throughout the night to reach Dost Mohammed, who learnt of the catastrophe within twenty-four hours. The Amir took it as a devastating blow and when his son Afzal Khan arrived in Kabul to confirm the dreadful news, having left behind all his elephants and camp paraphernalia, his father refused to receive him. The Amir called a council of war, in which he flew into a rage and ordered all the faint-hearted out of his sight. A last-hour attempt to negotiate a settlement with the Saddozai chief and his British allies ended in humiliation – Shah Shuja had his sights set squarely on Kabul and would not accept any of the Amir's terms. In desperation, Dost Mohammed gathered what forces were still loyal to him and rode out to meet the enemy. British intelligence reports gave the Dost's strength as 13,000 men. The Amir drew up his troops at Arghandeh, 24 miles from Kabul, but the situation was becoming more hopeless by the hour. The Kizilbash deserted the Amir's standard in waves and a number of his trusted lieutenants had gone over to Shah Shuja's camp. Their reasoning was hard to fault: if Ghazni had fallen in a day's fighting, what hope for Kabul? The Dost was left abandoned in the field, surrounded by a handful of followers numbering no more than 300 horsemen. On 2 August, cursing bitterly all those who had chosen to purchase safety by tendering their allegiance to Shuja, Dost Mohammed and his men turned their horses to the snow-clad Hindu Kush.

The following day Keane and Macnaghten wrote to inform Auckland that Dost Mohammed had fled westward, heading towards Bamiyan, and that a strong party had set out in pursuit. Unfortunately the British had been taken in by Haji Khan Kakur, a former governor of Bamiyan province and unbeknown to the British, one of the Dost's few remaining loyalists. This shifty individual led the troops a merry chase through the twisting hills until all hope was lost of overtaking their quarry. Few in the British camp suspected that Kakur embodied the Machiavellian streak that is not uncommon in the Afghan character, and which was one of the factors that caused the Army's eventual undoing. One man did see through the diabolical double agent, but his was not a welcome voice amid the high-spirited revelry that followed the fall of Ghazni and the rout of Dost Mohammed. It was Durand who spoke of Kakur's conduct as 'indicative of the intention of passing over to whichever side should prove victorious'.[28] The traitor was duly put behind bars, but the general and the Envoy were not about to let this little contretemps spoil their party. With an open road ahead to Kabul and final victory only a few days' march away, Dost Mohammed had now become very much a secondary objective.

Keane led the Army's uneventful tramp across the empty wasteland separating Ghazni from Kabul, under whose gates the entire force gathered on the morning of 6 August. 'It gives me infinite pleasure to be able to address my dispatch to your Lordship from this capital,' Keane wrote, barely able to contain his well-merited sense of triumph. 'The King [Shah Shuja] entered his capital yesterday afternoon, accompanied by the British Envoy and Minister, and the gentlemen of the mission, and by myself, the general and staff officers of this army.'[29] Keane then explained that Shuja 'had expressed a wish that British troops should be present on that occasion, and a very small party only of his Hindustani and Afghan troops'. That Shuja should choose to flaunt his British benefactors before a defeated Muslim populace bears witness to the man's colossal arrogance and capacity for self-deception. Durand saw through the charade when he wrote, 'On that day, he [Shuja] found himself again upon the throne and in the palace of his ancestors, but placed there by British bayonets, a puppet-king, an insult to his people and their chiefs.'[30] Kaye's description of the investiture adds a more picturesque note: 'The jingling of the money-bags, and the gleaming of the bayonets of the British, had restored him [Shuja] to the throne which, without these glittering aids, he had in vain striven to recover.'[31]

The moment was at hand for the triumphal entry into Kabul, and what a glittering procession it was to be. After a thirty-year absence, Shah Shuja rode through the main Kabul Gate, mounted on a white Persian charger and splendidly attired in black velvet, flanked by Macnaghten, Keane and Burnes. The latter was regally turned out in a cocked hat fringed with ostrich feathers and a blue frock coat with epaulettes no less magnificent than those of a field marshal. Burnes rode along seemingly unconcerned that the handful of people along the route of the royal procession would recognise him as the British Envoy, who had until recently enjoyed the trust and hospitality of their vanquished king. The party was escorted by a squadron of Light Dragoons and one of the

16th Lancers, along with a troop of Horse Artillery. Many British officers found it ominous that all this pomp and panoply did not rate a single cheer or hand clap, though the stillness in the streets of Kabul failed to blunt Shah Shuja's elation. No sooner had Shuja taken possession of the city, he sat down to write a letter to Queen Victoria, informing the young monarch, to whom he referred as his 'Royal Sister', that 'by the favour of God and the exceeding kindness of the British Government', he had now ascended the throne of his ancestors. To further demonstrate his gratitude, Shuja had taken it upon himself to create a new order, to be known as the Order of the Durrani Empire, divided into three classes. First-class orders were conferred on those who had taken a direct hand in putting him back on the throne, namely Auckland, Keane, Macnaghten, Cotton, Burnes and Wade. A list was drawn up of officers who would receive second- and third-class orders, while a medal was struck and awarded to every officer and soldier who had taken part in the storming of Ghazni. Shuja, never to be faulted for an excess of modesty, expressed his confidence that Victoria would be graciously pleased to permit the gentlemen and soldiers mentioned in his honours list to wear their decorations, 'so that a memorial of me may be preserved, and that the fame of the glorious exploits achieved in this quarter may resound throughout the whole world'.[32]

Macnaghten announced to the officers present that on this day, the aims set out in the Simla Manifesto had been fulfilled. In consequence, Keane sent a report to the Governor General confirming that the campaign had achieved its final victory. 'I trust we have thus accomplished all the objects which your Lordship had in contemplation,' he wrote, 'when you planned and formed the Army of the Indus, and the expedition into Afghanistan.'[33] This was not quite the case. The Army had indeed placed Shuja on the throne of his forebears, but the real question was yet to be addressed: how to keep him there. So far, this had not troubled anyone's thoughts.

Chapter 3

DANCING IN THE DARK

K abul lies on the river of the same name, at an altitude of 6,000ft, below the foothills of the towering Hindu Kush, from whose frozen peaks in the winter months rushes a harsh and snow-laden wind. From April to September, the city is a delight. Since the days of the Moghul emperor Babur, in the early sixteenth century, Kabul had been the summer capital of princely families from Persia and Peshawar, who flocked to this garden city seeking its refreshing air, like the rulers of British India on their annual pilgrimage from Calcutta to the hills of Simla. When the soldiers of the Army of the Indus made their first acquaintance with Kabul in early August, they encountered a city of orchards and gardens laden with pomegranate and mulberry, and the clear and rapid stream of the Kabul river. There was a welcome air of gladness to the scenery, in marked contrast to the burning plains they had crossed on the long passage from Kandahar. The British encampment was permeated with an air of gaiety and the men were content to spend the warm nights under canvas, filling their days with excursions to the hills close to Kabul and visits to historic sites like Baba Shah's tomb and the Alexander obelisk. With their strength now restored, the troops soon began to feel the urge to partake in physical activities, for as Revd George Gleig, Chaplain General to the Army, explains, 'Wherever Englishmen go, they sooner or later introduce among the people whom they visit a taste for many sports.'[1]

The long late summer days were spent in horse racing and cricket, both of which aroused a lively interest among the Afghans. On one racing day, Shah Shuja himself got into the sporting spirit by offering a jewel-encrusted sword as a prize for the winning horse. The

16th Lancers even had with them their pack of foxhounds. Cricket was less of a success with the native gentry. Gleig reports that the Afghans looked on with astonishment at the bowling, batting and fagging out of the English players. 'But it does not appear that they were ever tempted to lay aside their flowing robes and huge turbans and enter the field as competitors.'[2] The English, however, frequently engaged their Afghan hosts in wrestling matches and feats of strength, and caused no little amazement with their ability to bring down snipes and quails. The Afghans were only experienced in shooting at stationary objects, a pastime they were later to indulge to their hearts' content at the expense of the British soldiery. But for now it was fun and games, including a theatre with painted scenery and elaborate costumes, to regale the Afghans with performances of *Irish Ambassador* and other music hall comedies in vogue in those days. Once winter had set in, the people of Kabul turned out in utter astonishment by the riverbank to contemplate the British gliding across the frozen water on knife blades.

Some critics in England, the Duke of Wellington prominent among them, had warned that the Army's difficulties would begin where its military successes ended. For now, however, things went on as could have been desired. 'The Afghan chiefs professed, and acted as if they felt something like regard for their European invaders individually,' Gleig recalls from his own observations, 'though they never scrupled to tell them frankly, that as a people, they were abhorred.'[3] The English by and large treated the people of Kabul with respect and made proper allowances for their Koranic principles, with one fatal exception. Afghan women in 1839 enjoyed a degree of liberty that would have horrified the fanatical Taliban a century and a half later. The stifling burkha, where worn, was no prophylactic against promiscuity and purdah. The seclusion of women from public observation was largely disregarded in all but the most orthodox families. As the Persian proverb says, 'A Kabul wife in burkha-cover, was never known without a lover.' This laxness led many an English soldier to mistakenly believe that Afghan men, at least in the capital, took a tolerant view of their strikingly beautiful women's flirtations. Nothing could be further from the truth. Afghan wives were kept under the same heavy-handed regime of almost insane jealousy that prevails in other

Muslim societies, thus it is not surprising that the ladies of Kabul were only too delighted to receive the attentions of the gallant, fair-haired *feringhees* in uniform. 'They [the women] leave their homes on the pretence of visiting mother, sister or female friend,' recalls Atkinson, who was with the Army in Kabul, 'and remain as long as they like. In some of the walls facing the streets, there are loopholes, with tiny shutters, through which an Afghan beauty is occasionally seen glancing furtively at the stranger passing by, and as often the old long-bearded husband may be observed sitting grimly in solemn stupidity at a wider aperture below.'[4]

The British ruled in Afghanistan as in India, just and impartial in their formal dealings with the vanquished, but often with a disregard for the sensitivities of those whose country they had overrun. Fraser-Tytler also notes that the female factor undid all chances of building a close social relationship with the people. 'Many writers have emphasised the harm this intercourse did to our relations with the Afghans, and there is no doubt of the truth of this assertion in a country where outwardly at any rate the honour of their women is of fanatical importance,' he says. 'But the old proverb, "necessity is the mother of invention and the father of the Eurasian" applied in 1840 with the same force in Afghanistan as it did in India.'[5]

Numerous romantic liaisons were formed, some of which led to the altar, such as the celebrated marriage of Captain Robert Warburton to a niece of Dost Mohammed, an episode that met with outrage at the Afghan court, since the princess in question already happened to be married to one of the Dost's courtiers. Burnes himself was not immune to the charms of Afghanistan's fabled beauties, even in his earlier years at the capital. There was always a strong undercurrent of rumour that Burnes antagonised the chieftains by his affairs with Afghan women. Those who directed the Kabul mob that was to cut him down in front of his residence had no difficulty in exploiting these allegations. Burnes was reputed to have kept a mistress when he was assistant to the resident in Cutch. 'Many years later he was to acquire some notoriety for his successes with the ladies of Kabul,' writes his biographer James Lunt, 'and there is no reason to suppose that the ladies of Cutch were any more proof against his charms than the sloe-eyed Afghan damsels.'[6]

After several weeks of merriment, the time was at hand to take a decision on the future of the Army of the Indus. The first winds of autumn were stirring and behind this, the winter snows that would make the passes to India extremely rough going for a column of troops. The Simla Manifesto clearly stated that once Shah Shuja was secured in power and the independence and integrity of Afghanistan established, the British Army would be withdrawn. It was equally clear to all that Shuja, though installed in Kabul's Bala Hissar citadel, was neither secured in power, nor did Afghanistan bear any resemblance to a settled state. After the frosty reception Shuja had received on his return to Kabul, and with Dost Mohammed still at large and presumed to be rallying his forces in the hills, nobody put any store in the king's ability to retain power without the aid of British bayonets. Yet Auckland could not afford to leave such a large body of soldiers so far from home, troops that might be needed to put down pockets of insurrection in India and keep a watchful eye on the unpredictable Sikh kingdom in the wake of Ranjit's death. The decision was taken to leave half a dozen regiments in Kabul to defend Shah Shuja, while the Bombay army would be withdrawn by the Bolan Pass, and Keane would take a portion of the Bengal contingent into India by the route of Jalalabad and the Khyber Pass. A brigade under General Robert Sale would remain in Afghanistan, eventually to be forcefully garrisoned in Jalalabad. In spite of the jolly times that all had enjoyed, no regrets were heard in the ranks at the prospect of leaving Afghanistan. As he was preparing to depart Kabul, Keane turned to a fellow officer who was to accompany him on the march, and uttered the fateful words, 'I cannot but congratulate you on quitting the country, for mark my words, it will not be long before some signal catastrophe takes place.'[7]

The bulk of the Army of the Indus marched out of Kabul on 15 October, leaving behind a force of Bengal troops under the distinguished cavalry commander General Cotton. Of the two European regiments one, the 13th Light Infantry, was at Kabul, and the other, the 1st Bengal European Regiment, was at Jalalabad. The other seven were regiments of Bengal Native Infantry. This was now, in the eyes of the Afghans, starting to look more like an army of occupation. General Nott was despatched from Quetta to

Kandahar, a decision that later raised a great deal of speculation over the possibility of a very different outcome to the disastrous Afghan campaign, had the cantankerous yet highly effective Nott been allowed to take overall command. Weeks later, the sense of alarm and resentment among the local inhabitants was raised a notch when word got round that the British troops had sent for their wives and families.

From the Government's perspective in London, the Afghan question had been neatly tied up. The Russian threat had been effectively stopped, Herat was saved, Dost Mohammed was on the run, the Army had taken remarkably few casualties and Shah Shuja was seated on the throne of Kabul. So it was gongs all round: Auckland was given an earldom, Keane was created a baron, Macnaghten a baronet, Wade (as Burnes before him) received a knighthood, and a shower of lesser distinctions descended upon the subordinate officers. Several thousand miles removed from Whitehall, on the high Afghan plains, a different reality was taking hold. Night now came on with a definitely frosty edge, and the men could not remain much longer on the open wind-swept plains. Each day the snow-line on the distant mountains descended a little lower. The question arose of where to garrison the troops within the city walls. The logical stronghold was the imposing Bala Hissar fortress, whose massive walls and hilltop prominence rendered it by far the most defensible structure in Kabul. There was growing concern among the military, if not Macnaghten and the politicals, over what looked like the first signs of revolt. In the middle of August sedition reared its head in the vicinity of Kabul, when the Army discovered that Sikh elements were conspiring to restore Dost Mohammed who, with his sons Akbar Khan and Afzal Khan, thanks to the intercession of the Shah of Persia, had escaped from Bokhara, where they had been sent to imprisonment by Shah Shuja. The Dost rode hard to Khulum to gather an army of Uzbeks and advance upon Bamiyan with 7,000 men. More disturbing news came in from Khelat, which was reported to have fallen into the hands of Baluch rebels. Intelligence was also received that Yar Mohammed, the *vizier* of Herat, was preparing to attack Kandahar.

Durand, as military engineer, put forward a vigorous argument for the troops to take possession of the Bala Hissar, which commanded the capital and with a garrison of a thousand men and a few guns could have held out indefinitely against any besieger. The proposal made sense to all but Shah Shuja, who after giving his initial assent, suddenly changed his mind and obstinately refused the Army permission to occupy the citadel. In his misguided vanity, the British puppet-king reasoned that since the Bala Hissar overlooked his own palace, his subjects would be certain to see him as ruling in the shadow of the British conquerors. Macnaghten then threw a spanner of his own in the works by rejecting Durand's proposal to use the Envoy's own spacious, wall-enclosed quarters to house the British troops, with the native soldiers to be lodged in Shah Shuja's large square of stables. Macnaghten was not going to allow that. Durand had already constructed a row of barracks in the Bala Hissar on the assumption that his scheme would meet with the approval of Shah Shuja, who instead gave up the barracks to his harem.

In the late summer days of 1840 the decision was taken to build the cantonments, or fortified lines, to house the troops and their families at Sherpur, a mile north of the Bala Hissar. Lieutenant Vincent Eyre, one of the few British survivors of the Afghan disaster, describes the cantonments as an undertaking defying rule and precedent. 'The position fixed upon for our magazine and cantonment was a piece of low swampy ground, commanded on all sides by hills or forts', none of which was occupied by the British, Eyre writes in his memoirs. The perimeter, nearly 2 miles round, was far too long to be manned effectively by the garrison, while the watery ground was hopeless for the quick movement of artillery or cavalry. Eyre observes with acerbity that, 'The credit of having selected a site for the cantonments, or controlled the execution of its works, is not a distinction now likely to be claimed exclusively by anyone.' Eyre, who served as the garrison's deputy commissary of ordnance, expresses a stark wonder of how the Government could have, 'in a half-conquered country' left their forces in so extraordinary and injudicious a military outpost as the exposed cantonments.[8] This 'fortified position' consisted of a low rampart and a narrow ditch in the form of a parallelogram, 1,000yd long and 600yd broad, with round flanking bastions at each corner. The Mission Compound, which served as the residence of the Envoy, officers and assistants of the occupation force, was a death trap. Its very existence a mile away from the troops' quarters rendered the whole face of the cantonments useless for purposes of defence. Even more baffling was having the commissariat sited a quarter of a mile from the cantonments in an old fort that, in an outbreak, would be indefensible. The authorities claimed to be far too busy erecting barracks for the men to take time out to consider such minutiae. The Army had its barracks and bungalows, and there was coffee after the morning ride, the gathering round the bandstand in the evening, the impromptu dance and the occasional *burra khana*, or gala dinner party, in the larger houses. And so, 'as in the days that were before the flood, they were eating and drinking, and marrying and giving in marriage, and knew not until the flood came, and took them all away'.[9]

Macnaghten had good reason to be a worried man. 'Day by day the cloud over Kabul grew darker,' says the official military report. 'An open enemy was in the field, and the Sikhs were pushing their intrigues to the very gates of the Bala Hissar.'[10] The Envoy wrote to the Governor General, describing the perilous situation, and quoted a note from General Cotton, in which he said there was now no Afghan army, and that unless the Bengal troops were strengthened the country could not be held. This time, the day was saved by Dennie and Sale, who engaged Dost Mohammed's rebel force at Bamiyan and in Kohistan, respectively.

On the morning of 18 September 1840, Dennie's column entered the Bamiyan valley, where it was met by the blood-curdling shrieks of hundreds of ferocious Uzbek horsemen pouring down from the hills. The enemy's swords and long-barrelled *jezails* proved an ill match for the devastating fire that was laid down by Dennie's horse artillery guns. A round of deadly volleys left the field littered with the bodies of the dead and dying, men and horses. The remaining attackers were sent scurrying back to the hills, and Dost Mohammed himself owed his life to the fleetness of his horse. Such was the Dost's rage at having been treacherously deprived of his throne by his once trusted allies, that a fortnight later the former Amir reappeared in Kohistan in the eastern Hindu Kush, a hotbed of more or less permanent insurrection, not 50 miles from Kabul. The Dost's anger was inflamed by the fact that his entire family, with the exception of the two sons who had shared his imprisonment in Bokhara, were in British hands in India.

On 3 October Sale, with Burnes as Political Agent riding by his side, advanced to attack Julgah, a fortified position held by the Kohistan rebels. To Sale's great dismay, the might of British arms was repulsed by the defenders of this fortified village. It was only the Afghan fighters' decision to evacuate rather than try their luck against a second charge that avoided a British rout. From that day the Kohistan region was rife with reports of Dost Mohammed's whereabouts, as the elusive fugitive flitted from one mountain hideout to the next. This went on until early November, when a most remarkable thing happened. Burnes was fed up with the humiliating setbacks the British had endured in the field in the weeks following the Julgah disaster, and in consequence he wrote to Macnaghten saying that there was nothing left but to fall back upon Kabul. Dost Mohammed's thoughts were ahead of his enemies'. He reasoned that in time the British would redouble their efforts and send a more powerful force against him. Now was the time for him to retire from the conflict with grace and dignity, having proved himself capable of inflicting defeat on the *feringhee*. The Dost rode with a single horseman for twenty-four hours to Kabul, where he came across an English gentleman returning from his evening ride. This was Macnaghten, who was approached by the Dost and having ascertained his identity, found himself lost for words. The scene is described by Kaye from first-hand accounts:

> Throwing himself from his horse, Dost Mohammed saluted the Envoy, said he had come to claim his protection, and placed his sword in Macnaghten's hand. But the Envoy, returning it to him, desired the Amir to remount. They then rode together into the Mission compound, Dost Mohammed asking many eager questions about his family as they went.[11]

One can well imagine the Envoy's perplexity and the Dost's amusement in this unparalleled situation of a victorious adversary surrendering to his enemy.

After a few days' rest in Kabul, on 12 November 1840, Dost Mohammed was sent into exile where he eventually took up residence at Ludhiana, in the same quarters as his Saddozai kinsman who now sat on the throne from which the Dost had of late been ejected. The Amir did not suffer from want of company on his journey. Apart from his 9 wives and another 21 spouses of his sons, the royal progress was accompanied by 102 female slaves to look after the wives and another 210 male slaves and attendants, plus numerous grandchildren and other relations, making up a party of 381 people in total. The Amir was first sent on a visit to Calcutta, where he was joined by his son Haidar Khan, who had been despatched from Bombay. Bizarrely, Dost Mohammed was treated as a visiting dignitary at Auckland's banquets and gala balls in Government House. The Amir found the steaming climate of Calcutta not to his liking, so he persuaded Auckland to have him removed to Ludhiana with a personal allowance of 300,000 rupees per year to cover his household expenses.

During his ten-day stay in Kabul, the Dost could not help but take great joy in the British plight. Day after day, the war clouds gathering over Kabul grew denser and darker, though it would be another year before the storm broke in its full fury. The efforts at raising a regiment of Afghan infantry, which was intended to become the embryo of a national army to support Shah Shuja on his throne, ended in failure when a number deserted their colours and joined Dost Mohammed's rebels. The Envoy was almost daily in receipt of distressing news of insurrection everywhere south of the Oxus, while Kabul was crawling with conspirators sewing the seeds of insurrection. The Khyber Afridis who controlled the key passage between India and Afghanistan were in revolt, the Sikhs were pushing their intrigues right up to the gates of the Bala Hissar, while the Durrani tribes north-west of Kandahar were up in arms against Shah Shuja.

Soon after Dost Mohammed was packed off to exile in India, Macnaghten made his final preparations to accompany Shuja on a seasonal retreat to Jalalabad. Peshawar was historically the winter capital of the Afghan court but this was out of the question, for the city was, of course, still held by the Sikhs. It cannot be said that Shuja's return to power had fulfilled his expectations. It was a

melancholy set of circumstances for a man who deep in his heart
knew that he was nothing without his British masters. He would
spend hours on end sitting at a window of his palace below the
soaring ramparts of the Bala Hissar, whiling away his time, fearful
of contact with his hostile subjects. He complained to visitors that
his authority had been usurped by his allies, and those close to
him described him as nervous and irritable, and in failing health.
Durand tells us that 'everything appeared to him [Shuja] shrunk,
small and miserable, and that the Kabul of his old age in no respect
corresponded with the recollections of the Kabul of his youth'.[12] He
therefore greeted with relief the opportunity to escape the depress-
ing surroundings of the capital and retire to the warmer lowlands
of Jalalabad, where he spent the next five months contemplating
the sad predicament of a king whose rule barely extended beyond
his palace gates.

Into this unhappy scenario walked, or more accurately was carried,
William Elphinstone, the unwilling, newly appointed commander of
the British forces in Afghanistan. It was April 1841, and the 59-year-
old Elphinstone, suffering from gout, with one arm in a sling, had
made most of the journey from Calcutta to Kabul in a palanquin, a
fitting symbol of the crippled state of British India's Afghan policies.
Elphinstone is invariably the most heavily criticised of all the soldiers
and politicals who had a hand, directly or otherwise, in the downfall
of the garrison. Those whose misfortune it was to have served under
Elphinstone at Kabul, as well as the historians and administrators
who later sought to explain the causes of the Afghan disaster, struggled to find a kind word for the doddering Major-General, an officer
who was incapable of taking an independent decision. Auckland's
sister Emily Eden had nicknamed him 'Elfi Bey', perhaps unwittingly
after the ill-fated Mameluke ruler of Egypt. In his youth, Elphinstone
had performed outstanding acts of gallantry, most notably with the
33rd Foot at Waterloo, where he commanded with such distinction
that he was made a CB, a Knight of the Order of William of Holland
and of the Order of St Anne of Russia. Since 1839, he had been
in command of the Benares Division of the Bengal army. Alas, the

famous battle of 1815, a quarter of a century before, was the last time Elphinstone had seen active service.

Eyre describes him as a soldier with an illustrious past, who was now 'in want of confidence in his own judgement, leading him to prefer everybody's opinion to his own until, amidst the conflicting views of a multitude of counsellors, he was at a loss which decision to take. Hence much of that indecision, procrastination, and want of method, which paralysed all our efforts, gradually demoralised the troops, and ultimately, not being redeemed by the qualities of his *second in command* [author's italics], proved the ruin of us all.'[13] To Fraser-Tytler, Elphinstone was a person 'infirm in mind and body and ignorant of the country or people with which he was dealing, he was faced with a crisis requiring speed, decision and leadership, in all of which qualities he was deficient'.[14] Kaye, to whom must be ceded the last word on almost all matters concerning the First Afghan War, acknowledges what in those days could be taken as Elphinstone's few saving graces, for in spite of everything he was an old officer of the Queen's service, of good repute, gentlemanly manners, and aristocratic connections. 'But,' Kaye points out on a more sombre note, 'it must have been a wonder to him, as it was to all who knew him, what business he had in such a place. He had no Indian experience of any kind, and he was pressed down by physical infirmities.'[15]

Indeed, what on earth was Elphinstone doing in Kabul? Who had sent him there, and why? One person who was instrumental in sending Elphinstone to Kabul was Fitzroy Somerset, the future Lord Raglan. As military secretary at the Horse Guards, Raglan exercised considerable influence over army appointments. John Hobhouse, President of the Board of Control, had raised strong objections to Elphinstone's candidacy, thinking him too ill and weak-minded to take on the task. But Raglan was a friend of Elphinstone, and also of the Duke of Wellington, who declined to support Hobhouse's reservations. It will be recalled that Raglan also bore responsibility for the charge of the Light Brigade at Balaclava in 1854. The most that can be said in Raglan's favour in the Crimean episode, was that the debacle might have been the result of a misunderstanding of orders. But as commander of the expeditionary force sent to fight Russia, the buck stopped at Raglan's desk. Had his blunder at Balaclava and the appointment of a commander in Afghanistan occurred in reverse order in history, Wellington might have treated Raglan's judgement with greater scepticism.

Elphinstone's appointment was prompted by the resignation, on grounds of ill health, of General Sir Willoughby Cotton. Nott would have appeared to be Cotton's heir apparent, but the thought of the peppery, single-minded commandant at Kandahar running affairs in Afghanistan was anathema to Auckland, as well as to Macnaghten and the other politicals in Kabul. Nicolls favoured Nott's candidacy, but Nott had given offence to too many people, including Shah Shuja. Nott was something of a practitioner in feather-ruffling, as on the occasion he rounded on the 'thousand and one politicals' who had ruined the British cause and bared the throat of every European in Afghanistan 'to the knife of the revengeful Afghan'. Not to let anyone escape his sights, he summarily despatched Shah Shuja as 'the greatest scoundrel that ever lives'.[16]

The Government sought a man of a more docile nature, preferably someone opinionless and disinclined to make trouble for the Envoy and his entourage. Elphinstone's heart was not in the job, though he hoped that the move from the steaming plains of Bengal to the bracing uplands of Kabul might provide some relief for his gout, which unfortunately was not the case. But he took the post, for Auckland's offer had the distinct undertone of an order, and Elphinstone had been brought up to obey his superiors. To give Elphinstone his due, he spotted the weakness of the garrison's position the day he arrived in Kabul. His first recommendation, which was to build a proper fort for the troops, made perfect sense. The Government summarily rejected his request for £2,400 to carry out the works. Elphinstone went as far as to offer to buy some of the land surrounding the cantonments out of his own pocket, and level the orchards and gardens in order to clear a field of fire. From the start, Elphinstone was made to see that he was not expected to come up with initiatives. After all, the occupation of Afghanistan was already costing more than £1 million a year, well in excess of what Calcutta had budgeted when the Army was sent across the Indus. In Kabul alone, the Government had to bear the expense of maintaining four infantry regiments, two batteries of artillery, three companies of sappers, a regiment of cavalry and some irregular horse – a force of more than 4,500 men (it is important to keep in mind) fully equipped and in good order.

It is disputable to what extent Cotton's request to be relieved of his command was due to actual ill health, or a secret desire to be shot of a place that was starting to look like a death-trap. The first senior officer to walk away in open conflict with the Government was Brigadier Abraham Roberts, father of Lord Roberts of Kandahar, the hero of the Second Afghan War. Roberts, who commanded Shah Shuja's contingent, had had a bitter falling out with the Envoy, who rejected the brigadier's advice on the formation of an Afghan national army and dismissed his warnings of impending disaster as alarmist. 'His [Roberts'] clear insight into the dangers which were beneath our feet had been regarded as idle and imbecile fear,' writes Kaye, 'and the unwelcome declarations of his honest convictions as little short of mutiny.'[17] Roberts was replaced by Brigadier Thomas John Anquetil, a 60-year-old India hand with no qualms about taking on a command in Elphinstone's shadow.

If the choice of Elphinstone for Afghanistan was a calamitous error, the decision to send Brigadier John Shelton as his second in command fulfilled all expectations of disaster. Shelton was Colonel of the 44th Foot, a regiment that under his leadership had earned the enmity of the Indian Army for its refusal to fraternise with the native troops. Shelton's reputation was that of a morose, obstinate and irascible man totally lacking in respect for Elphinstone, whose gentle patience he pushed to the limit. This hostility between the chief and his second in command effectively undermined the decision-making process in Kabul at the worst possible time, for the crisis was now reaching boiling point. Shelton had lost his right arm in the Peninsular War, and a life of incessant pain caused by the crude surgical tactics of those days may be what darkened his character. A further misfortune was that Sale's brigade, the 13th Light Infantry, was due to return to India along with the 35th and 37th. These were seasoned India troops who had always maintained cordial relations with their sepoy comrades, the ideal soldiers to garrison an outpost that was soon to come under siege, making close proximity between Europeans and Indians a daily necessity.

By the spring of 1841, the cost of the continued occupation of Afghanistan was causing much anxiety in Calcutta and London. The East India Company was looking at an outlay that had spiralled to more than £1.25 million a year, though it has been said that Auckland was concealing a much larger deficit from the Secret Committee. The Board of Control was disgusted with the whole Afghan venture, which it openly denounced as a failure. Nicolls, the highest-ranking officer in British India, considered it a waste of money, tying down 25,000 men between Quetta and Karachi, plus nearly thirty political officers whose authority was resented by the army staff. The maintenance of Shah Shuja's forces alone accounted for nearly half that disbursement, an expense that did not gain much favour in Government circles where the unhappy Amir was increasingly regarded as excess baggage. After a little more than a year and a half on the throne, Shuja had failed to pacify his rebellious subjects.

Shelton had arrived in Kabul in a particularly foul mood, having been met with unforeseen resistance by the Afridi tribesmen on his passage through the Khyber Pass. The Durrani chiefs in Kabul were in a state of agitation, motivated by a rumour going round the bazaar that Shah Shuja was all in favour of a revolt that would free him from the British yoke. One of the seditious chieftains harboured a particularly deep grudge against Shah Shuja. Uktar Khan was nursing the double grievance of having been deprived of the governorship of Zemindawar province on the western bank of the Helmund, and having been roughly treated by the minions of Prince Timour, Shuja's heir apparent. General Nott, who was commander of Kandahar, sent a detachment with guns to chase him out of Zemindawar. The Afghan rebel was routed, leaving about sixty of his followers dead in the field, but the action served as yet another portent of things to come. Nott and his Political Officer, the famed orientalist and gallant soldier Sir Henry Rawlinson, were two men with a clear vision of where Auckland's Afghan policy was leading, but their warnings were not heeded in Kabul. Macnaghten in particular refused to acknowledge that the British power in Afghanistan was a chimera, and that opposition to Shah Shuja was growing stronger by the day.

The coming Afghan rebellion was not Calcutta's only source of concern. East of the Indus, the Punjab was rapidly deteriorating into anarchy. Ranjit Singh's heir, the weakling Sher Singh, was incapable of maintaining discipline in the Army. Calcutta took this with alarm, for the Government had relied on Ranjit to preserve stability in his kingdom, which shared a sensitive border with British India.

Two fatal policy decisions by Calcutta, both of which fall under the heading of cost-cutting, served to ignite the powder keg. The first was the order to retire Sale's brigade to India, the second the withdrawal of the subsidies, or more accurately, the bribes, that were dispensed to the tribal chiefs to keep open the roads between Kabul and the Khyber Pass.

Two subsequent uprisings broke out in the villages of the Zurmut and Ghudabund region east of Kabul, and once these relatively minor disturbances had been put down, at the beginning of October 1841, Sale was ordered to ready his men for the homeward march. The route via Jalalabad and the Khyber Pass was deemed to be peaceable, according to intelligence in the hands of the Kabul authorities. So confident was Elphinstone of the brigade's unmolested passage, based as usual on dubious second-hand information, that he refused Sale's request to supply him with serviceable rifles from the commissariat. The men's arms were, for the most part, unreliable flint and steel muskets that were in the habit of misfiring continually, and occasionally blowing up. The best of these old blunderbusses was just as likely to carry its ball wide of the mark as in a straight line. The Kabul garrison had in its armoury 4,000 perfectly new, unused muskets constructed on the detonating principle, but Elphinstone would not listen to the proposal. He reminded Sale that his men were on the first stage of their journey back to England, and that the rifles needed to remain behind for the defence of India. The old general's argument might have merited some justification had the weapons actually been used for this purpose. They were not, and when the Kabul mob finally broke out in open rebellion, 800 of these pristine rifles fell into the hands of the insurgents.

Sale's brigade began moving out of Kabul in stages via the Jalalabad Gate, starting on 9 October. The full column was made up of some 1,600 men of the 13th Light and 35th Native Infantry. The general was at first informed that he could expect a routine passage, that nothing would be exacted from his men other than the good conduct expected of British troops moving from one quarter to another. In reality, the retreat to Jalalabad became something of a dress rehearsal for the great calamity that was to befall the British force three months later. What had happened in the intervening period to change Sale's mission from that of an orderly withdrawal to a punitive expedition?

October 1841 marked the fatal turning point in the fortunes of the British force in Afghanistan. In late September, Macnaghten had summoned the Ghilzai, Kohistan and Kabul tribal chiefs to his residence for a meeting. Much to the Envoy's regret, and he was quite sincere about this, the Government in Calcutta had ordered a reduction in the subsidies paid for safeguarding the roads and passes to India. The shortfall was caused, first and foremost, by the expense of keeping Shah Shuja and his more than 800 wives plus retainers in the style to which they were accustomed. Macnaghten had objected to the retrenchment, pointing out that the stipends paid to the chiefs were simply compensation for abstaining from their immemorial practice of highway robbery, but he yielded to Auckland's pressure. Macnaghten informed the chiefs that thenceforth their subsidies would be reduced. The Envoy conveyed his fears to the Government, explaining that such a move was inviting dire consequences, for the maxim 'my word is my bond' held true among the Afghan tribes exactly as it did in the City of London. But Auckland, the Secret Committee and even Burnes closed ranks against the Envoy's superior judgement. Their argument was that the occupation of Afghanistan was proving to be too expensive an undertaking. Auckland explained, and with impeachable reason, that an early withdrawal of the entire Army was unthinkable, for this would trigger an instant uprising against Shah Shuja. Then standing logic on its head, the Governor General concluded that if the Army needed to be kept in place until stability was restored to Afghanistan, financial considerations dictated that this could only be achieved with a cutback in expenditure.

The immediate deficit amounted to 170,000 rupees (about £14,000) per year, which was to be made good in part from the allotments paid to the Ghilzai and Kohistan tribes, who would see their annual subsidies halved to 40,000 rupees. A document in the British Library India Office written anonymously by 'an Officer in the Honourable East India Company's Service', highlights the folly of this decision. 'There is a remarkable instance of honour amongst robbers furnished by the conduct of the tribes with whom we have just been engaged,' writes this officer, who was high ranking enough to be privy to Macnaghten's discussions with the chieftains. 'During the period of nearly three years, in which they have been in our pay, not one single letter or dispatch was ever lost on its way by this route to Kabul, and the transit of the whole merchandise passing the hills was as secure as if in one of our own provinces.'[18]

The assembled tribal leaders sat in silence as Macnaghten explained the Government's reasons for reducing their allowances. When he had finished speaking, the chiefs nodded and rose to leave as one, not uttering a word. They then convened a meeting of their own, in which they swore an oath on the Koran to support one another in their attempt to exact revenge on the deceitful *feringhees*. Within days, the deep gorges and formidable passes on the road from Kabul to British India had been turned into a no man's land. The tribesmen almost immediately managed to recoup half their losses by attacking a camel caravan on its way to India, carrying 20,000 rupees' worth of goods, as it passed east of Kabul at Tezeen. All communication with India was cut, leaving Kabul an isolated outpost inhabited and surrounded by an enemy that was gathering its forces to strike at the occupying Army. The long-barrelled *jezails* peeking from behind the stone breastworks that festooned the crests of the passes between Kabul and Jalalabad, were now in place not to safeguard British troops, but to fire on them. Even the Revd Gleig, who accompanied Sale's brigade, displayed an admirable sympathy for the wrongs suffered by those who despised the religion he preached. 'And hence arose, by degrees, distrust, alienation and hostility,' he writes, 'for which it were unfair to deny that there might be some cause.'[19]

Macnaghten pompously played down the seriousness of the revolt, which he dismissed in a letter to Rawlinson in Kandahar as a 'provocation', promising rather cockily that 'the rascals would be well trounced for their pains'.[20] Yet reports of imminent uprising were coming in from all quarters. Eldred Pottinger, Political Agent in Kohistan, rode down to Kabul to impress on the Envoy that a general revolt by the hill tribes was certain to break out in a matter of days. Reports now reached Kabul that Akbar Khan, the chief perpetrator of mischief, had moved forward from Khulum to Bamiyan and was inching menacingly closer to the capital, with murder in his heart.

It was under this ominous cloud that Sale set out to 'trounce the rascals' that lay in waiting in the passes. To deepen the general air of apprehension, it was feared that the entire Afghan strategy stood in danger of losing any semblance of coherent political leadership. In Britain, the Conservatives under Sir Robert Peel had come to power and a question mark hung over their support for the continued military occupation of Afghanistan. It was also widely known that Auckland, prompted by the defeat of the Whigs in the June election, had sent a letter to Hobhouse at the Board of Control in London, expressing his wish to be relieved of his duties before the end of 1841. Peel favoured as Auckland's successor Lord Ellenborough, an outspoken critic of the Afghan intervention. Then too, Macnaghten had been selected to take over from Sir James Carnac as Governor of the Bombay Presidency, the sweetest plum that the East India Company had to offer, short of the governor generalship itself. The Envoy's long exile in the harsh and now dangerous climate of Kabul was at last coming to an end. Alexander Burnes was the strong favourite to replace Macnaghten, a prospect that gave much gratification to the mercurial Burnes, but to few others in Kabul. Sadly, neither man was to see his political ambitions fulfilled, for the insurrectionist mob of Kabul had other plans for Burnes and Macnaghten. The Envoy was convinced that the local rebellion instigated by the tribal chiefs could easily be suppressed. So certain was the ingenuous Macnaghten that the Army would soon have matters under control, that he began making plans to depart Kabul on 20 October.

The first column to ride out of Kabul on 9 October was the 35th Native Infantry under Lieutenant-Colonel Thomas Monteith, who marched towards the passes with some artillery and cavalry details, as well as a detachment of Sappers and Miners under Major George Broadfoot, the eldest of three brothers, all of whom died sword in hand. This last unit boasted a curious, ragtag bunch of Hindustani fighting men who caused much astonishment among the regular troops. Broadfoot himself described his corps as being made up of '300 brave Hindustanis, 200 braver Gurkhas and 100 Afghan heroes'. Recruitment was on a no-questions-asked basis, following the advice given by a shrewd Afghan to take on men 'of broken clans, ruined, houseless, and with no other resources'.[21] Broadfoot mercilessly instilled in his corps an iron discipline, the men adored their commanding officer and they performed reckless feats of courage on the battlefield to gain his admiration. Each of these soldiers would be worth his weight in gold in the coming battle for the passes.

The operation got under way in a chaotic fashion that heralded the coming breakdown of military discipline. Before the brigade's departure, Broadfoot went to Monteith for guidance on what tools to take, but was told by the commander of the 35th that he had received no orders. Broadfoot then boldly marched to Elphinstone's quarters, where he found the poor gentleman so exhausted by the exertion of getting out of bed that it took him fully half an hour to prepare himself for visitors. He was unable to give Broadfoot any orders, so the next port of call was Macnaghten's residence, where he was subjected to a tirade on General Elphinstone's feebleness and was angrily told to take a handful of men with pickaxes, or to remain behind if he had misgivings about his superiors. If Akbar Khan, who by this time had brought his forces to within a few miles of Sale's position, knew the extent to which the defences of Jalalabad had been weakened, he committed a great tactical blunder by not taking advantage of such an opportunity.

Sale received orders on 12 October to follow Monteith's column, and in all haste, for the 35th had come under surprise night attack, with heavy losses, at Butkhak, a spot only 7 miles east of Kabul on the first halting place along the Jalalabad road. The men were ready for a fight, but given the lack of preparedness for any emergency in the Kabul command, all was improvisation. The troops had neither been informed of the situation on the road, nor whether they were embarking on a routine march to India or as an expedition for the relief of their comrades of the 35th, who were pinned down near the Khoord Kabul Pass. Nobody had had the foresight to make ready sufficient numbers of camels and other transport animals. Therefore the men, for the first time in Indian warfare, undertook to carry their own knapsacks, lightening their loads to the barest essentials, which came to one spare shirt, one pair of socks, one pair of boots, soap, towel and cooking utensils. The troops marched with forty instead of the standard sixty rounds of ammunition in their pouches, the remaining twenty to be carried on the pack animals, with the great risk of finding themselves separated from the transport in the narrow defiles.

Sale left behind in Kabul his wife, Florentia Sale, to look after her pregnant daughter Alexandrina and her wounded son-in-law, the garrison engineer Lieutenant John Sturt. Lady Sale was not only the lionhearted *memsahib* of the Afghan war, but also a truly outstanding heroine of the Victorian age. When Sturt fell mortally wounded on the retreat from Kabul, it was Lady Sale who ensured that her son-in-law received a Christian burial, the only victim of the massacre to be so honoured. It is through the journal left by Lady Sale, who was 51 years old when her husband Fighting Bob took his brigade to the passes, that we are left a superb blow-by-blow, eye-witness account of the Afghan campaign, from General Sale's march to Jalalabad, through the awful hardships of the retreat of the Army of the Indus, to the captivity and final deliverance of the British hostages who were being held by Akbar.

It was assumed that Sale's brigade would with little effort sweep aside the Ghilzais who had blocked the passes on the road home. Once that was accomplished, it was planned that Lady Sale would join her husband, and the infirm Elphinstone would be evacuated down the same road to safety. Elphinstone had already despatched a letter to Auckland, in which he expressed his wish to step down, being in his own opinion unfit 'body and mind' to remain in Kabul. Elphinstone and Macnaghten were so complacent regarding their imminent departure, that both men put their furniture up for sale by auction, fetching extremely high prices. Sale never suspected that this 'walkover' to clear the passes would in fact require seventeen days of pitched battles, the column fighting its way through at 4 miles a day, with the loss of thirteen officers and almost three hundred men before reaching Jalalabad. Sale's punitive expedition, as a prelude to the Army's full retreat along the same road, turned into the most severe fighting with the greatest losses that British troops had yet encountered in Afghan warfare.

Sale reached Monteith's camp where the doughty colonel proudly informed him that the raiders had been beaten off, but not before they had managed to abscond with eighty camels, a loss that threatened to play havoc with the column's further advance. On the evening of 12 October, Sale was able to report back to Elphinstone that 'the task of forcing the pass of Khoord Kabul and defeating the rebels posted within it has, this morning, been accomplished'.[22] The unembellished tone of Sale's memorandum disguised what had been a hard-fought engagement in the Khoord Kabul, the hellish defile that was soon to be littered with the bones of several thousand soldiers and camp followers of the retiring Army.

The brigade had started its slow advance towards the towering cliffs that enclose the pass at dawn on 12 October. An uncomfortable silence prevailed in the canyon-like gorge, similar to the stillness that descends on the earth before the onset of a cataclysm. The column was met by no opposition until the main body was well inside the pass, where in some places the walls are no more than a few feet apart, making retreat impossible. That was when the storm broke. With a round of deafening explosions, a hail of musket balls rained down from the rocks and precipices on either side. Revd Gleig, who was with the force, recalls:

> So skilful, too, were the Afghans in the art of skirmishing, that except by the flashes which their matchlocks emitted, it was impossible to tell where the marksmen lay. Rocks and stones, some of them hardly larger than a thirteen-inch shell, seemed to afford them excellent shelter. They squatted down, showing nothing above the

crag except the long barrels of their fusils and the tops of their turbans, and with such unerring aim were their shots thrown, that from the advance guard and from the body of the column men soon began to drop.[23]

Sale was one of the first to be hit by a musket ball, which splintered his ankle, his second wound of the Afghan campaign. Fighting Bob remained in his saddle and directed the operations until loss of blood forced him to hand over the command to Brigadier Dennie, the officer who had so skilfully led a storming party at Ghazni on the day Sale sustained his first injury. Sale gave orders for 200 of his trusted Afghan fighters to create a diversion by attacking the precipitous ridge on which the enemy had constructed their *sangars*, or stone breastworks. The rebels blocked the road through the gorge with a barrier put up with tree trunks and stone, behind which they directed an incessant fire at the oncoming column. Sale's own troops charged the barricade, while in a display of outstanding gallantry, two companies of the 13th and one of the 35th scrambled up the cliff faces on either side to dislodge the snipers at bayonet point. The entire brigade emerged from the eastern end of the 5-mile-long gorge at two o'clock that afternoon, having fought without a respite for seven hours.

Once the plains on both sides of the pass had been secured, Sale gave instructions for the sick and wounded to be carried back to Kabul. On the morning of 22 October the brigade was once more put on the march, advancing from Khoord Kabul towards Tezeen, the next staging post on the road to India, though few of the officers would have given odds on their making the crossing unmolested, if at all. From the bowl-shaped valley that debouched at the exit of Khoord Kabul, the column wound its way in a state of high alert across the plain, until they plunged into the next ravine, the Huft Kotal Pass. The crossing of this dark 17-mile corridor would require an all-day, nerve-racking march. The troops entered the shadowy chasm with terror in their hearts, barely daring to lift their eyes to the soaring promontories on either side, for fear of spotting the glint of long muzzles aimed at the exposed men below. Monteith had his flankers out, searching for signs of activity in the valley. They were called in as the brigade approached the entrance to the pass, to form a tight unit ready to deliver a sharp returning fire. Gleig, like the others, was keenly aware of their helpless position. 'It is hardly necessary to state that troops passing through such a ravine . . . however brave and disciplined they may be, feel that they are powerless,' he writes. 'They see that to change their formation is impossible, and that a few resolute men – indeed, that women or even children might, by rolling huge stones over the precipices, destroy them.'[24] Most of the men had never before experienced the destructive power of invisible snipers firing from behind the bullet-proof stones of hilltop *sangars*, a skill at which the Afghans excelled. To everyone's amazement and relief, apart from a handful of horsemen galloping back and forth along some of the more distant ridges, the enemy was nowhere in sight.

Two huge rocks rise like doorposts at the passage out of Huft Kotal, leading into the valley of Tezeen. The advance guard was nearly at this spot when the officer commanding the leading files suddenly threw up his hand and gave the order to halt his men – an Afghan war party had drawn up a few hundred yards ahead, whooping and waving their *jezails* above their heads. Monteith rode up and ordered the entire advance guard to close up and move forward, at which point the surrounding crags and hills were seen to be swarming with Afghans. The body of horsemen at the end of the pass had been placed as a decoy to lure the British cavalry forward and let loose a fire that in an instant would have emptied every saddle. The infantry immediately stood aside, right and left, to allow the guns to come up to the front at a gallop. The gunners unlimbered in haste, loaded and fired with such striking precision as to send the surviving horsemen fleeing in all directions. Dennie rode up to the front, where a young lieutenant, Edward King, a hero of the storming of Julgah the previous year, begged to have leave, with the company under his command, to drive 'the rascals' from the hill to which they had retreated and regrouped. Dennie, who was in temporary command of the force while Sale recovered from his wound, cast a glance over the scene and replied, 'Surely.' King and his men set off to rush the Afghan position, dispersing the enemy from the hill they held and scattering the remnants far and wide across the valley to ensure they did not pose a threat to the brigade's advance.

The troops were soon to find that they had underestimated the stubbornness of the Afghan insurgents. The main body pushed on, while the two companies sent out as skirmishers were kept engaged in a constant exchange of fire with marksmen on the hills. Ammunition was running short, making it steadily more difficult for the troops to keep their pursuers at a safe distance. To this day, the identity of the officer who issued the order to retreat remains a mystery. Instructions came up from the main body of the brigade for the troops to fall back by companies, one descending the nearest hill while the other, holding its ground, was to lay down a covering fire to keep the Afghans at bay. With empty ammunition pouches, the men misunderstood this as a signal to move back *en masse*, so that the retreat swiftly became a rout, soldiers racing across the open ground in a race for life or death. The Afghans took courage from what they perceived to be a panic run, and gave chase with *jezails* blazing and their Khyber daggers slashing left and right. King fell with a bullet in his heart, only moments before three fresh companies were sent up to regain the ground that the skirmishers had lost. Dusk was now closing in and just before darkness fell across the plain, the brigade's guns began blasting away at the attacking force. The Afghans had no stomach for artillery fire; indeed they had wreaked enough destruction on the force to claim a day of victory for the rebels. The weary defenders remained in position until eleven o'clock that night, when Sale sent out orders for them to return to camp.

Sale was piqued at the obstinacy of the Afghan insurgents and he was determined to teach them a lesson. The next day, before starting on the advance towards Jalalabad, the general instructed Dennie to take half the infantry, with a battery of guns, and attack a fortified stronghold of the rebel chiefs. Word of the impending attack got back to the Ghilzais and on 23 October, there appeared in Sale's camp a delegation of Afghans riding under a flag of truce, professing their desire to seek terms of submission from the Political Agent, Captain George Macgregor. The message from the Afghan camp was a mixture of threats and entreaties. If the British attacked, the insurgents would flee to the hills, destroying on the way their entire stock of winter provisions. The Army would find only scorched earth, with nothing left on which to feed the men or their pack animals. On the other hand, the Afghans had no wish to continue the fight, and asked for terms. The chief was even prepared to hand over high-ranking hostages as a guarantee of his honourable intentions. Macgregor read the letter that was handed to him, he took it to Sale's tent, and gave the general his opinion that the enemy had genuinely lost their taste for battle. True to their word, at six in the evening the Afghans delivered ten miserable-looking specimens to the British camp, none of which bore much resemblance to a fierce Ghilzai warrior. On 25 October, a sullen group of Afghans took a load of provisions and forage to the British lines. Their behaviour (several of them spat on the ground when they left the camp) aroused Sale's suspicions, and he instructed his men to stay on the alert. He issued orders for the troops to sleep fully armed and under cover of their breastworks. The plan was to resume the march at dawn on 26 October, led by an advance guard of the 13th Light Infantry, four guns, two companies of 35th Native Infantry and one company of sappers. The main body consisted of the strength of two regiments. The rear would be taken up by two guns, two companies of the 25th Native Infantry, one company of sappers and the remaining troops of the 5th Light Cavalry.

All went well for two days, but on the morning of the 28th, large parties of marauders on horseback began to appear in rocky bends along the road, falling upon anyone who had the misfortune to detach himself from the main body, and especially the native camp followers leading the supply camels. The harassment carried on unabated during the entire day's march, until camp was pitched and the brigands slipped back into the hills. Macgregor continued to reassure Sale that the chiefs would do their utmost to keep their word, and that there was no hostile feeling towards the English. The argument the Afghan chiefs were always eager to put forward, and usually in the most unctuous tones, was their inability to rein in the Ghazi zealots, who refused to a man to obey their tribal leaders. Sale, with reality staring him in the face, saw it differently: the Afghans had lured the brigade into the most inhospitable parts of the country, both in the harshness of its terrain and the savagery of its people, and it was now their intention to grab whatever baggage they could plunder from the column and kill as many troops as came within range of their *jezails* or striking distance of their knives. Lady Sale's diary entry for 23 October confirms her husband's suspicions, expressed in a letter carried back to Kabul by a despatch rider. 'Sale [note the Victorian formality] writes that the report is, that the people at Tezeen say they are unable to cope with us in battle, but that they intend to plunder and annoy the force on its way down.'[25]

Sale gave stringent orders for the corps to march in tight formation, with no camp followers moving ahead, no stragglers in the rear, and for the entire body to be able to form up quickly in case of attack. It was well that Sale took these precautions, for no sooner had the brigade moved out of camp, several hundred screaming Ghazi horsemen emerged from the hillocks and fell upon the column's rearguard, slashing and firing left and right. The marauders stalked the troops all day, rushing forth when the rearguard crossed exposed terrain, then dashing back to their hideouts to regroup and await their next opportunity. As always, the attacks came to an abrupt end as soon as the British pitched their tents. The rebels knew from experience that to expose themselves to the firepower of 2,000 disciplined troops and their despised artillery was to invite disaster.

The brigade marched in high spirits, for the stages were short, rarely exceeding 5 miles, and the only deprivation was the lack of forage suffered by the animals in this desolate landscape. The nights were bitterly cold, but the morning sun hitting the tents brought warmth to the men's numbed limbs, and with the promise of another fine day, the column moved on without a complaint in the ranks. The force was now approaching the Jugdulluk Pass, the last serious military obstacle to a safe withdrawal to Gandamak and from there to the town of Jalalabad, where the troops would find their well-earned rest. The pass sits on a plateau between 5,000 and 6,000ft above sea level, and from there the land spills rapidly down some 2,000ft to Gandamak and thence to Jalalabad, located in a balmy lowland valley less than 2,000ft high. The road from Jugdulluk to the pass runs uphill for 3 miles, and it was proving an exhausting task for the heavily laden camels and the gun horses. The way forward was made more taxing by small bands of marauders constantly attacking the rearguard. Nevertheless, the crest was won with small loss and the bugles sounded a halt before starting the painstaking descent to the village of Gandamak, 35 miles west of Jalalabad. It was necessary to send two companies of Gurkhas scrambling up the hills to clear the ridges of snipers. The sturdy Nepalese fighters clambered up several thousand feet, directing as they ran a deadly fire on the Afghans, all to the enthusiastic cheering of their comrades watching from the pass below. The officers commanding the three bodies of troops – advance guard, main body and rearguard – realised the folly of remaining within range of the breastworks that dominated the hills, so the bugles warned the troops to pick themselves up and move on to a more sheltered spot to pitch their tents. Before leaving their position, the troops were witness to a bleak reminder of Afghan brutality, to the dead as well as the living. One of the British officers, Captain Charles Wyndham of the 35th Native Infantry, had been killed in the day's action, and now the men looked on in horror as the Ghilzais, out of rifle range, proceeded to sever his head and set it up as a mark for target practice with stones.

The march was resumed the following day and by 29 October the brigade was in sight of the delightful valley of Gandamak, in which Shah Shuja had built a cantonment for two of his own regiments in a wooded area of fruit trees and abundant vegetation, watered by an adjacent stream. The force camped here for twelve days, during which time the only regrettable incident was the desertion of a number of irregular troops to the Afghan camp. It was all that Sale could do to retain the loyalty of the Khyber tribesmen who were to escort him safely over the notorious pass into India.

Once they had started on the last stretch of road to Jalalabad, the force had to fight off gangs of plunderers who kept up a steady harassment of the rearguard, leaving about 150 of their own men dead on the field as the day wore on. But it was a short march to the safe haven of Jalalabad, which was occupied without serious loss on the evening of 12 January.

The town lies on the right bank of the Kabul river, with some 20,000 inhabitants, a figure that has multiplied less than threefold in nearly two centuries. Jalalabad is not the sort of place that attracts much inward migration, lying on a crossroads between the bustling and more prosperous cities of Kabul and Peshawar. A contemporary document in the British Library India Office dismisses Jalalabad as 'a dirty little town . . . ' with ' . . . a mud wall, upwards of two thousand yards in circuit'.[26] When Gleig reached the settlement with the force, he wrote, 'Uninviting to the gaze of the ordinary traveller as this dilapidated city might have appeared, to the eyes of the brave but sorely harassed handful of troops . . . it offered many and great attractions.'[27] Just as well, then, that the men greeted their coming to Jalalabad with eager anticipation, for rather than a place of temporary rest, this was to be their home for nearly six months.

For now, there was to be little rest for the weary troops. The occupation of Jalalabad was what the townspeople had least wanted and expected. They were led to believe that the troops might stop to refresh themselves and their baggage animals, and then continue their march to India. Consequently, most of the citizens fled, in terror and disgust, before the column of red coats and their menacing guns. Scarcely was the brigade safely behind the walls, when a tumultuous mass of Afghans began gathering outside, baying for the blood of the *feringhees* who had taken possession of their town.

While the men rested, keeping a sharp eye on the movements of the Afghans outside the walls, Sale summoned the commandants of corps to a council of war to decide their next step. There was no question of abandoning their position, at least not until there was clarification of the situation at Kabul, from where a distressing piece of intelligence had intercepted Sale on 7 November, on the final stages of the march to Jalalabad. The point at issue was whether to keep possession of the whole town or concentrate the garrison in the citadel and hold that fortified position against what looked like the start of a drawn-out siege. On the face of it, the latter seemed the most sensible option from a strategic standpoint. But Sale was persuaded by other counsel, Dennie being the chief advocate, that a retreat into the citadel would give the wrong message to the Afghans, who might take it as a sign of weakness.

The next task was to sweep the Afghans from the heights outside the walls with a major show of strength, so that the troops might get on with the business of making ready the town's defences, a task that got under way using camel saddles as sandbags to reinforce the improvised entrenchments. The order was given for Monteith to lead a sortie the next morning, taking with him about 1,100 men and 2 guns, leaving slightly more than 700 troops for the defence of the town. 'The slightest reverse, it was felt, would tell,' recalls Gleig, 'and if by chance more than a reverse were to befall, the consequences must be serious.'[28] The infantry gathered at the Kabul Gate, the cavalry massed in their rear, and an order was issued for the artillery ranged along the wall to open fire. In spite of the devastating fusillade, the Afghans gave no ground until the troops charged forward from the gate, bringing down men and horses before them. The first objective to be taken was 'Piper's Hill', so named by the troops for a lone Afghan piper who stood bravely on the promontory playing 'his most unmusical instrument', with a reckless disregard for the shower of musket balls whizzing past him. The piper astonishingly escaped unhurt and the name 'Piper's Hill' sticks to this day among the local people. Once the enemy had been dislodged from the environs of the town wall and pushed back to the hills, the bugles sounded the recall and the whole force returned to Jalalabad in great spirits, leaving about two hundred of the enemy dead on the plain out of a force estimated at some five thousand. British losses on that day amounted to thirty-four killed and fifty-three wounded, not a negligible number considering Sale's limited manpower.

There was no doubt in Sale's mind that the garrison was in for a protracted siege. The general therefore deployed round-the-clock working parties to fortify the defences by filling in the breeches in the town wall and deepening the ditches that surrounded them. Sale ordered every tree that stood in the line of fire to be felled, thus depriving the enemy of cover, while every house and fort within firing range outside the walls was to be demolished. Parapets were put up along the ramparts and ten artillery pieces were run into the bastions and made ready for service. Foraging parties were sent out under heavy escort to requisition from the local villages supplies of sheep, grain and fuel. Within a few days Sale was satisfied that the town could withstand anything the Afghans could throw at it, and that the commissariat was stocked with sufficient stores to keep the men going for a month, albeit on half rations. The only provision lacking was brandy. Given the circumstances in which the brigade now found itself, all supplies of spirits had understandably been depleted. This had its positive side, for throughout the months of the siege not a single incident of fighting or crime was reported among the men, including the 13th Light Infantry, whose ranks were filled with men of a rough-and-tumble reputation.

Things remained quiet with no serious outbreaks of fighting until 28 November, but Sale and his commanders were not deceiving themselves: the garrison was in a state of siege. Worse, communications with Peshawar and Kabul were in such a precarious state that it could accurately be said contact had been broken between the two chief British strongholds on either side of the Afghan border. The only intelligence that got through were letters secreted in the clothing or travel baggage of native messengers, unsung heroes who put their lives at great peril by carrying information to the infidels holed up in Jalalabad. What news did get through brought no joy to the brigade, for the correspondence told of military disasters, uprisings and blockades across much of Afghanistan. This put the garrison on a state of high alert with the expectation of an imminent attack. The infantry slept with their weapons at the ready and the cavalry, with their horses saddled, next to them. After putting up for a fortnight with the steady harassment of the garrison's working parties, Sale's patience was running thin. He decided to take punitive action. At one o'clock on 1 December, after allowing the men time to finish their lunch, Brigadier Dennie rushed from the Kabul Gate with a column of 600 British and native infantry, two guns, some sappers and native irregulars and the entire troop of cavalry. Dennie's party was met with a sharp fire from the Afghans, but he valiantly swept round to the left of the gate, clearing the enemy from the rocky mounds on the main road to Kabul. The cheering troops next smashed in the door of a fort that had been left standing, and drove the besiegers across the plains. The 13th and the *jezailchis* irregulars fought like a force of nature as they chased the Afghans to the riverbank, where the guns opened up with a withering barrage of shrapnel and grapeshot. Many of the enemy were driven into the water, forgetting in their panic that most Afghans cannot swim. Those who weren't cut down by the murderous accuracy of the guns sank exhausted beneath the water. Having pushed the besiegers back about 12 miles from the gates of Jalalabad, the troops returned to the city in exceptionally high spirits, for the body count could not have been more in their favour: at least 150 enemy dead, while not one of Sale's men failed to return alive.

The outstanding victory Sale's brigade had achieved on 1 December was followed by a comparatively long period of inactivity. While the Afghans went away to lick their wounds, the troops busied themselves in strengthening the city's defences and adding to the stock of provisions. It was a melancholy period for Sale, who found himself with unwanted time on his hands to reflect on what had been his most tortuous decision in nearly half a century of military service. To understand the reasoning behind Sale's determination to hold Jalalabad rather than push on towards the Khyber Pass and home, it is necessary to retrace the brigade's steps to their arrival at Gandamak. No couriers had been able to make the dangerous crossing from Kabul for three or four days, and the camp was buzzing with rumours of some horrible disaster that had befallen the capital. At last, on 10 November a messenger reached Sale's camp after a harrowing twenty-four-hour journey through the passes, bearing a letter from General Elphinstone. The insurrection had spread to Kabul, which at first was thought to be a localised affray that would be put down in short order by the Army. This was not the case: heavily armed insurgents were rampaging out of control in the capital, putting the troops and their families at serious risk of being slaughtered. Elphinstone ordered Sale to turn his brigade around and return in all haste to the relief of Kabul. At the same time, Elphinstone despatched an order to Nott, who had sent a column under Major James Maclaren back to India via Shikarpore, requesting these troops to be diverted to Kabul, with the exception of that portion of the column which had already got beyond the Kojuk Pass.

Sale's wife Florentia, his daughter and son-in-law were with the besieged garrison. If he took the brigade back to Kabul, the combined infantry, cavalry and guns might well tip the scales against the insurgents. Sale called his officers together to give them the distressing news from Kabul, and to decide on a course of action. 'Some members of the Gandamak council of war, foremost amongst whom was [Major George] Broadfoot, argued vigorously in favour of the return march to Kabul,' writes Forbes. '[Captain Henry] Havelock strongly urged the further retreat into Jalalabad.'[29] Havelock, who was present at the storming of Ghazni, was Sale's personal staff officer and as such had no vote in the council. Later to become one of the heroes of the Sepoy Mutiny, Havelock argued that if the Kabul garrison was facing disaster, the blame lay with the politicals whose lack of moral courage had allowed the Afghan rebels to wrest the initiative. 'How was the garrison of the cantonment to be aided, since it apparently could not and would not aid itself?' quotes Havelock's biographer John Pollock. 'Yet, how again could it be in peril? It consisted of between five and six thousand men, having good artillery and immense munitions of war. Havelock pointed out that a hard winter had already set in and that if Gandamak was cold enough, the passes would now be freezing. The force was badly clothed, it had lost a great portion of its camp equipage, its camel drivers had nearly all deserted with their animals.'[30] For the brigade to retire to Kabul would be to invite almost certain destruction. Havelock's argument swung the vote. Indeed, his was but one of many voices, in India and at home, that later heaped bitter scorn on the Kabul garrison's failure to crush the rebellion.

The question now was whether to hold fast at Gandamak to await further clarification of the situation in Kabul, or to lead the force down to Jalalabad. Havelock once again took a leading role in convincing Sale to push on to Jalalabad, pointing out that water and provisions at their present position could easily be cut off by the Afghan renegades swarming about the plains. Macgregor had received reports that the tribes around Jalalabad were on the verge of occupying or destroying the town, which would leave the brigade isolated in the Afghan wilderness. Taking control of Jalalabad, on the other hand, would create a well-defended fortress which could serve as a safe staging post for the Kabul garrison on their return to India. The vote to continue the march to Jalalabad was by no means unanimous or without its critics. Durand, as might be expected, had little sympathy for Sale's decision to ignore Elphinstone's orders. Nott escapes his wrath, given that the Kandahar force was pushing its way through winter snows, which made a shift northward highly impractical. As for Sale, 'This decision was regretted by some of the ablest officers in his force. . . . Humanly speaking, Sale thus denied himself the honour and the satisfaction of retrieving the state of affairs at the capital.' Retiring to Jalalabad, Durand concludes, 'served no conceivable purpose except to betray weakness and still further encourage revolt. Had Sale maintained his position at, or near to Gandamak, he might have influenced the fate of Elphinstone's army, and one of the most disastrous retreats on record would have been spared to the British arms by the co-operation of his moveable column.'[31]

This was one of Durand's last salvos against the Government's bungled Afghan policy. He later served with distinction in the Second Anglo-Sikh War and in the suppression of the Sepoy Mutiny, after which he was rewarded with the post of Indian Foreign Secretary, and he continued to quarrel incessantly with his Cabinet colleagues. In 1870 Lord Mayo appointed Durand Lieutenant Governor of the Punjab, an office second in importance only to the Viceroyalty itself. In December of that year, during a tour of the North-West Frontier, at dusk he rode on an elephant to visit the town of Tank. Passing under an arch, his *howdah* was crushed against the roof of the gateway and he was thrown to the ground, his head striking a wall. He died on New Year's Day, 1871, and was buried at Dera Ismail Khan.

With painful resolve, Sale put his case to Elphinstone in a despatch from Kandahar dated 15 November 1841, explaining his decision to disobey his Commander-in-Chief's orders. Sale advanced some powerful reasons for taking this course: the destruction of his camp equipment, the fact that he was carrying upwards of 300 sick and wounded, and that lacking a single depot of provisions, the men would be incapable of scraping together one day's rations for the march.

If Sale was determined to sit tight at Jalalabad, Nott was equally set on holding firm at Kandahar and, in fact, had only received Elphinstone's supplication for help at the end of February, more than two months after it was despatched from Kabul. This gives an idea of the state of upheaval between the capital and the southern region, the heartland of some of most recalcitrant Pathan tribes. In any case, it would have been humanly impossible for Nott to have complied with the general's orders, for Maclaren's column never made it within striking distance of Kabul – the troops were forced to retreat to Kandahar in December, battling their way through raging blizzards. The Afghan chieftains in Kandahar likewise had gone to Nott, urging the commander to withdraw from the city. They assured him, somewhat too eagerly for the general's liking, that even having lost the support of the British Army, Shah Shuja remained in full control of Kabul. Nott dismissed the chiefs with a flat refusal to budge from Kandahar. He had come up against their double-dealing in the past, and so mistrustful was he of the enemy in his midst that the following month he saw fit to expel every Afghan from the city.

Sale and Nott had done the unthinkable, what in fact amounted to an act of mutiny, by blatantly disobeying orders from their superior officer. There was a sharp divergence in their motives, however, which illustrates the contrasting characters of the two generals, both seasoned veterans who were only eight months apart in age. Sale based his decision to take and hold Jalalabad, rather than retire to Kabul, on purely practical rationale: the passes were swarming with Afghan insurgents and he considered his force ill-prepared to fight its way back. Nott had obediently ordered Maclaren to proceed in all haste to Kabul, and the relief column was only beaten back by the weather. But when Elphinstone sent orders for the whole of the force under Nott's command to evacuate Kandahar and retire to India, Nott smelt a rat. He sensed that Elphinstone's orders, which were counter-signed by Pottinger, had been written under coercion. Nott would have happily led his men to Kabul, with a total disregard for winter obstacles, or to India for that matter, were he confident that his instructions came from a commander who was firmly in charge of the situation. Elphinstone was not, and Nott was right. The brigadier bluntly replied that he would not make a move without clear instructions from the Supreme Government in Calcutta. Nott and his Political Agent Rawlinson could later congratulate themselves on having disobeyed orders, when a communication arrived from the Governor General stating that in the best interests of British India, the Kandahar garrison was to stay put.

Sale and Nott could also draw on numerous examples of Afghan duplicity as grounds for refusing to abandon their positions. As Sale was to witness over the course of seventeen demanding days, the Afghan uprising was by no means confined to Kabul. But losing the passes and the surrounding countryside was a comparatively minor inconvenience compared with the humiliating capitulation and betrayal of the British garrison at Ghazni, one of the four main outposts held by the Army of the Indus. The citadel that British valour had carried by storm three years before was now besieged by the Afghan rebels. The force commanded by Colonel Thomas Palmer had come under attack in December, and for nearly three and a half months the regiment of sepoys had held out valiantly against vastly superior numbers. In mid-December the troops were forced to abandon their position and retreat into the citadel, where the local inhabitants revealed to the besiegers a subterranean passage that led under the walls into the city. The Indian troops, unaccustomed to the harsh realities of an Afghan winter, forced to survive on scant rations and having been deprived of their water supply, lost the will to fight. Palmer asked the rebel chiefs for surrender terms, and was offered safe passage to Peshawar, with colours, arms and baggage. For Palmer, the prospect of marching his men under escort to the warm plains of India and their families seemed almost too good to be true, as indeed it was. Many of the men might have wished to die a soldier's death. No sooner had the detachment evacuated Ghazni, the Afghans fell upon the troops, who put up a desperate defence for three days, until on 10 March a large number of sepoys had been killed and others taken into slavery, while the ten surviving officers were held as hostages.

On 28 February 1842, with nothing remaining of Elphinstone's desperate pleas for help but a voice of the dead echoing in the passes, with Nott and Sale struggling to hold their positions at Kandahar and Jalalabad, and with Palmer's sepoys facing starvation at Ghazni, an Indiaman anchored at Calcutta carrying on board the patrician figure of Edward Law, Earl of Ellenborough, the new Governor General of India. Ellenborough's mission, he told the East India Company directors before he sailed from England, was to restore peace to Asia, by negotiation or by force of arms. His first efforts met with success: Ellenborough put down a mutiny among the sepoys and increased reinforcements for the Opium War in China, which was later brought to a successful conclusion. Afghanistan was a tougher nut to crack. Ellenborough was bent on withdrawing all British forces from this turbulent land, and the sooner the better. But there was to be no question of a cut-and-run policy. The Governor General wrote to the new Tory prime minister, Sir Robert Peel, ' . . . the honour of our arms must be re-established in Afghanistan before it can be safe to contemplate as a practical course our withdrawal from that country'.[32]

Auckland's letter of resignation reached the Board of Control in October 1841. He left India in August 1842, an utter failure, the Government's Afghan policy in tatters. Auckland's tribulations were finally at an end and he was immensely pleased to be spared the burden of having to repair the damage done in Afghanistan, with which he could no longer cope. It is said that when he was told of the destruction of the British Army on the retreat from Kabul, he went into a state of shock. His aides feared that he had suffered a stroke but when Auckland recovered his composure, he spent hours pacing the Government House verandah, until he once again broke down that night and threw himself on the lawn, burying his face in the cool turf. His mood of despondency was reflected in a letter to Hobhouse, in which he confesses that 'the plans of public good and public security upon which I had staked so much . . . all broken down under circumstances of horror and disaster of which history has few parallels'.[33] Auckland achieved some personal redemption in his next appointment in 1846, as First Lord of the Admiralty, a post he had held twelve years earlier and in which he once more proved himself a capable administrator. It was little more than a caretaker role, however, for like many returning servants of the Raj, Auckland's health was broken and on New Year's Day 1849 he died suddenly, his earldom falling extinct since he had never married and left no heirs.

Hobhouse read through Auckland's letter in his sumptuous office of the New East India House in London's Leadenhall Street. This was an austere, classical stone structure, opened in 1800 to replace the great mansion house of Sir William Craven, Lord Mayor of London in 1610, a decade after the Honourable Company received its Royal Charter. The room was adorned with figures in relief, designed to indicate the nature of the business transacted within its walls: Commerce, represented by Mercury, attended by Navigation, and followed by tritons on sea horses, is introducing Asia to Britannia, at whose feet she pours out her treasures. Britannia's introduction to Asia west of the Indus was quite unlike anything the directors of the East India Company had expected to encounter.

Had Hobhouse any notion of the time-bomb ticking away under Kabul, it would have given cause to regret his encouragement of the military adventure in Afghanistan that was now about to culminate in a disaster so apocalyptic as to shake the Empire to its foundations.

Chapter 4

'Our Troops as Yet are Staunch'

If not for its tragic implications, Macnaghten's analysis of the cause of the Kabul insurrection would lend itself to comedy. The Envoy believed that the uprising had its source in a story put about by a rebel chief to his kinsmen, to the effect that 'it was the design of the Envoy to seize and send them all to London'.[1] The rebel leader in question, Amanullah Khan, had gathered his fellow conspirators together on the night of 1 November to forge a letter bearing Shah Shuja's signature, calling on the people of Kabul to put the infidels to death. How this ties in with the awful prospect of being packed off to London is not immediately clear, but the faked document achieved the desired effect. The Afghans hardly needed to look far to find any number of pretexts for staging a rebellion – having their subsidies slashed, their women falling into the arms of *feringhees* and, not least of all, their homeland occupied by a foreign army, had been fanning the flames of revolt for months.

Mohan Lal was a Kashmiri Hindu, a traveller, diplomat and author, who had accompanied Burnes on his early travels in Central Asia and later joined the British garrison at Kabul. He was an Indian *munshi* in the highest sense of the word: an educated linguist and interpreter. Lal was among the first Indians to receive a Western-style education at Delhi College, where he developed a lifelong affection for the British. This made him a valuable ally and source of information in the darkest days of the war. At seven o'clock on the morning of 2 November, Lal was shaken from his bed by an hysterical maid-servant, shouting through his bedroom door that the city was in chaos, with people fleeing their homes, carrying whatever possessions they could on their backs. It was a Tuesday, the third in the month of Ramadan, when the Muslim fuse is at its shortest after three weeks of fasting. Lal leapt out of bed in alarm, but not in surprise – he had been aware for some time of a plot being hatched to incite the residents of Kabul to revolt. Lal had alerted his close friend Burnes, who lived only a few houses away, to the threat of an impending uprising, urging him not to disregard the storm warnings. Burnes's reply was that on the one hand, Macnaghten had not yet taken up his post in Bombay, therefore Burnes lacked the authority to order the troops into the streets. Burnes also feared that any rash defensive action would be interpreted as a sign of weakness. Burnes's face suddenly went ashen, as with a shaking hand he laid aside a message that had just been brought in by a messenger. He stood up from his chair, and with a sigh he concluded that there was nothing left for the British in Afghanistan but to evacuate the country as soon as possible. 'Whilst I was talking with Sir Alexander Burnes,' Lal writes, 'an anonymous note reached him in Persian, confirming what he had already heard from me and from other sources, on which he said, "The time is arrived that we must leave this country."'[2]

On the morning of 2 November, Macnaghten was making final preparations for his departure to Bombay. Within forty-eight hours, Burnes would see the fulfilment of his burning ambition to take over as the Government of India's chief representative in Afghanistan. Burnes rejoiced at the prospect of becoming the most powerful British civilian authority in Afghanistan. He must have been making plans for a lavish celebration, breaking out his famed store of rare cognac, fine wines and hermetically sealed smoked salmon. Burnes was aware that Akbar Khan had arrived at Bamiyan from Bokhara, plotting some devilry in collaboration with his tribal confederates. Officers like Captain Colin Mackenzie and Lieutenant John Conolly, had been passed the word from local informers of unholy stirrings taking place in the city – indeed, the shopkeepers were terrified of being spotted selling their goods to the British. Burnes was warned by Mohan Lal of the gathering storm clouds. Taj Mohammed, another Afghan friend, came to him on the night of 1 November, with detailed intelligence on what was planned for the following day. A meeting had taken place at the house of Sydat Khan, presided over by the chief conspirator Amanullah Khan, with violence on the agenda. Burnes waved aside the scaremongers with the reassurance that once he took over the Envoy's job, he would restore the tribal allowances and all would be well. Taj went away shaking his head in dismay. Burnes the darling of London society, the much fêted Central Asian explorer, the man soon to be elevated to the stewardship of Britain's imperial destiny in Afghanistan, had been so blinded by success that he chose to shut his ears to the alarm bells. His biographer James Lunt writes:

> There can surely be no other explanation for Burnes's incredible stupidity. He knew the Afghans well enough by now to know how treacherous and cruel they could be. He had also been warned by Mohan Lal that he was a marked man, in some ways unfairly, since it was he whom the Afghans blamed for bringing the British to their country. But in other ways he had given some of them good cause to hate him. He had behaved high-handedly on more than one occasion, and his *amours* were notorious.[3]

Shortly before sunrise on 2 November, an armed mob began gathering in the streets near Burnes's residence. Shah Shuja's chief minister, Osman Khan, rushed into the house to warn Burnes that the rabble was baying for British blood: a full-blown uprising was in progress in the city. Those who hadn't armed themselves to attack the residence had bolted their doors and put up their shutters. The Afghan official pleaded with him to slip out and take refuge in the cantonments, while there was still time to make his escape. But no, even now Burnes refused to accept that his life was in peril. He was convinced that he could persuade the mob to disperse, or if that failed, that Macnaghten would send troops to his rescue.

About two hundred people were seen milling about the house, when Burnes flung open his balcony window to confront the mob. Burnes had the foresight, on hearing the racket outside, to fire off a note to Macnaghten requesting him to send a detachment of soldiers, in case of any need to intervene. He also sent two messengers to his sworn enemy Amanullah Khan, begging him to call off his followers. Only one of the messengers returned, barely alive. The other had had his head cut off at one stroke by one of Amanullah's men. Now Burnes stood on a gallery on the upper part of the house surveying the angry throng, and with his customary cockiness, he offered the insurgents a handsome reward to disperse and return peaceably to their homes. The answer came as Burnes was haranguing the crowd: a shot rang out and with a gasp, Lieutenant William Broadfoot fell from the gallery, a bullet through his heart. Burnes carried his lifeless body downstairs and later that morning, after the house had been ransacked and left in ruins by the maddened horde, a pack of pariah dogs closed in to feast on Broadfoot's remains. Burnes plainly saw there was no hope now but to defend himself: he ordered his 29-man sepoy guard to open fire on the mob. Meanwhile, the attackers had set fire to Burnes's stables and forced their way into the garden.

As Burnes was organising his desperate defence, Macnaghten's personal secretary, Captain (later General Sir) George Lawrence, returned from his morning walk to find the Envoy in a state of great anxiety, waving Burnes's note. Lawrence was the older brother of Sir John and Sir Henry, two officers who later gained fame as heroes of the North-West Frontier. Macnaghten had been locked in emergency talks with Elphinstone, who was recovering from a fall from his horse the previous evening. The old general, true to form, failed to grasp the gravity of the crisis, which threatened not only Burnes, but also the entire Kabul garrison. There was to be no relief column. Elphinstone was not prepared to risk sending the troops across the city, despite having at his disposal in the cantonments the 5th Bengal Native Infantry, a wing of the 54th, five 6-pounder field guns with a detachment of Shuja's artillery, the Envoy's bodyguard, a troop of Skinner's Horse and another of local horse, and three companies of Shuja's sappers. In short, enough manpower and guns to disperse the entire population of Kabul, if necessary. Widely spread and formidable as this insurrection proved to be, Eyre, a soldier on the spot, termed it an outbreak of discontent 'which military energy and promptitude ought to have crushed in the bud'.[4] Lawrence was outraged, to the extent that he got on his horse and at great risk to his own life he charged through the crowd of heavily armed rioters, racing to the gates of Shah Shuja's palace at the Bala Hissar. Shuja appeared genuinely perturbed by the disturbances taking place around Burnes's residence, and with good reason: the overthrow of British rule would inevitably seal his own fate. He despatched a detachment of native troops with two guns to restore order, but there was no support forthcoming from any of the British regiments. Shah Shuja's guard was beaten off with great loss, just managing to wrest the guns from the hands of their frenzied assailants.

Burnes and his brother remained with Broadfoot's body, begging for quarter as the flames extended to the room in which they had taken shelter. Mohan Lal, whose house stood close to Burnes's, now found himself in a tight spot. He had climbed to his roof to witness the spectacle in helpless despair, when musket balls began shattering his own windows. A section of the mob then turned its attention to this friend of the *feringhees*, who was seized by Shuja ul Daulah, one of the ringleaders of the insurgents and the man who was later responsible for the assassination of Shah Shuja. Mohan Lal was saved by Daulah's father, who pulled Burnes's friend away from the mob, took him to his house and hid him with his wives. The ladies restored Mohan Lal's composure with 'a sumptuous dish of rice pilaf' for breakfast.

Burnes had all but resigned himself to death. His brother Charles and whatever was left of the household servants and guards returned the Afghans' fire, while Burnes pleaded for mercy: his reply was a continual chant of 'come down to the garden'. At that point a Kashmiri merchant appeared in the room. This man, a complete stranger to Burnes, swore on the Koran that he was prepared to help him and his brother escape through the garden to a fort only a few hundred yards away. This was no time for explanations, it was their last chance. In their panic, the two brothers disguised themselves in native dress and followed their rescuer to the garden door. They took one uneasy step outside, when the Kashmiri suddenly shouted, 'Here is Sikander [Alexander] Burnes!' The wolf pack was on them in a flash. The knives kept falling on their lifeless bodies until nothing was left but a heap of carrion. Burnes was never given a proper burial and when the Army departed Kabul on 6 January, pieces of his body were still hanging from the trees in his garden.

Spurred on by their lust for blood and plunder, the insurgents charged the residence of Paymaster Captain Harold Johnson, who had taken the precaution of fleeing to the cantonments as soon as the rioting began. The mob ransacked the Treasury, and before making off with their booty they cold-bloodedly chopped to pieces every man, woman and child in the house.

Lawrence narrowly escaped with his life when he was sent back to the Bala Hissar to inform Shah Shuja that Brigadier Shelton had been ordered to occupy the fortress and prepare his troops for a possible assault on the insurgents. Lawrence was galloping through the narrow streets when an Afghan wielding a huge two-handed knife sprang from the shadows and lunged at him. The Captain spurred his horse out of the way, only to find himself under fire from some fifty Afghans who ran from the Lahore Gate to intercept him. Lawrence's escape unharmed was nothing short of miraculous – less fortunate, however, was Lady Sale's son-in-law, John Sturt. Lawrence was conferring with Shuja when the young Bengal Engineers Lieutenant rushed into the chamber, gushing blood from three stab wounds to his face and neck. Sturt had been attacked just outside the gates of the audience hall. His assailant was a well-dressed man, who escaped to an adjoining building where he was protected by waiting confederates who immediately shut the gates behind him. Fortunately none of the wounds were life-threatening, though had Sturt known of the fate awaiting him in the Khoord Kabul Pass two months later, he might have regretted forfeiting the luxury of bleeding to death in comfort. Yet his wounds were ugly enough – until late that night he was unable to open his mouth, his tongue was paralysed and he could not lie down, from the blood choking him.

Shah Shuja was genuinely horrified by the disaster that had taken place that morning. This was no surprise, for it was his protectors who were taking the brunt of the attacks, and by the afternoon of 2 November, the mob had wrested control of the city. Shuja knew that the next knife thrust could be aimed at his own heart. As for Sturt, Shuja arranged for him to be carried to the cantonments in his own palanquin, with a guard of fifty lancers.

Lawrence later reported that when he was given the order to occupy the Bala Hissar, Shelton seemed 'almost beside himself, not knowing how to act, and with incapacity stamped on every feature of his face'. He added, 'Brigadier Shelton's conduct at this crisis astonished me beyond expression.'[5] Shelton considered his force inadequate to cope with the insurgents, a truly astonishing comment given that he had under his command three companies of the 54th Native Infantry, Shah Shuja's 6th Infantry, four guns and a detachment of the 44th Foot. As proof of Shelton's pusillanimity, the rebels were so cowered by this formidable column that they huddled in the city's alleyways as Shelton's force proceeded unopposed at midday through the gates of the Bala Hissar. Once inside, Shelton was confronted by an angry Amir, wagging his finger at the brigadier and berating the Army for failing to take swift action to nip the uprising in the bud. Shuja's dismay was shared by many of the other officers, such as Eyre, who with much bitterness comments, 'The murder of our countrymen, and the spoliation of public and private property, was perpetrated with impunity within a mile of our cantonment, and under the very wall of the Bala Hissar.'[6] Mohan Lal says that had Shelton acted decisively and sent his troops against the mob, 'the life of Alexander Burnes would have been saved, and that movement would have not only preserved the lives of thousands, but even would have suppressed the insurrection at the moment, for the rebels had secured the means of escape for themselves, and would have fled on the appearance of our troops'.[7]

It must stand as a tragic irony that the chief rebels themselves fully expected the British to wreak vengeance on the plotters for the outrages that day. None of the chieftains ventured from his house for twenty-four hours for fear of being spotted as one of the ringleaders. The people of Kabul had been incited to riot to give a warning to the *feringhees* that they and their puppet-king were not welcome in Afghanistan, in the hope that they would pack up and abandon the country by the following spring. The uprising was not meant to be taken as a military challenge to the Government of India.

Shelton remained holed up behind the great battlements of the Bala Hissar for a week. During these days, as his troops kept up a desultory and ineffectual fire on the enemy, the brigadier began to formulate the plan that was to condemn the entire garrison to perdition. Shelton thought it hopeless to try to withstand a siege, and that the garrison's only hope for survival lay in a speedy retreat to Jalalabad, while there was yet time to lay their hands on provisions to carry the Army and its followers on the arduous trek through the passes. It was anyone's guess how much longer the garrison would be able to feed itself under those hostile conditions, with the commissariat stores sitting in a road commanded by a fort that was in enemy hands. Logistics aside, on a political level this would mean abandoning Shah Shuja to his fate and accepting the entire Afghan mission as a failure.

The military and political authorities had lost the initiative. The garrison was faced with three choices: they could dig in for a siege, try to rally the Army to strike at the insurrectionists or retreat to the safety of Jalalabad and thence to India. The first alternative posed an almost insurmountable problem given the garrison's weak defences, with the cantonments exposed to Afghan fire, and munitions and stores sited outside the defensive perimeter. As for the second option, it had been shown in the aftermath of Burnes's murder that the authorities were totally lacking in the moral fortitude needed to go on the offensive. So should they order a retreat while the force was still at full strength? The prospect of taking the entire garrison on a trek across the Afghan wasteland, with the first winter snows expected daily, was too dreadful a thought to contemplate. Kaye had no doubt that the question of why the Army failed to crush the uprising was 'one of the gravest that can be asked in the entire course of this historical inquiry'.[8]

With the Afghan rebels having taken over the streets of Kabul, what strategy did the top military authorities, Elphinstone and Shelton, in concert with the political Envoy Macnaghten, choose to follow? Their initial response to the crisis was characterised by inaction, rancour and procrastination. The news of Burnes's savage murder had the effect of shaking the garrison from its inertia – at least Macnaghten and the military commanders were engaged in much frantic talk about the need to do something. But even with Elphinstone 'infirm in mind and body', and unable to issue cogent instructions, there still seemed to be no way to come up with a collective decision on just what was best to do. Shelton was in despair with the growing conviction that the cause had been lost. Kabul was no different from other theatres of war in those days: it was virtually impossible for a commander to obtain an accurate and detailed picture of what was taking place outside his immediate field of operations. Shelton saw the enemy massed outside the walls of the Bala Hissar, but he had no idea if the rebellion had spread to the rest of the city. In fact, most of the violence had taken place at Burnes's and Johnson's homes. But as this had gone unchallenged, by nightfall the garrison was facing a general uprising, with the troops hemmed in on all sides of the cantonments, unable to move out a dozen paces from the gates without drawing fire from a neighbouring hostile fort. Lady Sale confirms that, 'In the cantonments all was confusion and indecision.'[9] The antipathy that existed between Shelton and Elphinstone came to a head that day, as the Commander-in-Chief and his second in command bickered over military strategy, while Macnaghten continued to make light of the revolt, right up to the moment he received confirmation of Burnes's assassination. When the Envoy was told of the murder, he took the precaution of vacating his residence and moving into the cantonments with his wife. Any doubts Macnaghten might have harboured about the severity of the crisis were dispelled later that day, when out on his horse to inspect the cantonment gates he came galloping back under a hail of musket fire. It was Elphinstone's response to the news of Burnes's murder, in a letter to Macnaghten, that set the garrison on a course to self-destruction: 'We must see what the morning brings,' he wrote, 'and then think what can be done.'[10]

Macnaghten must have been regretting his capitulation to Shah Shuja two years earlier, when he agreed to turn the Bala Hissar over to him instead of having the Army occupy the fortress with their families. Everybody was now crowded into the cantonments in as sorry a state as could be imagined. The Kabul river flowed a quarter of a mile away to the east, while to the south lay the bazaar village, a maze of squalid dwellings enclosed behind a low mud wall. A small fort, known as Mohammed Sharif's, commanded the cantonments' south-west bastion. This fort was attached to the Shah Bagh, or King's Garden, which was surrounded by a high wall. Elphinstone had previously proposed that this fort, as well as all the others within firing range of the cantonments, should be taken over by the British. The Government rejected this plan with the excuse that too much money was already being disbursed to the garrison. Under the current emergency and the need to protect the commissariat from attack, Elphinstone once again raised the issue of launching an assault on the fort, but now it was Macnaghten who dismissed this as an imprudent move. Elphinstone made no attempt to overrule the Envoy. The commissariat gate stood facing the entrance to the Shah Bagh, some 200yd farther up the road towards the city. About a mile away to the east rose the low crest of the Seeah Sang hills, and to the west of the cantonments, at roughly the same distance, was a higher range, with the village of Bemaru on its north-east flank, commanding a great part of the Mission Compound.

In the space of a few hours, a mob of several hundred unruly Afghans had spread panic in an overwhelmingly superior British fighting force. By withdrawing to the cantonments, the men in charge had given the enemy the upper hand and encouraged a widespread rising. The garrison was trapped, without access to its commissariat, facing a dwindling supply of ammunition and almost no chance of resisting a long siege. Of course, the alternative was for the troops to fight their way out and engage the insurgents, an undertaking that was still well within their capabilities. Penderel Moon describes moving the whole force from the cantonment as the lesser of two evils. He writes:

> This would not have solved the food problem, but within the walls of the citadel the troops would have been secure from attack and spared the fatigue of manning day and night a long line of rampart, and this would have enabled strong forces to sally out and obtain supplies from the surrounding country or even from the city.[11]

Sale had been vehemently opposed to this plan, which he believed would have entailed heavy losses. So with nearly 5,000 armed men under their command, Macnaghten and Elphinstone chose to send for help. But as has been seen, Sale would not, and Nott could not, come to the relief of the doomed Kabul garrison.

The British awoke that night to the crack of rifle fire coming from the Seeah Sang hills and the rumble of the cantonment drums beating to arms. Intelligence came in that a large body of men had been spotted coming over the hills. At three in the morning, the troops sprinted for their weapons and quickly took up positions on the ramparts to repel an assault by the Afghan insurgents. As dawn broke in front of the troops, the sight of the 'enemy' raised a mighty cheer in the garrison, for it was the 37th Native Infantry under the command of Major Charles Griffiths that appeared on the horizon. This young officer had been left behind by Sale at Khoord Kabul with instructions to wait for Elphinstone and escort the general and his party to India. Griffiths was the only man to respond to Elphinstone's summons for reinforcements. The firing that had alarmed the garrison was the last of the engagements the column was fighting with the Afghans, as it made its way back to Kabul. The regiment arrived in good order, having fought every step of the way through the pass and maintained a constant action against some 3,000 Ghilzais who harassed the rearguard all the way. The column was immediately sent to reinforce Shelton's troops in the Bala Hissar, an embarrassing demonstration to the reluctant brigadier that a strong detachment of soldiers could still command the city streets.

By evening, a large crowd of rebels had appeared between Mohammed Khan's fort and the commissariat, situated some 300yd from the cantonments. This gave the garrison cause for alarm, for they had only three days' food in store. The fort contained the whole of the Bengal Army supplies, including nearly 500 tons of grain, as well as all the medical stores. The loss of the commissariat would mean having to choose between surrender and starvation. But it also meant the loss of access to the heart of the city, thereby cutting off communication with Shelton's force in the Bala Hissar. The consequences of links with the Bala Hissar being severed were made painfully obvious at midday on the 3rd when an attempt was made to clear the streets of insurgents. Three companies of infantry and two horse artillery guns under Major Stephen Swayne were despatched into the city, which by now was alive with thousands of angry Afghans who had come streaming in throughout the night from the surrounding villages. The most that can be said for this half-hearted sortie was that the troops were able to beat a retreat in good order and with a minimum of casualties. The foray came to nothing, due to a breakdown in communications: the orders for Shelton to despatch a supporting contingent from the Bala Hissar failed to get through in time. Kaye decribes the lack of foresight in omitting to order out a proper contingent of troops which could have scattered the rabble off the streets. 'It is hard to say why a stronger force, with a fair allowance of cavalry, was not sent out in the first instance,' he writes. 'But the evening of this day, like that of the preceding one, closed in upon an inactive and dispirited British force, and an undisciplined enemy emboldened by impunity and flushed with success.'[12]

The rebels were confident they had gained the upper hand and they lost no time in exploiting their advantage to the fullest. The man most Afghans believed to be responsible for Dost Mohammed's overthrow and Afghanistan's occupation under an army of infidels, Sikander Burnes, lay dead in the garden of his residence. Now it was time to deal with the British soldiers and their families, cowering behind the walls of their cantonments. The chief conspirators saw no need to throw away hundreds of their followers' lives and risk an uncertain result by launching a frontal attack on the cantonments. They knew a formidable force was arrayed against them behind the low perimeter. Much better then to strike at the enemy's bellies rather than their guns. The commissariat was protected by a slender guard of fifty to one hundred men, according to various estimates. Mohammed Sharif's fort, still nearer the cantonments, had already been occupied by the Afghans, without a shot being fired in its defence. Communications between the cantonments and the commissariat were cut off by a swarm of insurgents holding the Shah Bagh gardens. The subaltern's guard, under Lieutenant Francis Warren of the 5th Bengal Native Infantry, found itself in imminent peril.

Early on 4 November, Elphinstone ordered the garrison's guns to open on another small citadel, known as Mahmud's fort, which stood on the banks of the Kabul river, between the cantonments' southern boundary and the broad open field leading to the city. The general would have been better advised to concentrate his firepower on the several hundreds of Afghans closing in on the commissariat compound. That afternoon, Warren sent an urgent message to Elphinstone, warning him that without reinforcements he would be forced to abandon his position in the face of far superior numbers. The insurgents spared no effort to deprive the British of their store of supplies. Warren reported that the enemy had begun to lay mines beneath the fort and move scaling ladders to the walls, and that some of his sepoys had deserted to the enemy. Elphinstone did eventually take action, but instead of reinforcements, he sent a party of infantry and cavalry with orders to provide cover for Warren's retreat. When word got round the cantonments that the commissariat was to be abandoned, it caused a furore in the ranks. A deputation of officers paid an urgent call on Elphinstone, entreating the Commander to recall the column and send a stronger force to protect the commissariat. The general almost always acted on the last words of advice he received, but in this case the delay cost the lives of several officers and many men of the escort party, who ran into heavy flanking fire from Afghan marksmen concealed behind loopholes in Mohammed Sharif's fort. Orders were despatched by runner to Warren to hold out to the last, though the lieutenant later denied having received these instructions. Elphinstone sent out two companies of the 44th Foot, under Captains Thomas Swayne and Thomas Robinson. Both officers were killed and several others wounded in the advance. The senior officer left in command ordered the column back to the cantonments in all haste rather than expose his men to this gauntlet of deadly fire.

The next day at dawn, the cantonments were alive with the snorting and stamping of cavalry horses' hooves on the cold ground and the jingling of their bridle bits, as a detachment of troops made ready to ride out to relieve Warren and save the precious provisions and hospital stores. The column stood poised at the gate, waiting on the command to move, when to everyone's horror Warren and his diminished contingent of sepoys were spotted marching towards the gate. The little garrison had abandoned the fort in the early hours by tunnelling under the wall to make good their escape undetected, abandoning all the Army's supplies to the enemy. Warren's decision was never challenged: Elphinstone was too mortified by the garrison's failure to send adequate reinforcements to point the finger of blame, and Warren was known to be an officer of great courage. During the brief siege, he had set an example of personal bravery by advancing alone under a hail of bullets to tear down an Afghan war flag from the commissariat gate.

The Afghans, whose strength was never estimated at more than some 2,000 armed fighters, busied themselves with looting the commissariat, which soon resembled a large ants' nest with each man taking away as much as he could carry – and all this plainly visible to a body of at least 4,500 battle-ready British and Indian soldiers. No orders were given for the troops to sally forth and cut down the rabble, the only initiative taken was to put the servants on half rations, and the authorities' reply to entreaties to storm the Bala Hissar, which was well stocked with provisions, was that the cantonments had cost too much in time and money to be abandoned. Moreover, Macnaghten was still determined to respect his agreement with Shah Shuja, even now that the rebels had forced him to desert his palace. Lady Sale tells of a report brought into the cantonments of a mine being laid under the palace, which was set to explode that same night, that is on 5 November. 'The King instantly left the palace, and took up his abode at the Gate of Haram Serai, where he remained during the rest of the siege,'[13] she wrote that day in her diary. From that day onward, until the garrison's final collapse, Shuja spent his time seated at a window commanding a fine view of the cantonments, sunk in a state of despondency as he watched the steady demise of his British allies.

The loss of the commissariat was not the only calamity to befall the garrison. Another store of provisions, this one containing the grain for Shah Shuja's troops, was kept on the outskirts of the city. The post was under the command of Captain Mackenzie, who had returned to Kabul the previous month after accompanying the advance guard of Sale's brigade as far as Khoord Kabul. The fort was in reality a very weak detached *godown,* or storehouse for goods and merchandise, that had been reluctantly put up after Shah Shuja demanded the original grain storage be removed from the safety of the Bala Hissar. Mackenzie fought furiously for two days against an overwhelming force of Afghans laying siege to the fort. Everything was against the little garrison, which was caught

1. A nineteenth-century view of Kabul. (*Courtesy of Royal Geographical Society*)

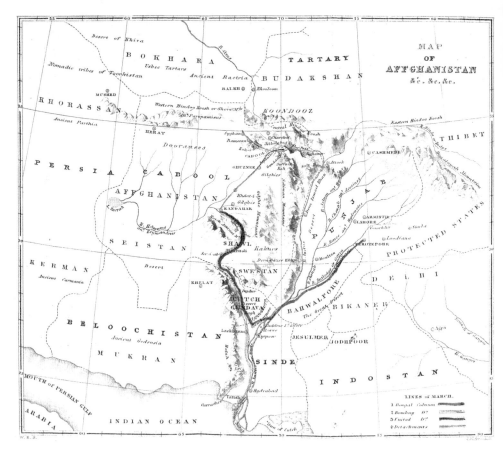

2. Lines of the march of the Army of the Indus in Afghanistan, 1838. (*British Library Board. All Rights Reserved. T.4803*)

3. Ahmad Shah Durrani, founder of the kingdom of Afghanistan in 1747.
(*Author's Collection*)

4. The Army of the Indus enters the Bolan Pass on the first stage of its invasion of Afghanistan. (*Courtesy of Royal Geographical Society*)

5. An Afghan tribesman. (*Photo by R.B. Holmes*)

6. Lord Ellenborough took over as Governor General in 1842 and was charged with cleaning up his predecessor's mess and redeeming British honour. (*Author's Collection*)

7. Sir William Macnaghten, British Envoy to Kabul, murdered by Akbar Khan. His head was displayed in the market square and his mutilated torso hung in the Kabul bazaar. (*Author's Collection*)

8. The Governor General Lord Auckland, who despatched the Army of the Indus to Afghanistan on the basis of deceit and miscalculations. (*Author's Collection*)

9. Shah Shuja ul Mulk, installed as the British puppet on the throne of Kabul and murdered by followers of Dost Mohammed. (*Author's Collection*)

10. The fortress of Ghazni, considered impregnable, taken by the British in 1838 on the march to Kabul. (*Author's Collection*)

11. Sir William Macnaghten receives the surrender of the Amir Dost Mohammed at the gates of Kabul. (*Courtesy of Royal Geographical Society*)

12. Akbar Khan, Dost Mohammed's favourite son and the leading conspirator in the uprising against the British garrison in Kabul. (*Author's Collection*)

13. Captain Colin Mackenzie, after his release from captivity in 1842. Some of the hostages grew fond of the Afghan styles of dress. (*Courtesy of National Army Museum*)

14. *Right:* Lady Florentia Sale, whose diaries told the horrific tale of the Army's massacre on the retreat from Kabul. (*Author's Collection*)

15. *Below:* Several of the British hostages in captivity in Afghanistan. (*Author's Collection*)

16. Pathan tribesmen waiting to ambush the rearguard of a British column. (*Courtesy of Royal Geographical Society*)

17. A skirmish in an Afghan pass. (*Courtesy of Royal Geographical Society*)

18. Major Eldred Pottinger, the hero of Herat, as a prisoner of Akbar Khan after the destruction of the Army of the Indus. (*Author's Collection*)

19. The house near Tezeen where Major-General William Elphinstone died. (*Author's Collection*)

20. Captain Thomas Souter of the 44th Foot, whose life was spared at the Gandamak massacre. He was wrapped in the regimental colours and the Afghans took him for a man of distinction whose life could command a high price. (*Author's Collection*)

21. General Sir Charles Napier, who placed the blame for the Army's destruction on Brigadier John Shelton, an officer Napier would have had shot. (*Courtesy of Geoffrey Roome*)

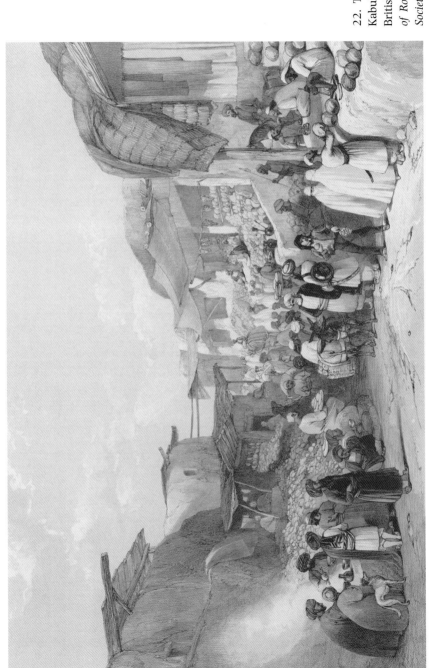

22. The Grand Bazaar of Kabul, demolished by the British in 1842. (*Courtesy of Royal Geographical Society*)

unprepared for the attack and found itself in dire need of water and ammunition. A great number of women and children were congregated in the building as well. Mackenzie fought valiantly against all odds until his ammunition was expended. After two days of relentless fighting, Mackenzie's men were dropping from exhaustion and his wounded were dying for want of medical attention. Despite his urgent pleas for help, no assistance was forthcoming from the garrison or the Bala Hissar. So in the dead of night on 4 November, Mackenzie fought his way back to the cantonments, taking a bullet wound on the way, in what Kaye heralds as 'one of the most honourable incidents of the war'.[14] The Afghans stormed the fort and carried off nearly 800,000lb of grain.

The garrison was seething with rage at Elphinstone's inexcusable failure to go on the offensive. The 44th had abandoned Mohammed Sharif's fort, to the amazement of the sepoys of the 37th who begged for a chance to redeem the Army's honour by taking the fort as well as the commissariat from the enemy. On 6 November, the fourth day of the uprising, Sturt stormed out of his mother-in-law's house in his pyjamas. He marched to Elphinstone's quarters with a request to bombard Mohammed Sharif's fort with his battery of 9- and 24-pounder howitzers. Permission was granted, but no sooner had Sturt taken the guns outside and swung them into place, an adjutant ran up with a message cautioning him not to waste ammunition, as it was in short supply. Sturt didn't know what to make of this remark, since the only commodity the garrison could count on in abundance was powder, which was reckoned sufficient to withstand a year's siege. He quite sensibly ordered his men to start shelling the fort, and damn the ammunition. It took two hours to blow a practicable breach in the walls, a feat achieved under a hot fire from the enemy's sharpshooters hidden in a couple of high towers that commanded the battery. The sepoys of the 37th and 5th were eager to advance under fire, and they did so with great courage. In a few minutes a storming party had carried the fort, but not without heavy loss. One officer who went down with conspicuous gallantry was Lieutenant William Raban. The young ensign led Her Majesty's 44th in the assault, and when the fort was taken he climbed to the top of the breach waving a British flag, and was shot through the heart.

The enemy made a dash for the hills behind the fort, pursued by a party of Anderson's Horse. Meantime, the 5th Cavalry charged the retreating Afghans who found themselves hemmed in on both sides. An intense clash broke out between the British troops, who were flushed with victory at the fort, and the rebels, who were desperate to break out of their encirclement between two cavalry corps. Lady Sale observed the engagement, as she did much of the fighting that took place near the cantonments during the siege. Her sharp, fearless eye would have earned her a place of honour among the doyens of war correspondents. She chronicled the Kabul rising with dash and held no punches wherever she saw fit to rebuke those in command for their follies. Of that day's engagement she wrote,

> From the top of our house we saw everything distinctly, the gleaming of the swords in the sun, and the fire of their pistols and matchlocks: fresh horsemen came pouring on to the assistance of the enemy from the back of the hill. They buried our cavalry and Anderson's Horse who, overpowered by numbers and a most galling fire, were forced along the ridge to the spot whence the first charge took place.[15]

A large number of Afghans had fled the fort to take up positions in the Shah Bagh. Eyre moved swiftly to dislodge the enemy from the garden by moving a 6-pounder gun into place at a large opening in the wall. He opened fire with grape and shrapnel, driving the enemy in panic from the wooded area. But a valuable opportunity was lost by failing to follow up the bombardment with an infantry advance, which could have held the ground permanently and re-captured the adjacent commissariat. The looters at this time had only been able carry away less than half the fort's stores. Brisk skirmishing continued throughout the day as the cavalry columns fought their way back to the cantonments, only just managing to rescue the 6-pounder gun which the Afghans, stealing up among the trees, had tried to carry away.

The failure to permanently reoccupy Mohammed Sharif's fort and the commissariat was demoralising for the troops, but more so for Elphinstone who took this as a sign that the moment had finally come when there was no alternative but to seek terms from the enemy. It hardly needs to be re-stated that the British, in numbers of troops and firepower, constituted a vastly superior force to what amounted to little more than an armed Afghan mob. Kaye was confident that the Army could have taken on and beaten a force five times its number. Yet the elderly general was so shaken by the enemy's success at spreading havoc, that on 6 November he began laying the ground for capitulation. 'It behoves us,' he wrote to Macnaghten, 'to look at the consequences of failure: in this case I know not how we are to subsist or, from want of provisions, to retreat. You should, therefore, consider what chance there is of making terms, if we are driven to this extremity. Shelton must then be withdrawn, as we shall not be able to supply him.'[16] Hardly the words to encourage fighting men to look to their commander for inspiration. The mood in the Bala Hissar would equally have kindled no fires among the sepoys, for by now Shelton had resolved that the only way forward was to turn back, that is, to India. Mohan Lal confirms this in his memoirs, 'He [Shelton] appeared from the commencement of the outbreak to despair of success, which produced a baneful effect in every fighting man. In short, he recommended to evacuate Kabul and to retreat to Jalalabad.'[17]

Even when several of the junior officers took matters into their own hands and went out to collect provisions from the surrounding villages, Elphinstone was not to be shaken from his despondency. These sorties were quite successful in procuring stores from the villagers, albeit at exorbitant prices, which nevertheless averted the prospect of immediate starvation in the cantonments. The main source of grain for sale was at Bemaru, about half a mile north of the cantonments, which was to become the scene of desperate fighting in the next few days. But with Elphinstone, there was seemingly no way to overcome an old man's pessimism: food there may be, but what of ammunition? The general was convinced that in three days of fighting the Army had used up enough ammunition to bring supplies down to a critical level. As has been stated, this was totally false, and the troops were moreover on top fighting form. Ellenborough himself later told the Secret Committee that there were abundant supplies of ammunition of all kind calculated for a year's use. As Lady Sale noted, two days after Elphinstone had begun to moot a capitulation, 'Our troops as yet are staunch, and if we are attacked, and succeed in repelling the enemy, we shall be able to keep our own until Sale's Brigade arrives.'[18]

Here we find two of the factors that made the garrison's downfall all but inevitable: Lady Sale was told that Macnaghten had sent out messages recalling her husband Sale, as well as General Nott but, like the rest of the British in Kabul, she was not yet aware that help would not be forthcoming. The garrison's fighting spirit evaporated once it became known that they were fated to stand alone against an enemy ever more inflamed by success. Lady Sale observed as well that the leaden sky above Kabul looked to be on the verge of discharging the first of its winter snows. This compounded the problem of obtaining provisions and scarce supplies of firewood, and few wished to contemplate the consequences of venturing out into heavy snowdrifts, if it came to a full retreat to Jalalabad. If, however, the authorities chose to open talks with the rebels, there could be no alternative but to quit Kabul. It was beginning to look, at least to the more fainthearted, that this was the only viable strategy. The Afghans were rampaging and looting with impunity, quick to take it for granted that victory was in their grasp once the enemy had lost the will to fight. There were those in Britain who spoke with shuddering accuracy of impending doom, among them the voice of the Establishment: 'There are many officers of sound judgement and experience here [in England] who have been through the Kabul campaign, and know the country well,' stated *The Times* in a leader, 'who think that not a single individual will return to tell the tale, since starvation is staring them in the face.'[19] Elphinstone and Macnaghten had no idea of just how alone they stood, for the Government of India itself, with the failure to send reinforcements from Jalalabad and Kandahar, now saw little chance of relieving the garrison before the spring. Ellenborough painted an exceptionally bleak picture to the Secret Committee in a report submitted a fortnight before the retreat, of which he knew nothing at the time. 'We must necessarily regard the position of our force in that city with great anxiety,' he said. 'It was divided, its means of supply were narrow and precarious, the whole surrounding country was opposed to it, and the season was approaching at which the passes of the hills would be closed by the snow.' The Governor General then laid before the gentlemen of the Honourable Company a fact which, if common knowledge 2,000 miles away in Calcutta, was damning in the extreme for men like Shelton who had the reality staring him in the face. 'The interval between the Bala Hissar and the cantonments is open, and a junction *could easily be made* [author's italics],' he reported. 'We must painfully await the result, for it seems to be physically impossible that troops could, before the spring, approach Kabul for rescue.'[20]

Even the Duke of Wellington, commenting afterwards on the course of the war, acknowledged that it was pointless to entertain any hopes for a military victory once negotiations were under way. 'After the first few days,' he told the House of Lords, 'particularly after the negotiations at Kabul had commenced, it became hopeless for General Elphinstone to maintain his position.'[21] By the end of the first week the rebel chiefs, much to their own amazement, had grown so confident of victory that they had nominated one of Dost Mohammed's cousins, Zeman Shah, as Amir. The insurgents now looked upon Shah Shuja's overthrow as a mere formality.

Macnaghten's thinking now shifted from military to political matters, in keeping with his position. The Envoy took the view that Elphinstone's weakness and lack of resolve ruled out any possibility of achieving military success. He therefore sought the good offices of Mohan Lal: would it be possible, he wondered, to tempt the cupidity of some of the tribal chieftains, by offering them bribes to come over to the British side? He sent two letters to Lal, addressed to the Ghilzai chiefs Khan Shirar Khan and Mohammed Hamzah, both of whom had taken part in the 2 November rising. 'You may assure them both,' Macnaghten wrote, 'that if they perform the service they have undertaken, the former shall receive one lakh [100,000] and the latter fifty thousand rupees.' The Envoy also tried to drive a wedge between tribal factions by asking Mohan Lal to enlist the support of Yar Mohammed, the rival of rebel leader Amin Ullah, by offering the former, one wonders with whose authority, the position of supreme chieftain. 'You may give promises in my name to the extent of five lakhs, and I fully approve your having raised 30,000 rupees for distribution among those disposed to assist our cause, but I would not advance more than 50,000 rupees before some service is actually rendered.'[22] Macnaghten had learnt too late the usefulness of money as a means of securing the tribesmen's loyalty. His largesse met with the same success as that of the man who hawked anti-earthquake pills in the streets of Lisbon in 1755. The insurgents had caught the scent of victory and, with faultless logic, they reasoned that the several hundred thousand rupees Macnaghten could lay on the table represented a pittance compared with the treasures that awaited behind the cantonments' walls.

The Afghan chiefs went away, ostensibly to consider Macnaghten's proposal. The Envoy was later told by Mohan Lal that the chiefs had agreed to support the British in their hour of need, on one condition: they wanted their money up front. It was an unconventional way of doing business, but in return they were prepared to offer a pledge on the Koran to obey Shah Shuja, make safe the road to Jalalabad, supply the garrison with provisions and openly espouse the British cause. It seemed too good to be true. Macnaghten suspected trickery, yet he acceded, for he had no other card to play. Some money was handed over to the rebels and they, still promising everything, began putting off the fulfilment of their promises, day by day. Macnaghten waited with growing despair for the chiefs to make good their word, while behind the Envoy's back the insurgents conspired with a powerful leader who had that week set up camp at Bamiyan. Akbar Khan had arrived from Bokhara to avenge his father's betrayal and drive the British and their Saddozai puppet from his homeland. Dost Mohammed's favourite son stood perched like a vulture on the hills west of Kabul, preparing to swoop down on the hapless garrison. Macnaghten had completely misread the character and intentions of his interlocutors, but at the same time he had at least sought a way out of the garrison's blind alley. Durand, who dispensed his words of kindness with an eyedropper, acknowledged Macnaghten's innate resolve in confronting the enemy, with what could be most generously described as a backhanded compliment. 'If Macnaghten be culpable for the effrontery with which he sought to blind and mislead others, as well as himself, as to the feelings of the Afghan people and the state of their country,' he writes, 'he proved free from that imbecile weakness which henceforward characterised the military leaders and their measures.'[23] To Macnaghten, in fact, fell the tragic duty of negotiating the retreat from Kabul, once Shelton and Elphinstone had lost all confidence in themselves and their men.

On 9 November, with the rebellion entering its second week, Macnaghten paid an urgent call on Elphinstone. The Envoy did not have the authority to issue military directives, but as the Supreme Government's representative he wielded a powerful influence in strategic matters. Elphinstone's health was now in a serious state of decay. Macnaghten was alarmed at the absence of firm leadership and the demoralising effect this was having on the troops. There was no shortage of able and robust officers in the ranks, but the Envoy was a man of procedure: he prevailed on the general to recall Shelton, second in command, from the Bala Hissar. There was no love lost between the two top commanders in Afghanistan and as for the troops, where feeble old Elphinstone was respected by the men as an honourable and brave solider, Shelton the bully and tyrant was the object of universal contempt. But he was tough and never shrank from a fight, and so a desperate garrison welcomed him into the cantonments with cordiality. What is most fascinating about Shelton's recall from the Bala Hissar, is that he made his way in broad daylight at the head of his men, bringing with him two guns, one company of the 44th Foot, Shah Shuja's 6th Infantry and several wagon trains filled with grain, and he made the crossing of the city totally unopposed. Shelton's bold march through Kabul should have made it evident to all that the Afghans had no stomach for an open clash with large bodies of well-armed, disciplined troops. It also begs the question of why the orders were not issued in reverse, and the entire garrison sent from the cantonments into the Bala Hissar, perhaps with Shelton's troops as an escort to clear the way of insurgents. The later retreat from Kabul was explained away on the grounds that it would have been impossible to protect the soldiers' families and thousands of camp followers between the cantonments and the Bala Hissar, a distance

of 1 mile through city streets, compared with a 90-mile trek across exposed terrain and snowbound passes on the road to Jalalabad.

Macnaghten's plan to place the two generals together under one roof, as it were, was not a felicitous one. It quickly became evident that there was to be no cooperation between these two men. Elphinstone complained of Shelton's high-handed treatment of a superior officer, while the brigadier asserted that he was thwarted in all efforts to organise the garrison's defence. Elphinstone complained that Shelton fairly bristled with insolence from the very day of his arrival: 'He never gave me information or advice, but invariably found fault with all that was done,' the general wrote, adding that Shelton seemed to be 'actuated by an ill feeling towards me'. Shelton argues otherwise: 'I was put in to command the cantonments, and consequently, in course of my inspections, gave such orders and instructions as appeared to me necessary. This, however, Elphinstone soon corrected, by reminding me that he commanded, not I.'[24] On the one hand, we have the bleating of a decrepit old man refusing to acknowledge his inability to command, one who in his own painful words was 'unlucky in not understanding the state of things, and being wholly dependent on the Envoy and others for information'.[25] But we cannot fail to censure a less than helpful Shelton, who might have smoothed his commander's feathers by displaying less arrogance and more tact. From that day, 9 November, to the garrison's retreat on 6 January 1842, Shelton bore a conspicuous part in the unfolding drama of Kabul.

Brigadier Shelton was not twenty-four hours in the cantonments when he was confronted with his first military challenge. Large bands of enemy on horse and on foot were spotted on the morning of the 10th, mustering on the Bemaru Heights to the west as well as the hills that commanded the garrison's eastern perimeter. A group of Afghans had taken possession of the abandoned Rikabashi fort, situated in a cultivated field within musket range of the north-east angle of the walls. From here, and concealed in the ruins of an adjacent house that had belonged to one of the non-commissioned officers, Afghan marksmen were easily able to pick off the soldiers manning the low works. It took some effort by an exasperated Macnaghten to prod Elphinstone into sending out a party to capture the fort. This was to be a major expeditionary force, a column consisting of 2,000 men under Shelton, backed up with horse artillery and mountain train guns. The force was ordered to hold itself in readiness, when an astounding thing happened: Elphinstone suddenly decided the sortie was too risky a venture and sent orders for it to be called off. Kaye reports that the general simply turned to his aide-de-camp and said, 'I think we had better give it up.'[26] One can easily imagine Shelton's rage when he brought his troops back into the cantonments. Giving Elphinstone's quarters a wide berth, he rode straight to Macnaghten's residence to demand the general's orders be overruled. The Envoy knew the garrison had provisions to hold out for at most another forty-eight hours, and unless the enemy were driven out of their new position, the British would be hemmed in on all sides. So it was agreed: Elphinstone's orders were to be countermanded and the attack would proceed as planned. The order to recall the troops to the cantonments had been given at ten o'clock that morning and the column was not sent out again until midday. This delay was to prove fatal, for in the intervening two hours the insurgents had gained enough time to take note of what was afoot and gather their forces to repel the attack.

The Afghans were in luck, for the assault got off to an inauspicious start when Captain Henry Bellew, assistant quartermaster general attached to the Bengal Army, volunteered to rush forward and plant a powder bag at the fort gate. The explosive failed to destroy the gate, blasting only a hole in the wall too small for more than two or three men abreast to pass through it. The troops fell in droves as they struggled to squeeze through the narrow aperture and what followed was a scene of total bedlam. The enemy fled from the rear gate, but the spirited advance of the storming party was checked by the surprise appearance of a large party of Afghan horsemen who quickly dispersed the panic-stricken infantrymen. A bugler of the 6th mistakenly sounded the retreat and it became a general scene of *sauve qui peut*. This was to be Shelton's day – the one-armed general lived up to his reputation for fearlessness under fire. Sabre in hand, he stood where the fire was the hottest and twice rallied his fleeing troops, until the heavy guns from the cantonments opened up on the Afghan cavalry. The men followed Shelton back into the fort, where the small party of British troops left behind was putting up a desperate defence. The fort was taken, but the engagement must be considered a missed opportunity. This was the first time since the start of the rebellion that a large body of troops had been brought into action. The Afghans could have been dealt a heavy blow had not the affair been mismanaged. Shelton had been given faulty intelligence regarding the location of the fort gate, and the force was too weak in cavalry to pursue the enemy into the hills. The capture of Rikabashi and its adjacent houses was a godsend for the troops and their families, albeit at a loss of 200 killed and wounded, in that it saved the garrison from the spectre of imminent starvation. Four smaller forts in the vicinity were found to contain nearly 60 tons of grain, but the troops were only able to bring in half that amount before dark. As expected, the rest was carried off by raiders during the night. The action also cleared the enemy from positions which until then were used as snipers' nests to harass the garrison.

Two days later the Army was back in the field, this time on the Bemaru Heights to the west of Kabul, where two guns were pouring a deadly accurate fire into the cantonments. Shelton was sent out to rout the Afghans and capture their guns, taking with him four squadrons of cavalry as well as infantry and two guns. The infantry breached the ridge but were forced back by the Afghan fanatics who fearlessly threw themselves against the British bayonets. A cavalry charge led by Anderson's Horse rallied the foot soldiers, and together they succeeded in putting the enemy to flight along the ridge. Eyre captured the enemy's 4-pounder, but the 6-pounder was lodged in an awkward position below the hilltop and with night closing in, he only managed to spike the gun. This was the last success the Kabul garrison was destined to celebrate before the Army's surrender and retreat.

Unknown to the British in their cantonments, almost from the start of the rising insurgent activity was taking place elsewhere, which shortly brought home the message that this was no local revolt instigated by a handful of hotheads in Kabul. On 3 November, a strong contingent of Afghan horsemen had begun attacking the Charikar garrison, located in the hills about 50 miles north of Kabul, a siege that was pressed without respite for ten days and nights. Then on the morning of 15 November, the British looked on with horror as two bloodstained and exhausted men rode in silence through the cantonment gate. Most remarkably, the two British officers had passed undetected at night through the streets and bazaars of Kabul. Major Eldred Pottinger, in Kohistan, had taken a musket shot to the leg, while the other rider, Lieutenant John Haughton, had lost his right hand fighting his way through to Kabul. These were the sole survivors of the Gurkha detachment that had occupied some fortified barracks at Charikar, whose defences were still under construction when the attack began. Pottinger's quarters were in an official government house 2 miles south at Lughman. Communication between Charikar and Kabul had been cut off in early November after the tribal leaders of Kohistan rose in revolt. Pottinger was determined to move the regiment out of their exposed position at Charikar, but this proved impossible given the large number of women and children accompanying the Gurkha troops. Pottinger then wrote to Macnaghten for help, unaware of course that the Kabul garrison was itself under siege. Some of the chiefs visited Pottinger to assure him of their loyalty, but he could not fail to notice the growing crowds of armed men taking up positions around the residency. On the morning of 3 November, Pottinger went out to negotiate with some of the lesser chieftains clustered in his garden. He was accompanied by Lieutenant Charles Rattray, the first British officer of the Kohistan detachment to fall. While Pottinger negotiated, the Afghans lured Rattray into an adjoining field and the lieutenant, sensing treachery, tried to make his escape but he was shot down as he ran. Pottinger fled into the residency and shut himself up behind the ramparts at the moment the Afghans opened fire. It was only through the last-minute appearance of a contingent of troops from Charikar that Pottinger's life was saved.

The troops returned to their barracks and woke on the morning of 5 November to find themselves besieged by a large force of Kohistani tribesmen. Given the barracks' weak defences, the Gurkhas and their commandant, Captain Christopher Codrington, were driven from their position by the overwhelming horde.

Codrington was one of the first to be cut down on that day. Seeing their commander fall wounded, the brave Gurkhas threw themselves at the enemy while Pottinger took on his former role as artillery officer and rolled out a gun to support the skirmishers. Haughton took charge of the little band of Gurkhas, who held their ground until nightfall put an end to the day's action. Codrington was carried into his house and joined by his men, where he managed to write a letter to his wife, and give Pottinger her picture for safe keeping. He lingered in great agony for two days, and was buried by his men even as the battle raged round the house.

The little contingent's numbers had been decimated in the first two days of the siege, but it was not a shortage of firepower, but of water that made the Gurkhas' position desperate. To remain cooped up behind their walls meant a slow death from thirst, while to attempt a breakout across open ground against an enemy that had swollen in number to the thousands was sheer suicide. The Afghans came forward and offered the Gurkhas terms: these were that the troops convert to Islam. Speaking for his men, Pottinger told the rebels that they had come to Afghanistan to put a Muslim on the throne, therefore the British had no quarrel with their religion. Pottinger and his men returned to their positions under a flag of truce, to await their dismal end. The situation was growing more desperate by the hour. On 10 November the troops scooped the last bucket of water from their stores and each fighting man was served half a wine glass. Some of the men organised sorties to draw water from a neighbouring stream, but on every occasion they were discovered by the Afghans, who shot them to pieces. Kaye quotes one of the Gurkhas as saying that they found some relief for their raging thirst by sucking the raw flesh of sheep. Some men placed the stomachs of the sheep in cloth and wrung them with all their strength to force out some moisture.[27]

The garrison was now left with only 200 men able to bear arms, each with thirty rounds of ammunition in his pouch. Pottinger and Haughton saw that their only hope lay in an attempt to break through the Afghan lines and take as many men as possible to Kabul. The men listened in sullen silence as Haughton explained the plan. Few expected to make it to the cantonments alive, yet they were Gurkha fighting men for whom a battlefield death was the only honourable alternative to capitulation. Pottinger led the advance on the night of 13 November, having spiked the garrison's guns, but discipline broke down the moment the men came into sight of the first pool of water. Pottinger and Haughton rode ahead, skirting the Afghan outposts and occasionally drawing fire when they eventually neared the city, which was surrounded by sentinels. The two survivors later found out that Captain Mackenzie had been preparing to march with 200 men to the relief of Charikar, an action that could have saved the force, which had perished almost to a man, along with their two remaining British officers, in the wild scramble for water on the retreat.

Macnaghten's state of despair over the loss of Charikar took a turn for the worse two days later, when confirmation came through from Macgregor, Sale's Political Officer, that the brigade commander had no intention of turning back to Kabul. All hope of relief was now lost, and the weather had turned cold and rainy, presaging the onset of deep winter. Yet Macnaghten stood almost alone among those in charge of the British garrison in his firm conviction that the Army must stay put and entertain no thoughts of venturing out into the snow-bound passes. He made his position clear to Elphinstone: a retreat to Jalalabad would be disastrous, the garrison's firewood, water and ammunition were in ample supply and, ever conscious of his moral duty, capitulation would be tantamount to throwing Shah Shuja to the wolves. Yet even in Macnaghten's determination to stand firm, one detects the same 'wait and see' vacillation that brings to mind Elphinstone's comment, 'We must see what the morning brings', when he was told of Burnes's murder. The Envoy writes to the general that it would be best to hold on as long as possible, 'in the hope that something may turn up in our favour'.[28] Shelton was the only one to advocate a withdrawal but Macnaghten, along with a number of senior officers, would not hear of retreat, while Elphinstone at this juncture had scarcely any opinions to expound. In the end, it was Shelton's voice that prevailed, and which brought calamity on the Army.

Early on 22 November, with the siege in its tenth day, a large band of Afghan horsemen and foot soldiers was spotted massing on the hill above the cantonments, next to the village of Bemaru about half a mile to the north, within musket shot of the British garrison. Macnaghten had a few days previous cut a deal with the village headman to supply the troops with provisions in exchange for a suitable bribe. The Afghan rebels, in turn, had set out to pillage the villagers and burn their houses as punishment for aiding the enemy. Major Stephen Swayne, the officer who the day after the uprising had been driven back when attempting to clear the streets of insurgents, now took two infantry wings and three cavalry detachments on a sortie to prevent the Afghans occupying Bemaru. The small force quickly advanced up the hill to find the entrance to the village blocked by a body of Kohistan fighters. Eyre was attached to the column and with the two field guns in his charge; he moved forward to find Swayne and his men pinned down in an orchard, under a very sharp fire from the houses. Eyre opened up on the summit of the hill, where the main body of enemy were gathered, but to little avail. Swayne's infantrymen kept up a steady and fruitless fire on the village for several hours. 'The cavalry were drawn up in rear of the gun on the open plain, as a conspicuous mark for the Kohistanis,' Eyre recalls with no little acerbity, 'and where, as there was nothing for them to do, they accordingly did nothing. Thus we remained for five or six hours, during which time the artillery stood exposed to the deliberate aim of the numerous marksmen who occupied the village and its immediate vicinity.'[29] It turned into an afternoon of shooting fish in a barrel for the Afghans, with heavy casualties inflicted on the cavalry, among men and horses, who stood helpless behind the gun. One can sympathise with Eyre's scorn for the strategic blunders committed that day (foremost among them was the failure to assess the enemy's position and strength before advancing on Bemaru, and leaving an entire cavalry squadron exposed in an open field) for during the operation, an Afghan musket ball pierced his left hand, terminating for the present his active service. The Bemaru action, in Kaye's words, marked 'one of the most eventful and the most disastrous in the history of the insurrection'.[30] Eyre puts it more conclusively: 'This day decided the fate of the Kabul force.'[31]

Macnaghten called a council of war at Elphinstone's residence that evening, with Shelton and a group of senior officers in attendance. The brigadier was for an all-out attack not only on the Afghans positioned on the hill, but also on the village to dislodge the enemy from the houses and grain stores. Shelton was right, in that occupying only the hill would encourage the enemy to hold the village with greater tenacity. Shelton's advice was overruled and it was decided to limit the action to an artillery bombardment of Bemaru. The force left the cantonments before dawn on 23 November under orders of strict silence, the only sound being that of the crunching of the horses' hooves on the thin layer of ground frost. For reasons that were never satisfactorily explained, the column took only one gun with them, which was placed in a field facing a village enclosure. This was in direct contravention of an army General Order by the Marquess of Hastings, that expressly forbade fewer than two guns to take the field under any circumstances. This order was well known to every officer serving in India.

Before first light, the gun opened up with grapeshot and was immediately answered by a deadly hail of musket fire from what houses and towers remained standing in the village. By daybreak it looked like the cannon fire had done the job, as parties of Afghans were seen scurrying from the village, leaving behind no more than forty men. Swayne was ordered to move in on the village and the hapless officer once again confirmed his talent for botching things by leading his men in the wrong direction. The assault party missed the open gate and instead found themselves bunched up against a small barricaded door in the village wall. Swayne's men began to drop under the Afghan musketry, the major himself taking a bullet in the neck. They had to withstand the enemy's accurate fire for half an hour before being recalled by Shelton, who had just spotted an enormous body of men, estimated at up to 10,000, heading in their direction from Kabul. Some of the officers gave the order to raise a *sangar*, or stone breastwork, on the ridge, which would have afforded adequate protection from the enemy fire. In fact, 100 sappers had been sent with the column for this express purpose – the order was never carried out. Instead, the men were drawn up into two squares, which had proved effective at Waterloo in repelling Napoleon's cavalry, but which at Bemaru provided red-coated targets for the distant fire of some of the world's best marksmen.

The troops were rapidly losing heart for the fight and what was worse, there were signs of mutiny. At seven o'clock that morning, when Lieutenant-Colonel Thomas Oliver ordered his sepoys of the 5th up the hill where the Afghans were pouring a sharp fire into the ranks, not a man would move. It was only when Oliver started off to rush the heights on his own that some dozen sepoys were shamed into emulating his act of bravery, which cost their commander his life.

The lack of a second gun was soon felt when after a short time, the vent of their only cannon became too hot to handle. Having lost the intimidating effect of artillery to protect them, by nine o'clock they found themselves almost surrounded by the enemy. The only gap in the encirclement was that facing the cantonments, drawing the men's eyes to the safety of the fortified walls half a mile from the scene of carnage. Shelton tried to rally the sepoys by offering 100 rupees to any man who would take the Afghan flag that had been planted about 30yd away behind an earthen mound. Nobody ventured out to claim the reward, all attempts to move the men forward were in vain. They began to run in the opposite direction, towards the cantonments. The second square some 200yd behind held, and this managed to rally the panic-stricken troops, but now the gun was in possession of the Ghazis. There was a short skirmish, in which the Afghans retreated, leaving behind the gun and taking with them only the horses and limber. The cavalry refused to give chase, seeing thousands more of the frenzied Afghans from the city pouring to their positions.

At noon, Shelton sent Captain Colin Mackenzie to move up Major James Kershaw's reserve that had taken up a position on a knoll. Kershaw replied that it would be better for Shelton to join him, for if he abandoned the hilltop their escape route to the cantonments would be cut off. By this time most of the sepoys of the second square and the artillerymen had fallen to the fire of the Afghans' *jezails*. Shelton saw the game was up and ordered the gun to be taken quickly up to Kershaw's position. Seeing this, the Ghazis rushed wildly at the disorderly body of troops and an utter rout broke out, with the men charging down the hill in the direction of the cantonments. The retreat, if it can be called that, was covered by a heavy fire from Shah Shuja's 6th Infantry in the Mission Compound. A troop of cavalry rode out to meet the pursuers and was badly cut up. There was no attempt to bring in the wounded, who were left in the field to endure the mutilation which the Afghans practised with such delight on their fallen enemies. Shelton commented after arriving in the cantonments that as far as he was concerned, the Bemaru debacle had put an end to all exterior operations against the insurgents.

'Our troops had now lost all confidence,' Eyre writes after the engagement on Bemaru Heights, 'and even such of the officers, as had hitherto indulged the hope of a favourable turn in our affairs, began at last reluctantly to entertain gloomy forebodings as to our future fate.'[32] For the moment, the garrison seemed to have even thrown away their chance of escape: the Afghans lost no time in demolishing a new bridge that Elphinstone, in a moment of lucidity, had ordered be built over the river adjacent to the cantonments. A small abandoned fort stood nearby and Shelton, recognising its strategic importance, had called for a small detachment to be posted there to defend the bridge. Even this simple precaution was neglected, with devastating results for the Army when the retreat finally got under way.

Into this scene of despondency now stepped the sinister figure of Akbar Khan, riding into Kabul under cover of darkness to deliver the death blow to his hated enemy, the British. His appearance in the city gave rise to great rejoicing by the insurgents, who fired salutes in his honour and treated the Barakzai chief as their leader. Kaye tells us:

> He had the wrongs of an injured family to redress. He had a kingdom to regain. He had been an outcast and a fugitive during two years of suffering and danger, because it had pleased the British Government to invade his father's dominions and to expel the *de facto* rulers of the country. And now he saw opening out before him a prospect of recovering the lost supremacy of the Barakzais, and restoring his exiled father to the Bala Hissar.[33]

Macnaghten was hoping that reinforcements might yet be sent from Kandahar, as there had been no news from that quarter. It was not until 18 December that the garrison learnt of Nott's failure to send a relief column to Kabul. The Envoy also thought it possible to keep a dialogue alive with some of the less fanatical tribal chieftains. This afforded another glimmer of hope that an honourable settlement might be reached allowing the force to sit out the winter unmolested in the cantonments. With Akbar, there was no compromising: Dost Mohammed's second son had a very different agenda in mind.

The defeat of the British force at Bemaru gave rise to renewed debate over the advantages and hazards of falling back on the Bala Hissar. All the officers realised that short of a retreat to Jalalabad, with provisions in the cantonments down to a few days' supply, this was their only chance of keeping 16,000 people alive through the winter. Shelton, as ever, despaired of holding out for the whole winter at Kabul and strenuously advocated an immediate withdrawal to Jalalabad. What the brigadier failed or chose not to take into account, was that if the insurgents stood back from attacking the Bala Hissar, with its rich store of arms and ammunition, to say nothing of the presence of the traitorous Shah Shuja, the reason had to be that they themselves knew that such an assault would end in disaster. A contingent of well-armed troops in the Kabul fortress could repel with ease any attacking force. Macnaghten, on the other hand, had always favoured abandoning the cantonments and taking a chance on regrouping the garrison behind the citadel's fortified walls. But he was beginning to waver, more disposed now to leaving the decision with the military. There is no record of Elphinstone having any opinions on the subject, apart from writing to Macnaghten to remind the Envoy of what he was already painfully aware – that food supplies were running short – and to express his concern over reports that water in the Bala Hissar was selling at a high price. This report was false.

The situation remained relatively stable from that day to the latter part of November, the quiet gloom that hung over the garrison broken only by the occasional burst of rifle fire from the sepoys manning the low battlements whenever a raiding party drew near to the perimeter wall. The insurgents from time to time shelled the cantonments from their hillside breastworks, without inflicting serious damage.

Macnaghten now focused his thoughts on another course of action, namely to open direct negotiations with the enemy. In this he could count on Elphinstone's full support, for the general, who could barely walk, longed to be back in the sheltered surroundings of India. The Envoy did not hesitate to act. He arranged a meeting on 27 November and sent two of his deputies, Captains George Lawrence and Robert Trevor (killed a month later in a similar parley with the Afghans), to meet the rebel leaders Sultan Mohammed Shah Khan and Mirza Ahmed Ali, at the destroyed bridge by the cantonments. Sultan Mohammed set the tone for the preliminary talks, which lasted two hours by the riverbank, by insolently declaring that as the Afghans had been victorious on the battlefield, it was their prerogative to dictate the terms of capitulation. The chiefs then asked to see Macnaghten, and the little party proceeded to the cantonments where the Envoy paced nervously in the guard room of one of the gateways. Macnaghten's face remained impassive, not betraying the sinking feeling in his heart as he listened to Sultan Mohammed spell out his demands. These amounted to nothing less than unconditional surrender: that the British deliver up Shah Shuja and his whole family, hand over all their arms, ammunition and treasure, and give themselves up as prisoners of war. Macnaghten resolutely shook his head – the terms were totally unacceptable, he said. 'We shall meet then on the field of battle,' said Sultan Mohammed. 'At all events we shall meet at the day of judgement,' replied Macnaghten.[34] The British now knew they could expect no quarter from the enemy.

Zeman Shah, who had been proclaimed amir by the insurgent chieftains, was an honourable and affable man, but there was no mistaking him for a moderate. The *fatwah* against the infidel invaders was read out in his name in all the mosques. Macnaghten took heart on learning that Zeman's nephew Osman Khan had been deputed chief negotiator to the British, taking this as a sign of willingness to achieve an amicable settlement. Akbar had no interest in extending the hand of friendship to his enemies, and his voice carried weight with the insurgents. He quickly saw that the surest way to defeat the enemy was by depriving them of provisions. He effectively denied food supplies to the garrison by threatening with death villagers who supplied any description of food to the enemy.

Akbar's tactics achieved the desired results: by 1 December the garrison's provisions had dwindled to eight days' supply. The animals, in particular, were suffering badly. The cattle were being fed on tree bark, the horses were found gnawing at the tent pegs and cart wheels. Lady Sale reports that she saw one horse bite off and devour its comrade's tail. A number of the men had taken to eating animals that lay dead of starvation in the streets, and found themselves in competition with the pariah dogs that gorged themselves on the carcasses of camels and horses. Some small quantities of grain were still being smuggled in and sold at extortionate prices by a few of the more daring villagers of Bemaru who were willing to take the risk. But this did not stave off the hunger now gnawing away at the entire garrison, which was also feeling the shortage of firewood. Needless to say, the Afghans took great pleasure in this misery, and Macnaghten quickly found out that there was to be no softening of the terms of surrender. The enemy completed the destruction of the bridge the British had erected over the Kabul river, torching the wooden structure before the eyes of the troops, who looked on helpless from the ramparts. Nearly 5,000 armed men stood ready, the ramparts were bristling with cannon, but no orders were given to fire at the brigands.

Several of the officers came to impress upon Macnaghten the urgent need to open talks with the rebels – if it was to be a retreat to Jalalabad, now was the moment to negotiate the garrison's withdrawal and gather provisions for what they calculated would be a five-day march. Before Macnaghten could make a fresh approach to the tribal leaders, the troops sustained yet another humiliation. On 6 December the Afghans launched an assault on Mohammed Sharif's fort. This little fortress, some 300yd from the cantonments, had been the scene of bitter fighting almost exactly a month previous, and was now held by a contingent of British and sepoy troops of the 44th and 37th. That morning a small Afghan raiding party stormed the walls, an assault that was witnessed by an outraged Lady Sale: 'The Afghans planted their crooked sticks, which served them for scaling ladders, got up one by one, pulled out the mud [blocking the window] and got in. A child with a stick might have repulsed them.'[35] The bewildered troops took flight as soon as they saw the enemies' heads at the window, abandoning their arms and ammunition as they ran from the fort. They fled into the cantonments and no effort was made to recapture the fort.

❖ ❖ ❖

Two days later, on 8 December, the die was cast. Macnaghten was brought a letter bearing the signatures of Elphinstone, Shelton, Brigadier Thomas Anquetil and Lieutenant-Colonel Robert Chambers (the latter two in command of Shah Shuja's forces and the cavalry, respectively), in which the four senior officers in Kabul appealed to the Envoy to open a dialogue for the Army's immediate retreat to Jalalabad. By a fateful coincidence, that was the day Maclaren's brigade returned to Kandahar after its unsuccessful attempt to march to the relief of Kabul. It would be several more days before the news reached Macnaghten, who did not need to be reminded that the garrison was at a critical juncture: food for the fighting men had dwindled to a two-day supply. The villagers would not sell grain to the British, and the Army would not fight for it.

Much against his desire to soldier on, Macnaghten now resigned himself to taking pen in hand to draft a treaty of capitulation on terms which he hoped were the least humiliating for the force and for the Government of India, to which he was accountable. On 11 December, having digested the dispiriting news from Kandahar, the Envoy rode out to meet the chiefs by the banks of the Kabul river at a spot about a mile from the cantonments. Macnaghten's negotiating party consisted of Captains Lawrence, Trevor and Mackenzie, with a small detachment of bodyguards. The chiefs of all the principal tribes were in attendance, and Macnaghten must have felt a shudder down his spine to be met by the merciless gaze of Akbar Khan standing in their midst. The Envoy kept a cool head as he read out, in fluent Persian, the text of his proposed treaty. The British, he explained to the chiefs, were prepared to evacuate not only Kabul, but all of Afghanistan as well, including a withdrawal of the Jalalabad, Ghazni and Kandahar garrisons, on the condition that the Afghans provided assistance in carriage and provisions. At this point Akbar Khan got up and shouted his defiance: there was no need to supply the British with provisions, for as far as he was concerned, they could leave Kabul the very next morning. Macnaghten ignored this outburst and continued reading. Shah Shuja would be given the choice of staying behind or accompanying the British. On the Army's arrival at Peshawar arrangements would be made for the return of Dost Mohammed, his family and possessions and, for the fulfilment of these conditions, the Envoy was prepared to give up four British officers as hostages. These men were to be freed and sent to India once the Dost had reached Peshawar on his return journey. Furthermore, the most influential of the chieftains would escort the British troops to Peshawar. Lastly, Macnaghten attempted to retain some of the high ground by stipulating that the Afghans would promise to remain well disposed towards the Government of India and refrain from entering into treaties with other powers, and that they should consider allowing the appointment of a British resident at Kabul.

The reading and subsequent discussions lasted two hours, after which the sirdars gave their assent to the terms, asking that the British abandon their cantonments within three days, on 14 December. The chieftains retired to the city, carrying with them an unhappy Captain Trevor as a token of the Envoy's sincerity. Trevor would not have allowed himself to be taken hostage had he known the grisly fate awaiting him at Macnaghten's next meeting with the chiefs. Even now, the Envoy in his naivety, was able to write in an unfinished report later found in his desk, 'We shall part with the Afghans as friends, and I feel satisfied that any government which may be established hereafter will always be disposed to cultivate a good understanding with us.'[36]

Shelton's troops evacuated the Bala Hissar on 13 December, in preparation for the Army's departure *en masse* to India. Their progress to the cantonments was held up by the packing of tons of provisions and supplies, and it was not until six o'clock on that evening that the 600-strong garrison cleared the gate. The next few hours came to resemble a prelude of what was to befall the Army on the road to Jalalabad. Once outside the fortress, an indiscriminate firing broke out from Shuja's angry troops on the walls, and the surrounding hills were seen to be bristling with armed tribesmen. Akbar Khan, who had promised the garrison safe passage to the cantonments, told the men they would have to call a halt until the morning. The body of troops spent a miserable night in the open, and the rearguard came under attack when they started off at daybreak. Akbar Khan, in contrast to his later actions on the road to Jalalabad, this time kept his word. He intervened to stop the tribesmen attacking the column, which made its way safely into the cantonments at ten o'clock that day.

Lady Sale's diary for 18 December foretells in one frightening phrase of the disaster lying in wait for the British Army: 'When we rose this morning the ground was covered with snow, which continued falling all day.'[37] By evening prayer, the snow lay many inches thick on the ground. Like a death knell, the words 'snow all day' rang with grim regularity in her diary entries from that day forward. Elphinstone issued instructions for the garrison to make ready to depart Kabul on 22 December. Macnaghten had now been given the news of Maclaren's return to Kandahar and thus relinquished all hope of rescue. The Envoy and Elphinstone sent letters to the major British garrisons in Afghanistan, ordering the evacuation of these positions, 'commencing their march immediately after the receipt of this letter, leaving all guns, the property of Dost Mohammed Khan . . . also such stores and baggage as there may not be the means of carrying away'.[38] The withdrawal with honour that Macnaghten had so desperately sought to obtain from the rebel leaders, was in the end to be a disgraceful capitulation. Nor did the sirdars abide by their pledge to feed the starving Army: despite payment being sent to the enemy, no cattle were sent in and shipments of grain were intercepted en route to the cantonments by roving bands of fanatics, without the Afghan chieftains lifting a finger to stop the plundering – nor, for that matter, with any move by the soldiers manning the walls. Foremost in Macnaghten's thinking was the need to keep on good terms with the enemy, now supposedly friends, to ensure that the garrison got away from Kabul unmolested.

Akbar Khan now induced his tribal comrades to turn the screws on the British by stiffening the terms of the treaty. The military chiefs were told that they must give up the small forts the troops

had occupied outside the cantonments, and they did so. The promised transport vehicles necessary to put the Army on the march
were withheld, causing the departure date to be pushed back, as
each day the snow continued to fall. There was now a permanent layer of about 5in on the ground. The chiefs then demanded
that the garrison surrender a portion of their guns and ammunition, and that Brigadier Shelton be delivered as a hostage. On
21 December Macnaghten held another meeting with Akbar Khan
on the plain between the cantonments and the city. The Envoy
agreed to hand over four hostages of which two, Lieutenant John
Conolly and Captain William Airey, were immediately given up. The
other two officers selected were Eldred Pottinger and the chief artillery officer, Captain Robert Warburton. Shelton, who had no interest
in falling into the Afghans' clutches, was spared. Macnaghten obliged
this generosity by sending Akbar his own carriage as a present.

The Envoy was cheered the next day, 22 December, when word
reached him that Akbar had quite inexplicably softened his stance,
seemingly moved to pity by the garrison's wretched state. The news
was brought by Captain James Skinner, who had been living under
Akbar's protection in the city. This officer was the bearer of proposals, as tempting as they were advantageous to the British position,
and just as false. Akbar sent a document in which he pledged to
seize Amanullah Khan, the most influential of the rebels, who was
to be delivered to the British as a prisoner. The Army would be
allowed to send a regiment to re-occupy Mohammed Sharif's fort,
and another to hold the Bala Hissar. Shah Shuja would stay on
as amir, and all that Akbar Khan asked was that he be appointed
vizier, or chief minister. Finally, the troops were to remain in their
present positions until the spring, at which time they could depart
Afghanistan under warm, sunny skies. Macnaghten eagerly signed
his name to the document, which Akbar proposed be ratified the
following day, and by doing so the Envoy sealed his own doom.
'That a scheme like this . . . should have for a moment deceived
a man of Sir William's usual intelligence and penetration,' wrote
Eyre, 'is indeed an extraordinary instance of infatuation, that can
only be accounted for on the principle that a drowning man will
catch at a straw.'[39]

On the morning of 23 December, Macnaghten had little time to spare for thoughts of the approaching Christmas holiday, as he made ready to attend his fateful meeting with Akbar Khan. After a hurried breakfast, which was to be his last, he sent for his staff officers Lawrence, Trevor and Mackenzie, who were to accompany him to the riverbank rendezvous. Colin Mackenzie heard for the first time, from the Envoy's lips, the background to this fresh round of talks. Mackenzie's first reaction was that Akbar must be plotting to ensnare Macnaghten in a trap. 'A plot!' the Envoy exclaimed irritably. 'Let me alone for that – trust me for that!' As they rode towards the city Macnaghten, sensing what was to come, uttered his famous words, 'At all events, let the loss be what it may. A thousand deaths were preferable to the life I have of late been leading.'[40] The Envoy did not view the occasion entirely without suspicion. To this end he had asked Elphinstone to have two regiments of infantry and two guns ready for action, if indeed a trap it turned out to be. He muttered with some annoyance as they rode out of the cantonments that the regiments he had requested had not yet been assembled. This was because Elphinstone had decided not to comply with Macnaghten's request, considering it too risky an action. The general sent a note ahead informing the Envoy of his decision, but it failed to reach him in time.

Macnaghten had on the previous day sent Akbar Khan a pair of handsome double-barrelled pistols and now he took along a black Arab stallion, belonging to one of the officers, which the Afghan had much admired. As they neared the meeting place, a crowd of armed men gathered by the roadside, looking on in silence as the little cortège cantered past. Macnaghten ignored their threatening presence, looking straight ahead at what he imagined to be his last hope to redeem British honour. He felt enough confidence to send back a small cavalry escort that had accompanied them from the cantonments. The spot agreed for the parley was a hilly area about 600yd from the cantonments, by the banks of the Kabul river. Akbar spread some rough horse blankets on the ground, where the snow was less thick, and when the Envoy and his party pulled up, he thanked him profusely for the gifts of the pistols and the horse.

The meeting began amicably enough, with the usual salutations and wishes for everyone's good health. The British party dismounted and seated themselves on the hillside, with Trevor and Mackenzie on either side of the Envoy, and Lawrence standing behind. One of the chiefs invited him to sit along with the others, but he would go no further than to kneel on one knee, as if readying himself to spring into action. Akbar opened the talks by asking Macnaghten if he were prepared to accept the terms conveyed to him on the evening before. The Envoy readily assented, but he was disturbed by the presence of such a large group of men around Akbar, whom he reminded that this was understood to be a confidential meeting. Some of the chiefs made theatrical gestures at beating off the crowd with their whips. Then Akbar rose to his feet and assured Macnaghten that everyone present was in the secret. This was the signal for the Afghans to seize the British officers, and a scene of utter mayhem broke out, one which today still obscures Akbar's role in the episode. The three officers were forced to mount horses behind Afghan riders and were immediately set upon by a mob of enraged Ghazis wielding sticks and daggers. Trevor was the unfortunate one: he tumbled from his horse and was swiftly hacked to pieces. Lawrence and Mackenzie got through and were whisked away at a gallop to Mahmud's fort. Macnaghten was wrestling desperately on the ground with Akbar and the last words he cried out were in Persian, *Az barae Khoda* – 'For God's sake!'

Those who witnessed the attack spoke of Akbar Khan drawing a pistol from his belt, one of the set that Macnaghten had sent him the day before, and firing point-blank at the Envoy. What is not known is whether it was the bullet that killed him on the spot, or if the poor man survived a few more moments to be despatched by the knife-wielding Ghazis who fell upon him like a pack of jackals.

The last despatch to reach Calcutta from the Kabul garrison brought the melancholy news of Macnaghten's assassination, which Ellenborough communicated to the Secret Committee. 'The last date of our intelligence, then received from Kabul, was the 25th of December,' he stated, 'when Major Pottinger reported the murder of Sir William Macnaghten, and the continuance of negotiation for the retirement of our troops from that place.' The Governor General conveniently laid the blame for the Afghan debacle at Elphinstone's feet, threatening the general with a court martial on his return to India. Ellenborough told the Secret Committee:

We have regarded the proceedings of Major General Elphinstone, as far as we are aware of them, with the keenest disappointment and displeasure, and we have requested the commander-in-chief to institute, when circumstances may admit of it, a full military inquiry into the Major General's conduct, and desired that the authority of the Major General over the troops serving in or near Afghanistan should wholly cease.[41]

Instead of reminding Ellenborough of his role in sanctioning Elphinstone's appointment, the directors of the Secret Committee wrongly treated his comments with silence, for what justification had the Government in sending a doddering, ill soldier to command an army of occupation, or failing to recall him at the first sign of ineptitude?

The Army's response to this outrage was no more encouraging. Macnaghten's murder took place within sight of the cantonments, in light of day, but no guns opened up on the mob and no orders were issued to send out a detachment of soldiers to avenge his death. A further and almost greater ignominy was heaped on the British when the Afghans set about performing their ritual mutilation. The Envoy's torso, along with Trevor's corpse, was paraded in triumph through the streets and later prominently displayed hanging from a meat hook at the entrance to the bazaar. Macnaghten's head was severed and impaled on a stake in a public square, and that night some thoughtful soul came to replace his glasses on his face. Mackenzie and Lawrence were locked away in a cell in Mahmud's fort, where later that day an Afghan appeared, bobbing up and down a human hand spiked on a pole. One of the fingers bore Macnaghten's emerald signet ring.

The hostages were woken at midnight and rushed off to Akbar Khan's house. On the way, their Afghan 'escort' relieved Lawrence and Eyre of their watches, rings and other valuables. Akbar received the officers from his bed, feigning a great show of courtesy, while still insisting with colossal cynicism that Macnaghten and Trevor were alive and well. It is not known what he intended to achieve by this deception and it was a few hours later that Skinner, who had just been released, gave them the truth. The next day Akbar accompanied the hostages to Zeman Shah's residence, where a violent argument broke out between the sirdar and the British officers in the presence of the rebel's amir. Akbar went into a rant, accusing the British of treachery and hostility towards the Afghans. This, he pronounced, rendered the terms of the treaty null and void. Akbar now demanded the surrender of all the married officers, their wives and children as hostages, along with the guns, ammunition and money held in the cantonments.

Major Eldred Pottinger, the second most senior civilian in Kabul, was designated Macnaghten's successor, and to the hero of Herat fell the unhappy task of negotiating the Army's retreat from Kabul. Pottinger was still bedridden, recovering from the wound he had received in his leg on his escape from Charikar. He made no pretence of being honoured by his appointment: 'I was hauled out of my sick room,' he wrote, 'and obliged to negotiate for the safety of a parcel of fools who were doing all they could to ensure their destruction, but they would not hear my advice.'[42] Pottinger's soldierly view was that the Army had no right to give up without a fight. Rather than squander precious time debating the terms of capitulation, Elphinstone and his staff ought to despatch a force to Kabul to crush the enemy and if need be, blow the place to pieces. It was common knowledge that Akbar and the chiefs did not intend to keep faith. Their treachery, it was strongly believed, would show its face the moment the Army abandoned its position in the cantonments – if not before. The word had been spread round the British garrison compound, probably by one of the Afghans who remained loyal to the British, that Akbar's intention was to abduct and enslave the women and children and murder all the men, except one, who would have his arms and legs amputated and be placed at the entrance to the Khyber Pass, a ghoulish warning to all infidels to keep out of Afghanistan. Apart from this macabre anecdote, there was an abundance of sensible reasons to treat the Afghans' undertakings as suspect, when not utterly worthless, but Pottinger was wasting his breath: he must have realised that there was very little fight left in the Army, and none whatsoever in its commanding officer. The enfeebled old man went so far as to canvas opinion from the married officers, as to which of them might be prepared to give up his wife and children to satisfy the rebels' demands. The general offered an inducement of 2,000 rupees per month to any man who offered to stay with his family. Major Philip Anderson spoke for almost all his brother officers when he replied he would rather put a pistol to his wife's head and shoot her. Lieutenant Sturt said his wife and mother-in-law, Lady Sale, would only be taken at the point of the bayonet. A dissenting voice came from Eyre, who said he would agree to the terms on the condition he were allowed to remain behind with his wife and child. Elphinstone then avowed he had no choice but to reject the terms. Pottinger found himself with his back to the wall. His powers were limited by having only been asked to assume the office of senior Political Agent, and that by default, without Macnaghten's authority as Government Envoy.

Pottinger was overruled and it was agreed to give the insurgents 1.4 million rupees, a sum that Macnaghten had offered as payment for guarantees of safe passage to Jalalabad. This writer can find no other instance in British military history of the commanding officers of a fighting force bribing their way out of a tight spot. Nevertheless, Macnaghten's secretary Lawrence was released from captivity on 29 December to prepare the necessary bills drawn on the Government of India. The treacherous Amanullah Khan's eldest son came into Lawrence's room at five o'clock in the morning, as the hour of prayer was being proclaimed from the city's mosques. He urged Lawrence to dress quickly and then had his men wind a turban round his head to disguise his European face, leaving only one eye exposed. An escort of 100 men accompanied Lawrence back to the cantonments, where he was almost tearfully greeted by the sentry who said the British never expected to see him return alive. Lawrence drew up the bills on the stipulation they should be cashed only on proof of safe arrival of the troops at Peshawar. Lawrence sent word ahead to the city's bankers, the idea being to prevent the bills being marketable in Kabul. A small consolation was that the chiefs were consequently able to raise nothing on these bills.

The six commissioned officers who had agreed to give themselves up were taken as hostages to Zeman Shah's house. The greater portion of the garrison's treasury and, to the disgust of the soldiery, five cannons were handed over to the chiefs. As the date of departure was repeatedly pushed back, the Afghans alleging insufficient time to make ready their escort party, few people in the cantonments spared a thought for the cheerless Christmas that had passed, much less the sombre New Year to come. Hungry, shivering families huddled round the faint heat of their fires, stoking the scant supply of firewood, their eyes cast mournfully away from the snow piling up on the ground. Lady Sale records that the thermometer at daybreak hovered below zero, never rising more than a few degrees above freezing. 'In the sitting room with an enormous blazing fire, at noon, 40°. Yesterday, with the same good fire, at 9 a.m., 11°.'[43] Prophetically, from this day, on which the British sealed the treaty with the Afghan insurgents, giving in to all the enemy's demands, her diary entries end almost invariably with the doom-laden words, 'Snow all day.'

A fresh blanket of snow had settled on the frozen earth on the morning of 6 January, Epiphany, as the Army began its slow march from the Jalalabad Gate. In an ironic twist, two days previous to the withdrawal from Kabul, the first brigade of General Sir George Pollock's relief force, consisting of 3,000 seasoned fighting troops, had crossed the Sutlej.

Chapter 5

BLOOD WAS FALLING,
BLOOD ON SNOW

T he Army had withstood sixty-five days of treachery and
depravation, and it was now to suffer the ultimate humiliation, by abandoning its position and giving up its weapons
to the enemy. The troops commenced the retreat without any sign
of the promised Afghan escort that was to protect them from the
rapacious Ghazi bandits. The well-meaning Zeman Shah had sent
Pottinger a letter warning of the dangers of leaving the cantonments without an escort. But once the entire force had been put
on the march, it gathered the unstoppable momentum of a tidal
wave of humanity. It wasn't until half past nine in the morning
that the baggage trains were wheeled out through a breech in
the low ramparts, which the previous day had been cut by Sturt,
the chief engineer. Until their very last hour in Kabul, the gods
of ill fortune seemed to have conspired against the British, who
missed the opportunity of an early start that might have seen
them through the Khoord Kabul Pass before sunset. Elphinstone,
through feeblemindedness or hostility, or both, had kept Shelton
in the dark as to the departure arrangements until the evening
of 5 January. The brigadier was stunned: that night he pleaded
with the general to give orders for the baggage trains to be loaded
and ready to move before daybreak. Nothing was done, and
Elphinstone in fact brushed Shelton's entreaties aside with disdain.
On the morning of departure, with the troops struggling to get
through the stream of camp followers who clogged the temporary
bridge constructed of gun carriages that had been laid across the
river, Captain Mackenzie found Elphinstone sitting on his horse,
observing the chaos in a state of bewilderment. All semblance
of military discipline was rapidly breaking down, with the camp

followers in a state of panic, pushing their way through the columns and seeking safety by intermingling with the troops. The Afghans had already begun looting and tearing apart the Mission House, with the Army not yet halfway out of the cantonments. The general's reaction to this mayhem was to despatch Mackenzie to the front of the column with an extraordinary order to call off the march. Mackenzie could see that Elphinstone was in no fit state to command, so he took it upon himself to persuade the general that a return to the cantonments would only throw the entire force deeper into confusion. Elphinstone, always happy to follow the last word of advice he received, gave his assent to carry on.

Brigadier Thomas John Anquetil commanded the advance guard, consisting of the 44th Foot, the Sappers and Miners, a squadron of the 4th Irregular Horse, Skinner's Horse, three mountain train guns and the late Envoy's escort. Anquetil had under his protection the British wives and children. Brigadier Shelton led the main column, with the 5th and 37th Native Infantry, Anderson's Horse, Shuja's 6th Infantry and two 6-pounder guns. Lieutenant-Colonel Robert Chambers took up the rearguard, composed of the 54th Native Infantry, 5th Cavalry and two 6-pounder guns. In all, well over 4,500 fighting men, with a swarm of more than 11,000 camp followers who were to prove the force's ruin.

The morning dawned clear and frosty, the snow lay nearly a foot deep on the ground, the thermometer stood considerably below freezing point. Eyre poignantly describes the ordeal that lay ahead on the first day of the withdrawal: 'Dreary indeed was the scene over which, with drooping spirits and dismal forebodings, we had to bend our unwilling steps. Deep snow covered every inch of mountain and plain with one unspotted sheet of dazzling white, and so intensely bitter was the cold, as to penetrate and defy the defences of the warmest clothing.'[1]

So laboured was the progress of this sea of humanity that after trudging through the snow for two and a half hours, the Army had only covered 1 mile, having to battle the Afghan skirmishers that began firing on the rearguard even before the last units were clear of the city. The first and costliest setback of the day was the river crossing. The plank bridge laid on top of the gun carriages would not allow the passage of more than a handful of men at a time. The camp followers refused to wade through the river, despite there being easy access to a shallow crossing only a short distance upstream. There was an overwhelming press of people and animals at the bridge, which in part accounted for the loss of nearly all the baggage on the spot, as well as a large part of the commissariat stores. When the rearguard came under attack, much was left on the plains by the terrified camp followers while Chambers' men, detached from the main body, had no choice but to defend themselves on open ground. The plight of those leading the retreat was hardly more enviable. The cold was so bitter and the snow-laden terrain so exhausting, in particular for the Indians who were less accustomed to such hardships, that men, women and children were lying down by the roadside to die. When they reached higher ground, those in Anquetil's column turned to see in the distance their cantonments in flames, with hordes of Afghans looting everything of value from the houses.

At four o'clock, Elphinstone halted the column and the Army began setting up camp for the night. They had advanced about 6 miles from Kabul, disregarding the advice of some friendly Afghans who had begged them to keep moving, at least to the more sheltered ground near the Khoord Kabul Pass. It would have made sound strategy to secure the pass before the insurgents had time to send their followers to intercept the Army. But this would have required the column to push on for another 9 miles through the snow, a feat quite beyond the strength of this exhausted, half-frozen multitude. It was not until two o'clock in the morning that the last troops of the rearguard stumbled exhausted into the bivouac area, where 16,000 people settled down to spend a miserable night in the snow, without tents or adequate clothing, with almost no cooked food, scooping out little shelters to protect themselves as best they could from the howling wind that blew across the plain. Shelton had already lost fifty of his men, along with his guns, to enemy attacks on the road. Dozens of frozen corpses lay strewn about, the bodies of those who had succumbed to the intense cold. There were many desertions during the night, desperate sepoys for the most part, who had flocked back to Kabul to meet an uncertain fate.

No bugles were sounded the next morning when the force rose like a disorganised mass of somnambulists, to move out without

orders, without leadership. They merely picked themselves up at
first light, those who did not lie among the scattering of corpses,
and trudged on towards Khoord Kabul. The first off were the camp
followers with the baggage carriages, followed closely behind
by many of the sepoys. The order of march was reversed, with
Chambers' rearguard taking the lead, but it became a desperate
struggle for the troops to push their way past the camp followers and hundreds of pack animals. Discipline came to an end as
the Afghans pressed in on the rear, carrying off the guns as they
pleased and killing all who put up any resistance. As the Army
advanced, a growing mass of Afghan Ghazis boldly made their
appearance on the hillsides that flanked the road.

Elphinstone's plan for that day was to take the column through
the Khoord Kabul Pass to the village of the same name. To everyone's dismay, after pushing on for 5 miles the order was given to
set up camp for the night at the village of Boothak at the entrance
to the pass, lying a foot deep in snow. This was an unwise decision
to say the least, since the Army was travelling with less than five
days' rations and with no forage whatsoever for the cattle. The reason for the halt was a letter that Pottinger had received from Zeman
Shah, in which the Afghan promised to send a party of horsemen
with food and firewood, and to have his soldiers disperse the Ghazi
tribesmen who hovered menacingly on the Army's flanks. As usual,
Elphinstone and Shelton were at loggerheads as to what action to
take. The brigadier, who was behaving in a more intelligent manner
than at Kabul, argued with faultless logic that since they had only
come 3 miles that morning, it was madness to stop now, with at
least another five hours of daylight before them. Their only hope for
survival was to press on as quickly as possible. If this required jet-
tisoning the camp followers along with the baggage in order to save
the Army, the women and children, then so be it. Another night out
in the snow without tents or food would destroy the troops. Shelton
now implored the general to continue the advance, but Elphinstone
was long past listening to reason. He was correct in declaring that
the force was in desperate need of food and warmth. But he was
wrong in believing that provisions would get through from Kabul.

Late that afternoon, a band of some 600 horsemen was spotted approaching across the plain. Far from being a supply column,

the body of Afghan cavalry made their appearance armed to the teeth and with Akbar Khan at their head. The British never found out what had become of Zeman Shah's provisions, or even if they had ever left Kabul. Captain Skinner was despatched under a flag of truce to enquire of the enemy's intentions. After a brief meeting, Skinner rode back to camp carrying a message from Dost Mohammed's favourite son, in which he had craftily turned the tables on the beleaguered force. The British had no one to blame but themselves for their wretched condition, he explained. Had he, Akbar, not implored them to hold tight in Kabul until a suitable escort was arranged? Yet being an honourable man, he had ridden out to offer his protection from the fanatical Ghazis, though his ability to constrain them was a matter of doubt. Elphinstone felt himself vindicated when Akbar said the force should remain the night at Boothak. The sirdar would supply the force with whatever it required, but the troops must stay put. Akbar had demonstrated his goodwill, so now the British should show theirs. They were to hand over more hostages until he received written confirmation that Sale had evacuated Jalalabad.

The Army discovered Akbar's true agenda the following day, the most tragic of the entire retreat in terms of lives lost. The doomed force now prepared to spend another night of suffering in the cruel snow, while Akbar's men quietly rode ahead to blockade the Khoord Kabul Pass.

At an early hour the following morning, leaving behind many corpses on the ground, the force picked itself up and began a confused march forward. By this point few of the troops, and certainly none of the camp followers, could spare a thought for the fate lurking in the corridor they were about to enter, a passage so narrow that the sun rarely penetrates its gloomy recesses. Three senior officers, Pottinger, Lawrence and Mackenzie, volunteered to give themselves up as hostages, which fortuitously saved their lives. It was proposed that the force push on to Tezeen, a village about 10 miles beyond the pass, there to await word of Sale's withdrawal. Food and firewood was a matter for later discussion: Akbar was now calling the shots. At this time of year, the stream that runs through Khoord Kabul becomes a mountain torrent, part gushing water, part ice, which the troops would be required to cross twenty-eight times to make it through the pass. The shivering multitude hunted for warmth and sustenance with the desperation of animals. The sepoys took to burning their caps and clothes, while the artillerymen broke into a store of brandy and drank themselves into oblivion. Lady Sale confesses to indulging in a small tipple herself to ward off the cold. She writes:

> For myself, whilst I sat for hours on my horse in the cold, I felt very grateful for a tumbler of sherry, which at any other time would have made me very unlady-like, but now merely warmed me, and appeared to have no more strength in it than water. Cups of sherry were given to young children three and four years old without in the least affecting their heads.[2]

This nonsensical belief in the warming effects of alcohol probably accounted for as many deaths that day as did the musket balls of the Afghan marksmen.

The Army came under attack as soon as the camp rose to commence the day's march. Major William Thain's contingent of the 44th valiantly defended the advance guard by driving off the Ghazis and positioning themselves on a height that commanded the road. The Afghans continued creeping up under cover of the ravines and hillocks, from which they relentlessly harassed the troops, spreading panic among the camp followers until the force got under way at midday. Hardly had they covered half a mile when the Ghazis let loose a ferocious attack from the hilltops, sending the slowly advancing stream of men and animals into wild disarray. It was here that Akbar showed his true colours. The chiefs who rode ahead of the first contingent of soldiers shouted in Persian to the fanatical tribesmen to cease firing at the *feringhees*. But Pottinger heard Akbar cry out in Pashtu, the Pathan language which he thought the British would not understand, for the Ghazis to slay them all. He alerted Mackenzie and told his brother officer that if he were killed, to remember that Akbar had called for the entire force to be massacred.

Many men fell even before the column entered the Khoord Kabul Pass. Lady Sale took a bullet in the wrist, three others having passed through her *poshteen*, or Afghan fleece, without doing her any injury.

Her son-in-law Sturt, who rode back to look after a wounded Major Thain, had his horse shot out from under him and before he could pick himself from the ground received a severe bullet wound in the abdomen. Several of the children were carried off by the Afghans, others were saved by mothers who defended their young with their own bodies. One of the wives, a Mrs Mainwaring, was threatened by a sword-wielding Ghazi horseman. Spotting her plight, a gallant sepoy grenadier galloped up and shot the Afghan dead. He conducted the woman and her child through the pass until he himself was cut down. From that point, Mrs Mainwaring was forced to walk for miles through deep snow, picking her way over the bodies of the dead and dying, her baby clutched to her breast.

It can be argued that on this morning, once Akbar's evil intentions had been put beyond doubt, there was still time for the Army to turn round and fight their way back to the Bala Hissar, a distance of around 10 miles. The sacrifice would have been terrible, but far preferable to the miserable doom waiting in the passes. Most of the men would have rejoiced at the call to fight, had the proper leadership been there to give the command. But the commanders in question, in Lady Sale's favourite expression, were hopeless 'croakers'.

Once inside the dark canyon of the Khoord Kabul, the Army had passed the point of no return. The tribesmen knew this, and as soon as they had the main body and the baggage escort in their sights, the bullets began whizzing down by the hundreds. The column's progress into the Khoord Kabul Pass had all the trappings of a funereal procession, and its depiction by contemporary writers is impregnated with sombre eloquence. 'Onward moved the crowd into the thickest of the fire, and fearful was the slaughter that ensued,' noted Eyre in his journal.[3] Kaye wrote in similar terms, 'Into the jaws of this terrible defile, the disorganised force now struggled in fearful confusion.'[4] Men were dropping every few paces from the relentless fire that rained down from the flanking escarpments. Most of the sepoys had abandoned their weapons, while the British soldiers were too numbed with cold and fatigue to put up any resistance. The Afghans fired indiscriminately, knowing that the Army had lost its ability as well as its will to put up a fight. The British officers who had been taken hostage later gave an account of marching through the pass near evening, behind the force, when they came upon a sight of horror. The bodies of their comrades had been stripped and many of them mutilated. There were children cut in two, Indian women as well as men lay lifeless in the snow, some frozen to death, others chopped to pieces, many with their throats cut from ear to ear. That day, the bodies of some 500 fighting men and more than 2,500 camp followers were left in the pass.

By nightfall, the remnants of the column were clustered close together on the open ground, settling in to face another night of misery. It was snowing heavily when Assistant-Surgeon Alexander Bryce, who would himself not survive the retreat, dressed Lady Sale's wound. He extracted the musket ball from her wrist, and also attended to Sturt's horrendous stomach wound. Florentia Sale could see by the expression on the surgeon's face that there was no hope for her son-in-law. He died the next day in great agony, in the arms of his wife, the daughter to whom Lady Sale touchingly refers throughout her narrative as 'Mrs Sturt'. Lady Sale was one of the more fortunate that night, for someone had found a tarpaulin under which she, along with Sturt, the other ladies and their husbands huddled. The sepoys and camp followers tried to force their way not only into the makeshift tent, but into its occupants' beds as well. A bed to be understood in this case being a fleece laid half on the snow, with the other half wrapped round its owner. She recorded in her diary:

> Many poor wretches died round the tent in the night. The light company of the 54th Native Infantry, which left Kabul thirty-six hours previously eighty strong, was reduced to eighteen files. This is only one instance, which may fairly be taken as a general average of the destruction of our force. More than one half of the force is now frost bitten or wounded, and most of the men can scarcely put a foot to the ground.[5]

On 9 January, the 12,000 or so survivors rose like automatons from their beds of snow to resume another day's march. The men straggled behind, with hardly any order in the ranks, allowing the camp followers to trudge aimlessly along in advance. The disorderly throng that clogged the road was the Army's chief tactical nightmare. But on this morning it hardly mattered, for within an hour of starting, when the column had covered less than a mile, Elphinstone recalled the entire force to camp. The general paraded the wreck of his regiments to hear Captain William Grant explain the reason for the sudden volte-face: Akbar Khan had sent a messenger with a proposal that all the married men, with their families, place themselves under his protection. The sirdar would guarantee them honourable treatment and safe escort to Peshawar. Elphinstone was no doubt genuinely concerned for the welfare of the women, some still weak from childbirth, others in the final weeks of pregnancy. Horrifying as it sounds, some had nothing to wear but the nightdresses they had on when they fled the cantonments. Others had scarcely tasted food since departing Kabul. There was loud protesting in the ranks when the letter was read out, but on this occasion Elphinstone stood firm. He was not a leader of men, but he was a gentleman. Pottinger, before being taken hostage, and remembering that Akbar's own family was being held prisoner in British hands in India, sanctioned the proposal. The Political Officer hoped that if for no other reason, the sirdar might be restrained by considerations of self-interest. So Lady Sale, Lady Macnaghten and the other widows and wives of the British officers, along with their husbands, a party of some thirty in all, were led away to safety – but not to Peshawar. Moreover, Akbar's promises to send food and fuel remained unfulfilled. Without provisions and firewood, many more victims were that night consigned to a miserable death. The families were taken away to a small fort about 2 miles distant at Khoord Kabul village, all of them grasping to the faint hope of somehow being escorted to Jalalabad. Lady Sale and sixteen others were herded into a filthy, windowless room. At midnight an Afghan came in to serve them some mutton bones and greasy rice, which they gratefully devoured.

The following morning, 10 January, marked the force's fifth day of exposure to the rigours of an Afghan winter. Preparations for the march got under way at daybreak against the usual backdrop of pandemonium. Everyone's greatest fear was to be left in the rear, hence the camp followers' wild mêlée to push to the front of the column. The 44th Foot could muster only about a hundred men fit to bear arms and these, along with some fifty troopers of the 5th, hustled the mob aside to take up position as the advance guard. It was not until ten o'clock that the first units moved out, keeping a watchful eye on the groups of Afghans scurrying ahead on the ridges towards a small rocky gorge on the road called Tarakie Tungie. This led to the start of a 2,000ft climb to Huft Kotal, or hill of seven ascents, the other side of which the road meandered down into snow-free ground.

The Afghans attacked as soon as the column stopped at the mouth of the gorge, set between the spurs of two precipitous hills. Many of the officers and men of the advance guard were suffering from snow blindness and in their disorientation, they marched straight into the incessant volley of fire. By the time the troops had struggled to the top of Huft Kotal to begin their descent to the village of Tezeen, the gorge behind them was choked with corpses and the dying. The sepoys and camp followers abandoned all they were carrying, including their weapons, and fled for their lives. This was a golden opportunity for the Afghans to rush down on their unresisting victims. The butchery was appalling: when the remnants of the advance guard waited for the rear to join, they discovered to their horror that they were almost the only survivors of the column that had marched from Khoord Kabul a few hours earlier. Less than 300 troops, composed of 50 horse artillerymen, 70 of the 44th and some 150 cavalry troopers, were all that were left of the whole Kabul force. The bodies of the soldiery strewed the road as far as the Khoord Kabul Pass, the defile itself impassable from the piles of dead bodies. Roughly 4,000 troops and 8,000 camp followers had perished since the force departed Kabul, yet the men were to face three more days of this torturous existence before they found relief in death.

As the little band of troops contemplated their end, Akbar Khan drew up with a party of horsemen. Elphinstone ordered the troops to make ready for an attack, but the sirdar raised his hand in a gesture of peace. Captain Skinner, one of the few commissioned officers left, had previously acted as go-between for Akbar Khan and was probably the man best acquainted with his conniving ways. He stepped up to Akbar's horse, barely able to contain his anger, and demanded to know why the sirdar, supposedly the most powerful of the tribal chieftains, had done nothing to stop the slaughter. The British had agreed a treaty with him, handing over hostages and captives as had been agreed on both sides, and the Afghan had in turn guaranteed their safety. Now the corpses of an entire army, along with thousands of camp followers, lay rotting on the Afghan plain.

Akbar returned a pained look, expressing his deep regret at what had occurred. But, he said, despite his efforts he had found it impossible to restrain the frenzied Ghazis, who refused even to obey the commands of their own chiefs. Akbar barely made any effort to disguise his hypocrisy. The only alternative now, he intimated, was for the soldiers to lay down their arms and place themselves under his protection. The sirdar's own men would escort them safely to Jalalabad, a promise of which the men had now grown weary. As for the several thousands of camp followers still scattered about the countryside, Akbar regretted that these people were too great a burden to take on. They would have to be left to their fate. When Skinner related these outrageous terms to Elphinstone, it was decided that the force would turn its back on Akbar and his worthless assurances, and continue the trek to Jalalabad.

Once the column made its descent to Tezeen, the men were met by the grotesque sight of hundreds more dead camp followers, those who had pressed on ahead of the troops past the summit of Huft Kotal, only to be massacred by the Afghan fanatics waiting at the foot of the hill. At four o'clock that afternoon, Shelton's rearguard joined the rest of the exhausted soldiery in the Tezeen valley. Akbar and his followers had taken a short cut over the hills and were already waiting in the vicinity of the British camp. In spite of all the evidence to the contrary, Elphinstone still hoped for a negotiated settlement with the Afghan chief which would allow the remains of his Army to continue on to Jalalabad. To this end, he sent Skinner out for another conference with Akbar. The Afghan saw no need to offer compromises to a vanquished enemy. His answer remained unchanged: surrender your arms and give yourselves up to us. Even Elphinstone now saw that all hopes for negotiation were at an end. As evening shadows crept across the valley, the general summoned his few remaining officers to a meeting, in which it was decided to make a 22-mile dash to Jugdulluk under cover of darkness. With any luck, which had so far been in scarce supply, they might make it through the treacherous pass by morning.

It was impossible to camouflage the movements of so large a body of men in an open valley, so word was sent through to Akbar that Elphinstone's intention was to advance only 7 miles to Seh Baba, alleging this to be a more comfortable spot to spend the night. That evening, the column renewed its march, and as always their progress was fatally held up by the assemblage of camp followers. There was some heavy firing on Shelton's rearguard from marksmen holed up in a network of caves some miles from Tezeen. A few of the officers fell by the wayside, but the bulk of the force managed 17 miles that night, limping into the village of Kutter Sung at eight o'clock on the morning of 11 January.

The Afghan insurgents now showed themselves at their most pitiless: Shelton had to contest every inch of ground under an intense fire from the surrounding heights. The terrain provided no cover and there was no turning back. 'It was now evident,' wrote Eyre, 'that the delay occasioned by the camp followers had cut off the last chance of escape. From Kutter Sung to Jugdulluk it was one continued conflict.'[6] The depleted advance guard made it to Jugdulluk at about three o'clock that afternoon and took shelter on high ground behind some ruined walls of the village. From this position they could see Shelton in the distance, struggling up the road. The brigadier was urged on by the cheers of the men pinned down ahead of him. The walls afforded the troops little sanctuary from the musket fire, but the real source of their distress was thirst – it was maddening to be only a few yards from a stream, which held instant death for anyone who ventured out to fetch water.

Akbar now had the effrontery to summon Captain Skinner to his encampment, even as the Afghan's kinsmen who crowned the surrounding heights continued to pour volley after volley on the troops. Skinner dutifully made his way to Akbar's tent, returning two hours later with a message inviting Elphinstone, Shelton and Captain Johnson to a meeting with the sirdar. To the troops' despair, Elphinstone agreed to see Akbar, handing over temporary command of what was left of the Army to Brigadier Anquetil. The sirdar received the three men with exquisite courtesy, fed them a sumptuous meal of mutton and spiced rice, served them sweet tea and sat them before a roaring fire, by which time the British officers had fallen completely into the Afghan's hands.

Captain Johnson had a fluent command of Persian and acted as interpreter in the conference. Through him, Elphinstone implored Akbar to send food and water to the famished troops. The sirdar falsely swore he would carry out the general's wishes but in the meantime, he informed Elphinstone, Shelton and Johnson that they could consider themselves hostages to the evacuation of Jalalabad. Elphinstone would not hear of it: the veteran of Waterloo summoned up his courage to declare that he would prefer death to being separated from his troops in the hour of danger. Akbar reassured him that all these matters could be amicably resolved in the morning. He then offered them the irresistible comfort of a warm tent for the night.

The three unwilling hostages awoke on 12 January to the tumultuous din of Ghilzai tribesmen flocking into Akbar's camp. They had come to feast their eyes on the enemy chiefs whom the illustrious sirdar had tricked into captivity. At nine o'clock, after a luxurious breakfast, the three officers were led before the Ghilzai leaders to negotiate the Army's fate. The talks went on all day and the atmosphere was growing uglier by the hour. Akbar needed to deploy all his powers of persuasion to restrain the chieftains – their utterances of hatred for the infidels threatened imminent violence. The angry tribesmen were placated by an offer to disburse among them 200,000 rupees, Akbar giving his personal guarantee that the money would be delivered to the chiefs. Still no progress was made, and at seven o'clock in the evening the captives' ears perked up to the crackle of gunfire coming from the direction of the pass. Treachery was rife below as well as up in Akbar's camp. Skinner had been told that a rider was on his way in with a message from Akbar Khan. The soldiers took heart in the hope that the messenger might bear some good news from their officers, perhaps even a guarantee of safe conduct to Jalalabad, though secretly they no longer put any faith in Akbar's word. As the horseman drew near, he pulled out a pistol and put a bullet through Skinner's face. The officer lingered in great pain for six hours and, after his death, what was left of the force saw that nothing was to be gained by further delay but death by thirst or musket ball. Elphinstone had read their thoughts. He directed Johnson to use his good offices to despatch a note to Anquetil, instructing the brigadier to have the troops ready to march at eight o'clock the next morning. The Afghans saw to it that the message never got through, and meanwhile Anquetil had taken matters into his own hands. That night, leaving the sick and wounded to their fate, the men picked their way down the path into the Jugdulluk valley to pursue the trek to Jalalabad. Of the original force, there remained only about 120 of the 44th and 25 of the artillerymen. Even now the troops had to put up with the encumbrance of a far greater number of camp followers, who clung to the fighting men for protection. As they marched, the Afghans stole in among the teeming drove, slashing with their daggers at the unarmed men and dashing off with all the plunder they could fit into their saddlebags.

What was left of the column now faced a 3-mile uphill trek to reach the infamous Jugdulluk Pass at dusk, a place to be entered with extreme trepidation, and not at all at night. Watch fires blazed on the hilltops and the men knew they were exposing themselves to the deadly *jezails* of the Ghazis who lined the steep escarpments on both side of the pass. Nearing the top of the defile, the force was brought to a sudden halt by a barricade of logs and boulders in their path. The Afghans were there, patiently waiting in the cold darkness. They opened up with their muskets, throwing the camp followers into a panic-stricken scramble for cover. For Kaye, the battle in the Jugdulluk Pass hammered the final nail into the Army's coffin. 'The massacre was something terrible to contemplate,' he recounts. 'Officers, soldiers and camp followers were stricken down at the foot of the barricade. A few, strong in the energy of desperation, managed to struggle through it. But from that time all hope was at an end. There had ceased to be a British Army.'[7] Twelve officers fell in the pass, among them the column's commander Brigadier Anquetil. A few men and several officers bravely scrambled over the barrier, bayoneting the Ghazis who charged them in a fury. At daybreak, a party of some twenty officers and forty-five soldiers of the 44th, with a pack of some three hundred camp followers jostling the troops, reached Gandamak. A smaller party of soldiers had pushed on ahead to a spot near the Sourkab, a tributary of the Kabul river. There was a dispute over which road to take to Jalalabad, and the one finally chosen ran over the hills adjacent to the Sourkab, past the village of Futtehabad, about 15 miles west of Jalalabad.

The remnant of the 44th arrived at Gandamak on the morning of 13 January in a state of total despair, with not more than two rounds in each trooper's pouch. Major Charles Griffiths, of what had been the 37th, was the most senior officer left. He formed up the men in a square on a little hillock, determined to fight to the end. When they reached this spot, parties of Ghazis began gathering around the soldiers, who were outnumbered by a hundred to one, according to reports by the handful of survivors. Most of the men were already wounded, but they were determined not to lay down their arms. The Afghan horde started to close in on the little band, when a messenger broke out from the massed enemy to inform Major Griffiths that Akbar Khan awaited him in conference. No sooner had he ridden off with the Afghan, the enemy began closing in on the troops, all the while entreating them to give up their weapons and accept the hand of friendship. When the soldiers refused, the Afghans began snatching at their rifles, and then the Ghazis withdrew to higher ground to begin picking off the officers and men at will. Their ammunition exhausted, the men still stood fast, driving back the waves of fanatics at bayonet point. It was only a matter of minutes before nearly all the men lay dead or dying on the blood-soaked ground. One final rush finished their work, though along with three or four privates who had fallen wounded, the Ghazis spared Captain Thomas Souter. The Afghans never showed any mercy to British officers, but in this curious case Souter had wrapped the regimental colours round him and the enemy took him for a person of distinction, whose life could command a high price. The fortunate captain and his men were handed over to Akbar, who sent them off to the north-east on a one-month trek to a fort in the Lughman valley.

The group of mounted officers that had ridden out of the Jugdulluk Pass ahead of the 44th escaped the carnage at Gandamak. They reached Futtehabad in safety as the massacre was taking place a few miles behind them. Some had perished on the road, but six survivors rode into the small cluster of houses that afternoon, where the farmers took pity on their wretched state and offered them food. They thanked their kind hosts and sat down for a rest when several of the villagers crept up on the unsuspecting officers and plunged their knives into two of them. The others rushed for their horses and galloped off in the direction of Jalalabad. Of the four who made good their getaway, three were overtaken and killed within 4 miles of the Jalalabad garrison.

The tale of Dr William Brydon's remarkable escape has assumed pride of place in the annals of military folklore, and rightly so. In 1839, at the outbreak of war with Afghanistan, Brydon was posted to the 5th Native Infantry as an officer in the East India Company's Army Medical Service. When the bulk of the Army of the Indus withdrew from Afghanistan, Brydon remained behind with the occupation force in Kabul. Now riding alone across the barren plain, Brydon knew he was only a couple of miles from Jalalabad and so he spurred his pony on as fast as the exhausted beast could carry him. Just as his heart was lifting with the thought of salvation at hand, he spotted a party of about twenty men drawn up in the road, each clutching a handful of large stones. To turn back would have doomed him to the same fate as his slain comrades. The Afghans carried no firearms and were obviously local villagers, so Brydon reckoned that if his pony held out, there was just the slimmest of chances of cutting his way through the group of men. With great difficulty he spurred the pony into a gallop and taking the reins in his teeth, he rode straight into his attackers, slashing his way through with his sword. Brydon quickly put himself out of range of their knives and only took a couple of bruises from flying stones. Less than a mile down the road he was met by another similar party blocking his way. He made straight for them, but was obliged to prick his pony with the point of his sword before he could get it into a gallop. Brydon's own account of his escape, published as an appendix to Lady Sale's journal, gives a hair-raising description of the final dash to Jalalabad. 'Of this party, one man on a mound over the road had a gun, which he fired close down upon me and broke my sword, leaving about six inches in the handle,' he writes. 'But I got clear of them, and then found that the shot had hit the poor pony, wounding him in the loins, and he could now hardly carry me.'

Brydon rode slowly on, until five horsemen appeared on the road, wearing red tunics. He took them for a party of irregular cavalry from Jalalabad, but they were Afghans, leading away the horse of one of the murdered officers who had ridden with Brydon. He tried to get away, but his pony was literally on its last legs and could hardly move. One of the Afghans broke away from the group and closed in quickly on Brydon, thrusting with his sword. Brydon just managed to deflect the blow with the bit of sword left on the hilt, which broke off and fell from his hand as the Afghan galloped past. When his attacker raised his arm to strike again, Brydon hurled the handle of his sword at him, forcing him to swerve. The blade fell on Brydon's left hand. 'Feeling it disabled, I stretched down the right to pick up the bridle. I suppose my foe thought it was for a pistol, for he turned at once and made off as quick as he could.'[8] Brydon then felt for the pistol he had been carrying in his pocket – tragically it had dropped out along the road. Suddenly he felt himself drained of energy, nervous and frightened at shadows, barely able to sit his saddle as his pony struggled to put one hoof in front of another. Brydon was losing blood from wounds to the knee and to his left hand. He had also received a near-fatal blow to the head from an Afghan knife, being saved from death only by a copy of *Blackwood's* magazine rolled up under his forage cap.

At that moment the sentinels on the ramparts of Jalalabad, looking out over the plain that extended northward and westward from the town, spotted a small dot approaching. Earlier that day, Brigadier Dennie confided to Sale, like an oracle of doom, his conviction that the Kabul force had been entirely destroyed. 'You'll see, not a soul will escape from Kabul except one man, and he will come to tell us that the rest are destroyed.' The evidence of that prophecy was now before their eyes. 'Did I not tell you,' Dennie exclaimed, 'here comes the messenger.'[9] Brydon approached the walls on his dying pony, whose head drooped low as it dragged itself slowly onward. The rider seemed in as desperate a plight as his horse. His head was bent forward upon his breast, the reins had fallen from his nerveless grasp, and he swayed in the saddle as if he could barely retain his seat. As he came nearer, and lifted his face for a moment, he was seen to be frightfully pale and haggard, with the horror of an untold tragedy in his bloodshot eyes. That horror was immortalised in Lady Elizabeth Butler's celebrated painting of Brydon's arrival at Jalalabad, *Remnants of an Army*, now part of the National Army Museum's collection in London. A detachment of the 13th Light Infantry galloped from the gate to escort Brydon into the fort, where his wounds were dressed and he was given a hearty dinner. The pony was put in a stable and almost immediately it collapsed, never to rise again. That night lanterns were suspended from poles at different points about the ramparts to guide stragglers into the fort. From time to time, the bugles sounded the advance. Not a soul came forward, not that night nor on the two nights following, on which the beacons were lit.

Brydon was the sole survivor of the Kabul force to reach Jalalabad in safety. But there were others, still alive, who had lived through the barbarous massacre of the troops and camp followers. As the ragged troopers of the 44th were battling every inch of the way to their doom at Gandamak, the hostages were being led off in the opposite direction, to the little fort at Khoord Kabul. Their state of exhaustion and the unspeakable privations they had endured on the march were such that even the indomitable Lady Sale acknowledges she was in no state to take a stand on Akbar's proposition to lead the captives out of danger. 'There was but a faint hope of our ever getting safely to Jalalabad, and we followed the stream,' she records in her diary. 'But although there was much talk regarding our going over, all I personally know of the affair is that I was told we were all to go, and that our horses were ready, and we must mount immediately and be off.'[10]

They started off towards Tezeen on 11 January under an escort of about fifty Afghan horsemen. Akbar Khan's soldiers told the British officers to be prepared to use the swords they had been allowed to carry, as an attack might be expected from the Ghazis lying in wait in the hills. The scenes of carnage which the band of captives encountered on the road were so gruesome that even the likes of Florentia

Sale felt horrified by the sight. She confessed to be sickened by the smell of blood from the mangled bodies, who had been stripped and left naked in the snow. The piles of corpses were so thick that it required some care for the party to guide their horses so as not to tread on the bodies. Lady Sale counted fifty-eight British dead on the road that day. Numbers of camp followers were found stumbling about, still alive, frostbitten and out of their senses with misery. Those who could still speak cried out for food and water, which the prisoners were unable to supply. None of these poor wretches, the agony of despair depicted in every face, were to survive the next few days. The British prisoners retraced their steps along the same road on which the Army had advanced a few days before, to spend a reasonable night at Tezeen. The next morning they continued on their journey, meandering along a rough track that followed the river to a little fortress belonging to the conspirator Amanullah Khan. The men and women were crammed together into one room, with no complaints from a group of fastidious Victorians desperately in need of warmth. At this place, recalls Lady Sale with her customary scathing wit, an old hag sold them chapattis at three for a rupee – until she perceived her customers' semi-starved state and raised the price to a rupee each.

On 13 January, as the 44th was making its last stand a few miles behind at Gandamak and Dr Brydon rode alone into Jalalabad, the unsuspecting hostages were approaching Jugdulluk, the first stage of an odyssey of captivity that was to last more than eight months. They reached the village that afternoon after a harrowing struggle over mountain paths that even the baggage camels found difficult to negotiate. The last 2 miles of road were lined with corpses, including that of the much-admired Captain Skinner, all stripped and lying side by side, just as they fell. A few tents had been pitched at the settlement, in which Lady Sale's party discovered Elphinstone, Shelton and Johnson, who a few days before had fallen into Akbar's trap at that very spot. Here the hostages got their first news of the catastrophe that had befallen the Army. In stunned silence, they crept into their makeshift shelters, but few managed to get any sleep that night, their thoughts tormented by visions of the many thousands left dead in the snow.

The hostages, now gathered together in one group, embarked on a four-month voyage that was eventually to take them to Shiwaki, a small fortification about 2 miles from Kabul. Akbar knew it was only a matter of time before the Government of India despatched a punitive force to Afghanistan and he was anxious to move on quickly. The last thing he wanted was to lose the hostages, who represented his only bargaining tool. The morning after their arrival at Jugdulluk, the prisoners moved out in a northerly direction under the escort of a squadron of Irregular Horse. To the rage of all the prisoners, these troopers turned out to be Indian Army deserters who had gone over to the Afghan rebels during the retreat. The British prisoners were force-marched 25 miles that day up a steep and narrow gorge to the top of the Budurnuk Pass, the most difficult they had yet encountered. It was an exhausting day of ignominy that ended on an even sourer note when on reaching a small fort at dusk, they were refused admittance and found themselves obliged to set up a bivouac in the open air. George Lawrence and Lady Macnaghten were the only ones in the party travelling with baggage, so as on previous occasions, they arranged their trunks to form a windbreak for the women and children.

The prisoners were given no respite: waking stiff with cold and with their stomachs crying out for food, at first light they were marched to the Panjshir river, and from its confluence with the Kabul on to the verdant Lughman valley, heading westward to an unknown final destination. They passed a large shrine, which legend has it was the tomb of Lamech, the father of Noah, a holy site to which Shah Shuja had made a pilgrimage two years previous. Shortly afterwards they arrived at Tirghuri, a large village the likes of which they had not laid eyes on since the retreat from Kabul. The streets were lined with market stalls and the village housed a large number of resident Hindu shopkeepers, who took pity on the bedraggled travellers, providing them with food and drink. They halted here, and it being a Sunday, the British captives joined together in divine worship for the first time since their captivity.

Like Lady Sale and Vincent Eyre, Lawrence kept an account of his days as a hostage. He describes the Sunday service as melancholy but deeply emotional, 'frequently interrupted by the tears and long drawn sobs of some of our number'. But all was not well in the village. Shots were heard during the prayer service, and there were reports of deaths. This turned out to have been an attack by brigands, who were beaten off by Akbar's men. Lawrence learnt of this in the evening, when Akbar came to inform him that 'he had been forced to cut off the ears of some plunderers'.[11] The sirdar said there was no time to lose, for the Ghazis would be back in strength before long. With barely a day's rest to restore their strength, the following morning saw the hostages back on the road, carrying with them a swelling burden of wounded and sick British soldiers, who now numbered about fifteen. The idea was to trek higher up the valley to a place of greater security. As they left the village, Akbar and his men were hard pressed to drive off the swarm of Ghazis who closed in around the column, probing for a chink in the wall of horsemen to rush in and finish off the British prisoners.

As they plodded up the valley slopes, Akbar approached Lawrence with a devastating piece of news that confirmed what everybody had darkly suspected all along: the Army was totally destroyed and only one man, a Dr Brydon, had made it to Jalalabad. 'Akbar Khan, to our horror, has informed us that only one man of our force has succeeded in reaching Jalalabad,' records Lady Sale. 'Thus it is verified what we were told before leaving Kabul, that Mohammed Akbar would annihilate the whole Army, except one man, who should reach Jalalabad to tell the tale.'[12] The word quickly spread to the others and it was a sullen, downcast party that tramped into the newly erected fort of Budiabad, the property of one of the rebel chieftains, Mohammed Shah Khan. Here, at least the prisoners were able to indulge in a measure of privacy, if not comfort, of which they had so far been deprived. To everybody's relief, the women and their families were allotted separate quarters from the officers and lower ranks, which in itself came as a vast improvement over the alien communal life they had shared in the past week.

Once they were settled in, Akbar Khan paid a visit to the ladies to whom he unctuously explained that they were to consider themselves his honoured guests, that they would lack nothing he could supply them with and that as soon as the road was safe, the entire party would be sent to Jalalabad. His meeting with the men was equally solicitous. When Lawrence complained that one of Akbar's men had been hurling abuse at him, the sirdar told Lawrence he could have the offender's ears, if he so pleased. Akbar then asked Lawrence to draw up a list of whatever his 'guests' required in the way of food, and this would be furnished without delay.

There then occurred a strange phenomenon, one which could stand as perhaps the earliest recorded incidence of 'Stockholm Syndrome', a psychological response in which over a period of time, an abducted hostage begins to manifest feelings of loyalty to the hostage taker. The most extreme case was that of Mrs Wade, who out of fear or by some dark psychological twist, converted to Islam and became the concubine of an Afghan chieftain. She turned so violently anti-English that she betrayed her own husband, one of the captives, by revealing to the Afghans that he possessed two pieces of gold which she had herself sewn into his boot. Of all the prisoners, Lady Macnaghten had the most reason to despise Akbar Khan, her husband's murderer, yet inexplicably, she requested Lawrence to make Akbar a gift of the fine grey horse he rode, which had belonged to the Envoy. This could have resulted from a burst of emotionally charged gratitude, though in the final analysis, Akbar had offered to provide his prisoners with nothing more than a few basic human necessities. Then it was Lawrence who came forth and handed the sirdar a gold-plated revolver and a diamond ring, both of which he had saved from the Government stores. When Akbar and several of the other chiefs departed the following morning, Lawrence sent him off with a silver hookah, and Lady Macnaghten presented him with a fine pashmina shawl he had greatly admired. Lawrence duly handed over a list of the daily supplies of sheep, flour, rice, cooking fat and firewood the captives would require, and this time the sirdar was as good as his word. Lawrence brought up the subject of money, as by now the rupees they had taken from Kabul had been spent on purchasing provisions along the way. Akbar again complied, handing over 1,000 rupees to Lawrence to purchase whatever extra provisions they required from the villagers along the way. The sirdar even refused to accept a receipt, saying such things were only required among traders, not between gentlemen. For now, the hostages were worth more to him alive than dead.

Akbar felt the need to cover his tracks, just in case things were to go badly for him when the British relief force crossed into Afghanistan, as surely it must. He went to see Pottinger, knowing him to be the chief political representative among the captives. Pottinger's word would carry credibility with the military authorities, so Akbar requested him to write a full account of the Kabul insurrection to be sent to Macgregor at Jalalabad, reckoning that the relief of Sale's garrison would be the first objective of a British force marching from India. Akbar's credulity was remarkable, since he genuinely believed that he would come out of this report smelling of roses. Pottinger, for one, suffered no symptoms of Stockholm Syndrome. Hence Akbar flew into a fit of anger when he read Pottinger's version of the uprising, which portrayed the sirdar as the treacherous insurrectionist that he most clearly was. Akbar endeavoured to persuade Pottinger to tone down the letter so as to give a more favourable impression of himself, particularly with regard to his kindly treatment of the hostages. Pottinger's letter to Macgregor is not known to survive, but it is safe to assume that the final draft bore no resemblance to a whitewash. Pottinger was understandably ill-disposed towards Akbar, whose men had inflicted the leg wound he received on the road from Charikar, and which had yet to heal properly and remained a source of constant pain. Akbar, for his part, had good reason to be concerned for his own safety: Lawrence received a letter that day from Jalalabad, telling of the massive relief force assembling at Peshawar under General Sir George Pollock, that was preparing to march on Jalalabad. The tide was about to turn.

Along with this heartening letter came a packet of newspapers, along with a bundle of clothing collected by the troops at Jalalabad. The hostages were now furnished with some basic comforts of life and for the first time since their captivity, they settled down to enjoy a few days of relatively mundane existence. This period of calm came to an abrupt end on the morning of 19 February, an unusually close and mild day. 'About 11 a.m., when I was exercising the children at drill, I felt the ground suddenly convulsed under my feet,' writes Lawrence, 'and immediately the ladies rushed out of their rooms, large masses of the lofty walls falling in on all sides, and the whole fort seeming to rock to and fro.'[13] Lady Sale was reading a letter from her husband General Sale that morning, encouraging her to keep up her spirits as no relief was expected before April, when disaster struck suddenly and without warning. 'For some time I balanced myself as well as I could, 'til I felt the roof was giving way,' she says. 'Our walls and gateways, and corner towers are all much shaken, or actually thrown down. We had at least twenty-five shocks before dark, and about fifteen more during the night, which we spent in the courtyard.'[14] Lady Sale and her companions spent the better part of a month coping with a constant wave of aftershocks, fearing the next big tremor that could bury them all.

The earthquake spread panic across eastern Afghanistan, an omen of cataclysmic events in store for Akbar Khan and his cadres of Afghan rebels. At Jalalabad that day, Colonel Monteith had climbed to one of the bastions and was sweeping the horizon with his telescope, when all at once the earth began to tremble violently, and there was a rumbling which some of the troops described as the sound of hundreds of heavily laden wagons rolling over a rough track. The whole of the plain around the fort began to heave like billows on the ocean surface – a second later, walls and houses came tumbling down, not sparing the parapets and all the defensive works it had taken the garrison three months to erect. Monteith himself was buried under the ruins, yet escaped death. In fact, his mishap provided the only levity of that disastrous day. Sale and Havelock spotted Monteith's wig, covered with dust, under a heap of timber and rubble. Sale pulled at it, and was shocked to hear from under the debris a cry of pain and Monteith's voice shouting for whoever it was to stop tugging at his hair. Once the dust had settled on the ruins and the officers were able to gather their thoughts, they realised that the garrison now lay exposed to an assault by Akbar Khan, whose army stood scarcely 6 miles from what had been the ramparts. That night the troops maintained a watchful vigil over the plain, which shuddered nearly hourly with aftershocks. Almost immediately following the earthquake the men, pickaxe and shovel in hand, carried off a small miracle by working day and night to fill in the breaches and rebuild the walls to an even stronger state than before, so that a few days later when Akbar made his move, he met with a surprise.

Thirty miles away, the hostages were indulging in great, if discreet, celebration, on hearing from a Hindu merchant just returned from Jalalabad that Akbar Khan's assault on the garrison had failed. Lawrence recalls having warned the sirdar when he left their camp that he was wasting his time and men by riding off to attack Jalalabad. To which Akbar gave a shrug and the laconic reply, 'Never mind, Sale and his garrison will soon be with you.'[15]

Life once again entered a tranquil stage for the captives, the only incident of note being an attempt on Akbar's life by one of his servants, who had been given a 100,000 rupee bribe by Shah Shuja to do the job. The assassination attempt failed, the man was caught and roasted alive for his trouble. On 10 April the hostages were told to pack their belongings and prepare to depart Budiabad. But no sooner had they proceeded 4 miles on the road, a group of horsemen rode up at full gallop, waving their turbans with cries of 'Bravo! It is over!' and ordering the party back to their old quarters at Budiabad in all haste. The reason given was that there was no longer any danger of a British attack, for Sultan Jan, one of Akbar's confederates, had annihilated Pollock's force in the Khyber Pass. The British hostages were stunned – was all hope of freedom finally to be abandoned, with nothing to look forward to but a life of misery as slaves of an Afghan warlord? 'The story was told us in so detailed and circumstantial a manner that for a time we really were inclined to believe it to be true,' writes Lawrence.[16] The party trudged back to camp in an abyss of despair. But their anguish was short-lived, for it emerged that the tale was a hoax. The march had been halted when a row broke out among the chieftains, causing Akbar to fear his enemies would seize and murder the British prisoners, thereby depriving the sirdar of his trump card. The sirdar's dismay over the impending British advance had spread to the valley's entire population, who began bundling their families up to the hills for safety.

The next day saw the hostages off again, this time in earnest, the little caravan traversing some rugged hills in a westerly direction towards Kabul. Several hours into the march, they crossed a shallow rapid to enter a valley blossoming with gentian, forget-me-not and other varieties of flower. It was the first greenery they had seen for weeks. Here they came across Akbar Khan, reclining in a *nalkee*, a litter for persons of rank, on a knoll by the roadside, looking ill and careworn, his arm bound up from the assassin's knife-thrust. Akbar smiled wanly and beckoned to Lawrence to join him, for he had tidings to share with the English. In contrast to the previous day, this tale of a clash with the British was wonderfully true. Akbar spoke in a soldierly manner of the crushing defeat he had sustained at Jalalabad, how his force had been taken by surprise by the British cavalry, with Sale himself at their head on his white charger. The sirdar was forced to flee on horseback and narrowly managed to escape capture, having spent some anxious hours at a river crossing while his men knocked together a raft to take him across.

The march continued for another week, and then on 23 April tragedy struck on the way from Tezeen to Kabul. General Elphinstone was in a weakened state, suffering from a leg wound as well as severe dysentery. He could no longer take the strain of marching under a heavy downpour since departing Budiabad. The party had reached Tezeen on 19 April, where one of the officers' wives, a Mrs Waller, gave birth to a baby girl, whom she appropriately named Tezeena. The prisoners were moved out again on short notice and the upheaval proved too much for Elphinstone. The evening of the 23rd found the senior officers gathered round Elphinstone's makeshift camp bed, where the old general lay shivering violently and rapidly losing his grip on life. Everybody present in the room took pity on the pathetic figure of the dying soldier, a victim of the errors of others – all, that is, except for Shelton, who vowed that if he survived he would lay the blame for the disaster squarely on Elphinstone's shoulders. Summoning what little strength he yet retained, Elphinstone asked for the prayers for the dying to be read out, and also whispered to his batman Moore of the 44th to bring him a bowl of hot water and clean shirt. Once washed and changed, Elphinstone requested Moore to lift his head. The batman, who was in tears, obeyed, and at that moment the general expired. 'He repeatedly expressed to me deep regret that he had not fallen in the retreat,' writes Lawrence. 'His kind, mild disposition and courteous demeanour had made him esteemed by us all, although his death to him was a most happy release.'[17] Sadly, Elphinstone's tribulations were not to end with his death. Akbar consented to send the general's remains for burial to Jalalabad in the charge of his batman Moore, who travelled disguised as an Afghan. On

28 April word arrived that the coffin had been seized on the road by a party of Ghazis, who stripped the body naked and pelted it with stones. Akbar was incensed at this outrage and despatched a rescue party to bring in Moore and the general's body, which was then repacked and forwarded on a raft down the Kabul river to Jalalabad, where it was interred with military honours. His failings notwith-standing, a fitting epithet for the old general could be taken from the Prologue of Chaucer's *Canterbury Tales*:

> He never yet no vilonye had sayde
> In al his lyf, unto no manner of wight.
> He was a very perfit gentil knight.

The hostages spent nearly a month in this place, until on 23 May they were taken off to their final rest stop at Shiwaki. Here they were at last given roomy, clean and comfortable quarters in a compound less than a hour's walk from Kabul, where fighting was raging between the Saddozai and Barakzai factions. But before they commenced the march to Shiwaki, a dispute arose between Akbar and the prisoners, who demanded the ladies be furnished with camels for the journey. The degree of familiarity between warder and prisoners had deepened to an extent to which Akbar merely remarked with good humour, 'Well, you are strange prisoners!'[18] And the plucky hostages got their way, though they had to content themselves with mules to ride, as there were no camels to be found. They soon came upon the corpses of the ill-fated Army, many of them recognised as friends, most of them reduced to skeletons, a stark reminder of the fate awaiting the hostages themselves had they contrived to stay behind with the troops.

The party was led to within sight of a city whose ruler, the British puppet-king Shah Shuja, was no more. Weeks before, as the Barakzai clansmen and supporters closed ranks round the beleaguered Amir, Shuja had begun firing off desperate letters to Macgregor at Jalalabad, between January and March, pleading for help and, as was his wont, money. All that Macgregor, who had troubles of his own, could offer was encouragement to hold on for a while longer, as Pollock's relief force would not be long in coming. That was on 9 March, but by the time the letter was delivered to the Bala Hissar, the Saddozai ruler had only a few days left to live. Shuja thought he had appeased his enemies, notably those of the Barakzai faction, by offering to personally lead his soldiers in support of Akbar Khan at Jalalabad. Rising early on 5 April, Shuja arrayed himself in royal apparel and lifted into a chair of state, he proceeded towards his camp, which had been pitched at the foot of the Seeah Sang hills east of Kabul. Shuja ul Daulah, the son of Zeman Shah, had stolen out of the Jalalabad Gate before dawn with a party of Afghan marksmen to set up an ambush on the road. As the royal procession passed the spot where the assassins lay in waiting, they opened fire on Shah Shuja, striking down several of his bearers. Shuja ran for his life, casting aside a leather bag filled with precious stones, the royal treasure he had thought to take with him in case affairs went badly on the battlefield. The assassins chased after and cornered him, and he fell to his knees pleading for his life. Daulah strode casually up and put a bullet through his brain, and then cast the corpse into a ditch. None of the assailants spotted the bag of gems, which was later picked up by an Afghan peasant who had witnessed the murder from a nearby field. He examined the jewels, which he believed to be bits of worthless coloured glass, and later happened to show them to a trader in the village of Charsu near Kabul. The wily merchant offered him a trifling sum for the treasure, which he eagerly accepted. Unfortunately for the buyer, another person spotted the transaction and denounced the trader to Daulah, who had the man lashed to the mouth of a gun and threatened to be blown up if he did not give up the gems. Thus fell Shah Shuja's property into the hands of his assassin.

It is open to question whether Shah Shuja had been playing a double game. Some sources claim that he had struck a secret pact with Macgregor by which Shuja's forces, rather than rallying to Akbar's banner, would link up with the 'Army of Retribution' coming from Peshawar. It was even reported that Shuja had confirmed to Sale in writing that he was on his way with all the troops he could collect to meet General Pollock's force at Jalalabad. The story has it that this letter, if it ever existed, was intercepted and delivered to Akbar Khan, who immediately ordered Shah Shuja's assassination.

Shuja's soldiers would have made little difference to Akbar's fate at Jalalabad. Having been routed by Sale on the battlefield, Akbar was now in a more conciliatory frame of mind. The score or so of British prisoners held in his custody gave him an upper hand and the chance to buy some time. His demands were accordingly scaled back, and he was now willing to settle for an exchange of prisoners, along with an undertaking by the British to evacuate all their forces from Afghanistan. Pollock had a few weeks previous sent a message agreeing in principle to pay a ransom of about £20,000 for the hostages. Akbar now instructed Lawrence, along with Captain John Troup and a handful of Afghan soldiers, to ride to Jalalabad to obtain these terms in writing from the general, whose column had fought its way to arrive at Sale's besieged garrison on 16 April. The two men started at three o'clock in the morning on 31 July, riding through the night to avoid the ferocious sun that in summer months sends the heat on the Afghan plain soaring above 115°F. Fourteen hours later their exhausted ponies took them to Tezeen, where they rested, and on 2 August they reached the fort of Jalalabad. Sale reports that the moment he entered Pollock's tent with his letter from Akbar, he could see in the general's stern countenance that the march on Afghanistan was already too far advanced to entertain any prospects of a negotiated settlement. Akbar had somewhat ingenuously written in his message, 'The General must fix a day on which he will depart', which prompted the terse reply, 'I will not be dictated to.'[19] Sale took the bad news back to Akbar on 10 August where he found the sirdar preoccupied with matters of internal strife. Akbar was in a weak position politically. All parties were jealous of one another, and especially of the rising power of Akbar Khan. Amanullah Khan, the chief instigator of the Kabul uprising, had transferred his unstable affections from Akbar's family to Shuja's once again. 'Kabul politics were such that no one was much surprised by this defection,' writes Norris. Amanullah now switched his support to Shah Shuja's third son Prince Futteh Jang, who took possession of the Bala Hissar and demanded all the British hostages be handed over to him. 'Civil war was imminent, and many of the more peaceable citizens left Kabul for the country,' says Norris. 'By now Kabul was the scene of daily fighting between the factions.'[20] Amanullah took refuge in the Bala

Hissar and Akbar began a determined siege of the great fortress. Akbar's men had gained the upper hand, and the sirdar was about to be recognised as Futteh Jang's chief minister, with Amanullah as his second in command, when Zeman Shah stepped into the fray, claiming that he alone was the rightful ruler of the Barakzai faction and that Akbar had no right to treat with Futteh Jang without his authority. This was the chaotic state of affairs in Kabul when Lawrence handed Akbar Pollock's letter. The sirdar gave Lawrence a menacing look as he flew into a rage. 'I had thought you English were men of truth,' he shouted, 'that your word once given was as good as law. I now see I was in error, and so ends all my hopes of an amicable arrangement, and now it must be war.'[21] What Akbar did not know was that the course of the war had already been decided, for Pollock was in receipt of orders from the Government that effectively killed all hopes of a compromise: having relieved the Jalalabad garrison, he was now to lead his force to Kabul. The exaltedly christened Army of Retribution was preparing to do precisely what its name implied. Pollock's advance into Afghanistan, however, had in no way resembled a walkover.

Chapter 6

THE EMPIRE STRIKES BACK

When Sale found out that his wife had been taken hostage by Akbar Khan, it was all his fellow officers could do to deter him from ordering the immediate evacuation of Jalalabad and retreating to India, in compliance with the sirdar's demands. Many feared that Pollock would not arrive in time to save the garrison being overwhelmed by Akbar's army. The sirdar's camp was out of range of the garrison's guns and the Afghans had occupied the Peshawar road as well as the ground outside the Kabul Gate, cutting off communication with India. The only way of getting messages through was with *cossids*, or native runners, many of whom showed extraordinary bravery in slipping through Akbar's lines, and paid a terrible price for their courage. One unfortunate *cossid* was caught with a note secreted in a cake, and was marched to within sight of the garrison's walls and choked to death with his cake. Another was sent back to Sale with his ears and nose cut off.

The garrison dug in for an indefinite siege, and naturally their main concerns were for provisions and ammunition. Foraging parties were sent out under escort, with varying degrees of success, to collect sheep and grain for the men's rations. More ingenious tactics were called for to ensure a supply of ammunition. This problem, Pollock tells us, was addressed in the following way: 'Afghan musket balls were picked out of the parapet walls for re-use, and a block of wood, carved into the figure of a man, dressed in Sale's spare uniform and showed over the ramparts with a sword which waggled when a string was pulled, for several days brought a shower of bullets for collection.'[1]

Several stormy councils of war were held in Sale's quarters in the Jalalabad fortress. In these sessions the brigadier and his

175

Political Officer Macgregor advocated a withdrawal at all costs to Peshawar, fighting their way through the Afghan lines if necessary. Macgregor detailed the dangers and difficulty in which the garrison was placed. Broadfoot vehemently opposed any form of capitulation and found a staunch supporter in Monteith. He maintained that however weak the measures taken for their relief, the council had no grounds for thinking that the Government had abandoned them. He reminded the officers assembled in the room that reinforcements were being pushed forward to Peshawar and that every consideration mitigated against a retreat. Dennie stood behind Sale, mainly out of his dislike of Broadfoot, and found an ardent backer in Captain Augustus Abbott, both of whom tried to put down Broadfoot by ridicule. Amid much muttering and tight-lipped glances, the first meeting was adjourned for the night. When the council reassembled the next day, the room soon rocked with shouts and insults, after which only Sale and Macgregor were left in favour of a withdrawal to India. Sale, tired of the sniping, announced that he was prepared to abide by a majority decision. The timing of their rapprochement was fortunate for on the next day, 13 February, a message arrived which caused considerable embarrassment to the feuding officers. It was a letter from Pollock, saying that he had reached Peshawar and was determined to relieve Jalalabad. The garrison was duty-bound to hold its ground and did so for the next few weeks, always in the anticipation, day by day, of the approaching tramp of Pollock's cavalry and the creaking of the gun carriages in their wake.

In early April, a second report was brought in from Sale's spies in the enemy camp, this one of a far less encouraging nature. The Army of Retribution had been routed in the Khyber Pass, Pollock's forces were fleeing in disarray, the British were now completely at the mercy of Akbar's Afghan troops, who were calling themselves the true liberators of their country. Throughout the night of 6 April, Akbar's artillery thundered across the valley with a salute to the victory of their kinsmen, the Khyber Afridis. The men of the garrison were distraught with a feeling of impotence, which soon gave way to a rising tide of anger and demands for revenge. 'It was on the same day, and through similar channels, announced to me, that the Afghans were sending reinforcements to aid in defending the frontier passes,' writes Sale.[2] By similar channels, intelligence came in claiming that a revolution had broken out in Kabul, that Akbar was intending to retreat to Lughman, along with several more conflicting bits of information. Sale decided to take the offensive. Only 500 sheep were left in the garrison to feed 2,000 troops, and ammunition was becoming scarce. Sale called another council of war and this time the vote was unanimous. The plan was to relieve the blockade of Jalalabad and clear the plains of hostile tribesmen in order to hasten Pollock's advance. The troops were overjoyed with the prospect of launching an attack on Akbar's camp, though they knew the Afghan army outside the gates outnumbered the British by nearly four to one.

Sale's plan for this offensive, which was to become one of the most glorious actions of the British in India, was to form three columns of infantry. In the centre were 500 men of the 13th Light Infantry under Dennie, one of the heroes of Ghazni. On the left flank was the 35th Native Infantry, another 500 troops led by Monteith. The right was taken by a company of the 13th, another of the 35th and a detachment of Sappers and Miners, the whole of this column commanded by Havelock. Only twelve men were left in the fort as a guard to each of the gates, while the camp followers armed with pikes manned the walls. The force stood poised at the Peshawar and Kabul gates in the chilly darkness before dawn on 7 April. Orders had been given that no bugle or drums were to be sounded to announce the advance. Akbar's tents stood on the banks of the Kabul River, about 2 miles south-west of the fort's Kabul Gate. This was protected by a dry bed where the river's course once ran, and between Jalalabad and the camp stood half a dozen forts held by small Afghan detachments. Sale knew this was going to be a crucial battle, for both sides would fight with the fury of a last stand. If the British were defeated, Jalalabad would be lost and the survivors slaughtered in ritual Afghan fashion, or taken into slavery. Akbar Khan, on the other hand, was playing his last card in his struggle to evict the *feringhees* from Afghanistan, and he could expect little sympathy from his rivals should the day go badly for him.

At first light, the gates creaked open and the password 'Forward' was given. The troops rushed out to find that Akbar, far from being taken by surprise, had formed his entire force in battle order. The right flank of his army rested on one of the forts, the left on the Kabul river and a battery of Ghilzai marksmen held some ruined works about 800yd from the Jalalabad perimeter wall. The main action of the day was on the Kabul front, where the eastern sky was starting to show streaks of light. Havelock's column quick-marched past one of the old tumbledown forts, taking no notice of the more than 200 skilled Afghan marksmen quartered inside. A few men fell wounded from some sporadic musket fire as the column pressed on, until Havelock could see in the distance the Afghan host, their armoured horsemen waving green and yellow war banners. Some enemy cannon opened fire on the British column. These were Elphinstone's guns which had been captured by the enemy on the retreat from Kabul.

The orders were to go straight for the main body of the enemy and not to waste time with the forts scattered on the plain. These were to be dealt with after the overthrow of Akbar's army, should they continue to offer resistance. But contrary to plan, Sale had thrown Dennie's column against the fort on the left flank to silence what he believed were a handful of snipers inside the walls. Dennie led his troops at a gallop straight for the fort and finding an aperture wide enough to penetrate the defences, the men poured through the outer wall. What they had not expected to encounter was a murderous fusillade from a strong Afghan force protected by the defences of the inner keep. Dennie was one of the first to be hit, taking a musket ball through his sword belt. Once the fort had been cleared of resistance, two orderlies led Dennie, slumped over his saddle, back to Jalalabad. He was dead before they reached the Kabul Gate. Sale was quietly, if severely, censured by many of the men for his rash decision to divert Dennie's column to the fort, but the general glosses over the incident in his report: 'Colonel Dennie, of Her Majesty's 13th Light Infantry, received a shot through the body, which shortly after proved fatal.'[3]

Monteith's horsemen charged the Afghans before them, who broke and fled in a panic. Havelock's column found itself in an exposed position amid the deafening din of battle. He formed his men of the 13th into a walled enclosure and the sepoys into a square outside it to await the charge of the Afghan horsemen, now gathering speed half a mile away. Havelock placed himself in an exposed position where he could command both parties, an act typical of the man's legendary bravery. His courage was buoyed by a deep religious faith, so that after the battle he exclaimed, 'I felt throughout that the Lord Jesus was at my side.' One young soldier of the 13th later remarked, 'He was as calm under fire as if he stood in a drawing room full of ladies, a man fit to live or die.'[4] Havelock ordered his men to hold their fire as the screaming Afghan horsemen levelled their lances. But one of the sepoys let off his musket, frightening Havelock's horse which threw him and galloped riderless back to Jalalabad. Three quick volleys broke the charge, with the ranks behind tumbling over their fallen comrades and horses of the first wave. The survivors turned and fled, leaving the field covered with bodies. On that day, Shah Shuja was assassinated outside the Bala Hissar, a symbol, as Pollock was to find out, of the Afghans' determination to resist even in defeat.

Sale's victory was complete, with an ample supply of baggage, artillery, ammunition, arms and horses falling into British hands. The British casualties numbered eighty-four, against nobody knew how many losses on the enemy side, for as usual the Afghans took enormous personal risks to remove their fallen comrades from the field. Akbar galloped off to Kabul with the wreck of his army, and this was the tale of defeat which on 11 April, the distraught sirdar shared with Lawrence. Ellenborough issued a proclamation hailing the battle as one of the most outstanding actions of British warfare, and ordered a twenty-one gun salute to be fired at every principal army garrison in India. 'The defence of Jalalabad,' he said, 'maintained for a period of nearly six months of severe fatigue, suffering and privation of every sort, has thus terminated with one of the most brilliant victories which has, since 1815, crowned the British arms.'[5]

Ninety miles to the east, in the desolate and rugged hill country that is home to the similarly spartan Pathan tribesmen of the Khyber Pass, there was no talk of retribution. Pollock had reached Peshawar in February at the head of a powerful army composed of the 3rd Light Dragoons, the 9th Foot, a British Horse Artillery battery, 5 native cavalry regiments, 8 guns of the native artillery, 4,000 native infantry, the usual complements of Sappers and Miners, 400 Pathan *jezailchis* and a large Sikh contingent of 24,000 men with 20 guns. On his arrival in the Sikh city, the general found to his dismay that the leading brigade, with Brigadier Charles Frederick Wild commanding, had been soundly trounced in the Khyber Pass and had retreated in disorder to Peshawar, with many desertions by the sepoy troops and morale at a low ebb.

Swiss-born Wild, who became British by naturalisation, had reached Peshawar in December 1841, with four native infantry regiments and a detachment of gunners under his command, but no guns. The Government had naively placed faith in its allies and despatched Wild's advance column on the assumption that guns could be borrowed from the Sikh garrison in that city. The Commander-in-Chief in India, Sir Jasper Nicolls, held back the Horse Artillery, which should have accompanied Wild's force, in spite of Ellenborough's later request for guns to be sent. Nicolls was of the opinion that guns could be of no use in a mountain pass. With this diminished force, Wild was expected to replenish the magazine, treasury and commissariat at Jalalabad, a task equivalent to making bricks without straw.

Since the death of Ranjit Singh, the Sikhs were beset with internal troubles of their own, leaving them with little enthusiasm for the British cause in Afghanistan. Wild managed to acquire only four rusted pieces of ordnance that had the habit of knocking their carriages to pieces when fired, and with these in tow he prepared to fight his way through the Khyber Pass. This celebrated pass had never in history been forced by arms. Asian conquerors like Tamerlane and Nadir Shah at the head of their enormous hosts had bought a safe passage through it from the Afridis. The Moghul emperor Akbar in 1857 lost 40,000 men in attempting to take his army through it, and others such as Aurangzeb had met with disaster in the terrible defile. Now an ill-equipped band of British soldiers was marching in to confront the same stubborn Pathan tribesmen, waiting behind their stone breastworks above the road to rain musket fire and boulders on the invaders.

'This place was the most desolate looking spot I ever beheld', was how Lieutenant John Greenwood described the Khyber Pass, who was fortunate to be with Pollock's 31st Foot that followed Wild's hapless column. 'It was a large stony plain without a particle of vegetation of any kind, and bounded on all sides by bleak rugged hills which seem to frown upon us in defiance.'[6]

General Paolo di Avitabile, the Italian mercenary who commanded the Sikh garrison at Peshawar, was of the eccentric habit, every day before breakfast, of having a few local men hurled from the top of the minaret of the city's Mahabat Khan mosque to keep the unruly tribesmen in line. Avitabile believed in a firm hand and if these morning punishments failed to temper the troublemakers' spirits, there were other ways of keeping his defiant subjects under the thumb. A letter from a newly arrived officer of the 9th Foot to his family describes in vivid detail how the Italian general dispensed rough justice. He writes:

> The city of Peshawar is the most splendid place I have seen since I left Calcutta, but there is one thing that detracts from the beauty of the scenery. It is surrounded by gibbets, some of them having the remains of as many as 20 or 30 poor wretches hanging from one gibbet, some suspended by the feet, others by the hands. These are the Khyberees [Afridis] our people are going against. They give them no trial, but execute them immediately they are taken.[7]

Fortunately, Avitabile was sympathetic to the British and as a fellow European with first-hand knowledge of the Khyber and its perils, his advice was worth heeding. The Italian endeavoured to dissuade Wild from entering the pass. Avitabile cautioned Wild not to rely on his Sikh troops, for the men he could provide would be of little worth. This proved to be the case when they refused to advance to Jamrud at the mouth of the pass, and marched back to Peshawar carrying with them one of Wild's guns. The brigadier understood the risk he was taking, but there were compelling reasons for him to move ahead. For one thing, there was a well-founded fear that time lost in advancing on Afghanistan worked to Akbar's advantage. If the sirdar's troops were allowed to cut off the road between Peshawar and Jalalabad, it would require a force of thousands instead of hundreds to dislodge them. With this danger in mind, Sale and Macgregor had written to Wild pleading for the relief force to advance at the earliest moment. Wild saw no alternative to an immediate attack on the Khyber.

It was as foretold. The 53rd and 64th Native Infantry moved out on 15 January, slowly marching towards Ali Musjid, a fortress 5 miles within the entrance of the Khyber Pass. This garrison of two small forts, standing on the summit of an isolated rock, has always been regarded as the strategic key to the pass. It was of immense importance for Wild to take this fort, which in fact had been previously garrisoned for a time by a small detachment of local levies of the Yusufzai tribe, no friends of the Khyber Afridis. The native troops were under the command of a Mr Mackeson, of whom little is known apart from his kinship with the Peshawar Political Officer, Frederick Mackeson, who was assassinated by a Pathan fanatic in 1853. Mackeson held no recognised place in government or the Army and he was so disabled by illness that he had to be carried about in a litter to organise the fort's defences. Ali Musjid's high and isolated position renders it almost impregnable, but its one weak spot is the lack of a water supply, and this became Mackeson's chief problem when his little band of troops came under siege. Mackeson's fertile imagination soon came up with a solution. He was witness to the Afghans' obsession with recovering their fallen comrades, so whenever his troops repulsed an attack, he would send out a party of his men to recover the enemy corpses, which he then exchanged at the rate of two goat-skins of water for each body. It is a wonder that the wily Afghans did not think of poisoning the water. It was only when the garrison's food supply ran out that Mackeson was obliged to lead his men quietly out of the fort at night, when he succeeded in escaping to Peshawar. There is no record of what became of Mackeson after his successful defence of Ali Musjid, and it was a great pity that his services went unrecognised. There were few more gallant episodes in the entire Afghan war.

Wild's force did not fare so well in the Khyber Pass. The objective was Ali Musjid but the fatal mistake was to split the force, sending the 54th and 63rd Native Infantry ahead at midnight on 15 January, with Wild at the head of the rest of the brigade set to follow the next day, bringing up the baggage, cattle and provisions. The force was approaching Ali Musjid at seven o'clock the next morning, having had only one shot fired at them on the overnight march, when the Afridi warriors began to show themselves on the surrounding heights. These tribesmen were driven off by the sepoy skirmishers at a cost of only two or three wounded, and for the moment all looked hopeful once the fort was secured. A 'young officer' attached to Wild's column later wrote, 'This evidently shows that the rascals were taken by surprise, and that if we had all gone on together, we should have now been with Sale in Jalalabad, instead of having been obliged to retreat and evacuate the fort.'[8]

Wild attempted to link up with the two columns the next day, taking with him three regiments of Sikhs who formed his advance. They were forced back by a ferocious barrage of fire from a large body of Afridis waiting at the entrance to the pass. As Avitabile had forewarned, the Sikhs quickly took to their heels and threw the regiments behind them into confusion. At this the entire force fell back in disarray, Wild himself taking a bullet to the mouth. Despite his wound, the brigadier managed to rally his men to forge ahead and join the advance columns, only to find that the Afridis had erected an immense stockade of rocks and thorn bushes across the path where it narrows to 10ft across. The tribesmen opened fire through loopholes cut in the barricade, through which they laid down a deadly barrage. Wild launched a desperate charge at the stockade, which was finally taken with a large number of casualties inflicted on the enemy. Once through, the brigadier saw that to advance further with his depleted and demoralised soldiers would be to court disaster. He sent orders ahead to Ali Musjid for the garrison to evacuate the fort the next day. On 16 January, as the sepoys abandoned the fort, the Afridis let loose with their *jezails*, a powerful weapon accurate to about 500yd, or nearly twice the range of the smooth-bore British-issue Brunswick rifle. The result was a frantic scramble for cover, followed by a dash back to Peshawar, many of the terrified pack animals throwing their loads on the way, and with the bullocks in a stir of confusion, lurching about and blocking the road. The retreat, if one can call it that, turned into pandemonium, with men, bullocks and camels crammed into the narrowest part of the defile, making an easy target for the tribesmen's long-barrelled rifles. Wild was severely wounded, yet he made a valiant attempt to maintain discipline, but to no avail as the columns fled in disorder back down the road to Peshawar.

Nothing was to be done now but to wait for the arrival of Pollock's army, marching up from the Punjab. Had Wild resisted the pressure to march and delayed his attack by a fortnight, the Khyber Pass would have been taken with the aid of Pollock's mighty force. The general reached Peshawar on 5 February, sorely dismayed by what he found. The garrison was in a shambles, with some 1,000 men in hospital and the numbers rising rapidly. Apart from the wounded, most of the troops were down with typhus and gastric ailments. Pollock and Wild had also to contend with a widespread collapse in morale among the native soldiery, which led to four of the five sepoy regiments vowing they would not follow their commanders a second time into the Khyber Pass. The Hindu troops had been enlisted for service in India, and argued they could not go beyond their natural borders without losing caste. There were agents from Wild's brigade who held nightly meetings with their Hindu brothers, denouncing the British as colonial exploiters and urging the men to desert. There was even suspicion that Gulab Singh, minister to the Sikh ruler Sher Singh, had instigated the sepoys to rebel and was carrying on a friendly correspondence with the Afghan chieftains in Kabul.

The need to get the sick back on their feet and enforce discipline in the ranks ruled out Pollock's hopes of an immediate advance on Jalalabad. As a result, the newly arrived regiments remained inactive in Peshawar and there followed a painful period of delay for the British ranks, who were anxious to march to the relief of their comrades at Jalalabad. With nearly 2,000 men now out of service due to sickness, Pollock had no choice but to await reinforcements from the Punjab. Fortunately, he did not have too long to wait, which was just as well given the mutinous state of the sepoys, and the growing impatience of the British troops. The first contingent of dragoons marched into Pollock's camp on 30 March and on the following day, the general ordered Wild to launch a second assault on the Khyber Pass, with the eccentric General Sir

John McCaskill covering the rear. The memory of Wild's unfortunate first attempt to force the pass was still fresh in his mind and he was determined to avoid the same mistakes. He wanted his column to be lightweight and mobile, to enable the troops to advance quickly and react in good order to the sort of surprise sniping tactics that were the Afridis' speciality. Consequently, Wild reduced his baggage to a minimum, and he himself shared a tent with two of his staff officers. He had spent the days prior to the attack rallying support among his Sikh allies and inspiring confidence in his sepoy troops.

Everything was in readiness, yet the force that eventually moved up to Jamrud at the mouth of the pass resembled more a massive host than a flying column. The main body was made up of the grenadier company of the 9th Foot and two squadrons of the 3rd Dragoons comprising the British contingent, with detachments of the 26th, 30th and 33rd Native Infantry, along with the customary Sappers and Miners. Aside from nine pieces of artillery, the column was transporting all the treasure of the force on camels and a large supply of ammunition, protected by a squadron of the 1st Native Cavalry. The commissariat stores were escorted by two companies of the 53rd in advance and the 1st Cavalry covering the rear. Then came the baggage and camp followers, along with camel panniers for the sick and wounded, covered by a squadron of Irregular Horse and a squadron of the 1st Cavalry. And that was only the main body, for the rearguard was no mean fighting force in itself: three foot artillery guns, the 10th Light Cavalry, two squadrons of Irregular Horse, two of the 3rd Light Dragoons, two horse artillery guns, three companies of the 60th Native Infantry, one company of the 6th and another of Her Majesty's 9th Foot. Pollock was taking no risks on a repeat of the first disaster in the Khyber Pass. Two infantry columns were instructed to climb the heights on either side of the pass once the mouth had been breached. This was crucial to preventing the Afridis firing at Wild's force from above as it marched through the defile, which in places narrows to a few feet in breadth.

The massed body of troops got under way at three o'clock on the morning of 5 April. The weather had cleared after several days of heavy rain, which had mired the gun carriages in the soggy ground and left the men huddling miserably in their tents. Crowds

of banner-waving tribesmen were gathered on the nearby hills surrounding the entrance to the pass, and as the morning dawned
the positions of the two forces were revealed to each other, sig-
nalling the first bursts from the Afridis' matchlocks. The British
discovered that the enemy had thrown up a formidable barrier of
mud, stones and tree branches across the road. The initial fear was
that this was going to be a re-run of Wild's previous encounter,
since the guns had little effect on the barricade. Wild and Pollock's
advantage lay in the sepoy flankers who scrambled nimbly up the
hillsides, taking the tribesmen completely off guard. There was no
time for the Afridis to muster their men to repel the troops. Once
the light infantry had swept the hills and the heights were secured,
it was a relatively simple task to knock down the roadblock and
let the guns open up on the enemy positions, with deadly effect.
The artillery quickly made a mockery of Nicolls' claim that guns
would be useless in a narrow pass. Wild must have looked on with
bemused anger as the showers of shrapnel blasted the Afridis from
behind their hilltop sangars.

'No General could have wished his plan of attack to be carried out with better effect,' says Kaye. 'They [the Afridis] had not
expected that our disciplined troops who had, as it were, been looking at the Khyber for some months, would be more than a match
for them upon their native hills.'[9] Pollock was on the verge of making history, the first time that an armed body would successfully
fight its way through the Khyber Pass. What stands out as most
remarkable about this feat of arms is that it was accomplished with
comparative ease, the Afridis having lost their taste for artillery fire.
The greatest problem Pollock faced was conveying his long burden
of baggage wagons up the winding road, which zigzags for miles
between towering cliffs until it reaches the village of Landi Kotal on
the summit. The general was compelled to move forward at a slow
pace, with the march up to Ali Musjid occupying the greater part
of the day. The heat was intense and the troops suffered greatly
from thirst. But once they had gained the fort, which the enemy
had evacuated that morning, the men expressed their pride in having won back their battle honours. Avitabile had warned Pollock
before he marched from Peshawar that he was heading to certain
destruction. The Italian commander was proven wrong, and now

the general could take pride in having accomplished the first part of his objective with so little loss of life and no loss of baggage.

From Ali Musjid, the column moved up through a tapering half-mile cleft that required half a day's work to pull through the guns. Lieutenant Greenwood recalls that he was jammed for six hours by the press of baggage animals that had to be led through in single file. The spot was so narrow that half a dozen tribesmen from above could have annihilated the whole of the column with boulders. Greenwood's regiment, the 31st Foot, camped about 12 miles past Ali Masjid that night, at a place called Lal Beg Ghuri where the pass widened out and was less threatening. A great number of Afridis were congregated on the distant hilltops, waving their banners and beating their war drums, but making no attempt to oppose the force.

The entire column moved past Landi Kotal, which stands atop the Khyber at 3,518ft, without encountering any serious resistance, and the following day proceeded down to Landi Khana, the last market town before abandoning the pass and entering Afghan territory. The only incident of note that the 31st experienced, apart from a few sharp exchanges of fire, was the loss of a number of camels that had been left to graze on the hills. The camels were eventually recovered from five Afridis, who were taken and shot. The native troops, as Greenwood records, could give as good as they got when it came to barbarous activities on the battlefield. 'The slain were soon decapitated, and the sepoys carried their heads into camp in triumph stuck on the points of their bayonets,' he writes. 'Among the Khyberees who fell was a woman who I believe was killed by accident. But she was fighting in company with the others and a bag of bullets, I heard, was taken from her person.' Greenwood asked one of the sepoys how it was that they killed the woman. 'Sahib,' he said, 'she must have been killed by mistake, but as for males, I have lost twelve brethren in this cursed pass, and I would bayonet a Khyberee of a month old at his mother's breast.'[10]

By 15 April, Pollock's rearguard had emerged from the Khyber Pass and the entire Army was camped within 7 miles of Jalalabad. Sale's troops burst into cheers of jubilation at the news of Pollock's great success in the pass and his imminent arrival at the lately beleaguered garrison. The following day the band of the 13th Light Infantry went forth to greet their comrades. Hearty greetings were exchanged on both sides after which the band, in keeping with time-honoured usage, turned about and began to play the troops in. It was fitting for the musicians, perhaps tongue-in-cheek, to march the last two or three miles to Jalalabad to the cadence of the old Jacobite air, 'Oh, but ye've been lang o'coming!'

The Khyber Pass had been forced and Jalalabad relieved in masterful fashion. Now it was time for the Army of Retribution to live up to its name. Pollock at Jalalabad and Nott commanding the Kandahar garrison were men of markedly different backgrounds and temperaments. Both were in their late fifties and had arrived in India at the turn of the nineteenth century, but that is where the similarities ceased. Pollock was a cosmopolitan Londoner and aristocrat, a reverent soul who kept a Bible by his side. He was a calm, imperturbable, sensible and efficient man, but bereft of anything resembling an inspiring personality. Nott, on the other hand, was a Scots yeoman, a dour and self-reliant disciplinarian, quick to criticise the conduct of his superiors and on intimate terms with few. What both men shared in common was an ardent desire to get on with the job, which meant marching on Kabul to avenge the deaths of 16,000 British subjects before withdrawing from Afghanistan. The newly landed Governor General, Ellenborough, took a different view. Though he first advocated the relief of Ghazni, the small garrison of Khelat-i-Ghilzai and Kandahar, and possibly reoccupying Kabul, he soon became conscious of the legacy left by his predecessor Lord Auckland, and became eager to evacuate the British Army from Afghanistan at the earliest possible date. Ellenborough was alarmed by the capitulation of the Ghazni garrison and also the defeat of General Sir Richard England, the commander of the Bombay brigade who had been despatched to the relief of Palmer at Ghazni and Nott at Kandahar. The column had marched from Quetta on 26 March, with only two incomplete infantry battalions and small detachments of cavalry and horse artillery, England having decided not to wait for the rest of the

brigade to catch up with him. Two days later he met serious opposition at Haikalzai where the Afghans held the heights. England's
column was routed with about a hundred killed and wounded.

Ellenborough's view of the situation, as expressed in his first
meeting with Nicolls, the Commander-in-Chief, was that of first
importance was the security of the troops and the last act should
be a blow at the Afghans. Nicolls informed Pollock that only three
conditions would permit him to delay his return to India. Firstly,
it was necessary to liberate the British held captive by Akbar,
and secondly, a lightly equipped force should be sent for their
rescue. Lastly, in the unlikely case that the Afghans attempted
an attack on the force, Pollock was to strike such a blow as to
cause them to remember him for years to come. It was not until
July that Ellenborough tacitly sanctioned the move on Kabul.
The affair was settled with a wink and a nod. Kaye contends that
Ellenborough 'was shaken in his determination to bring back the
armies to the provinces by the clamour that, from one end of
India to the other, was raised against the obnoxious measure of
withdrawal. In this conjuncture, he betook himself to an expedient unparalleled, perhaps, in the political history of the world.'[11]
Ellenborough reminded Pollock and Nott of their instructions
to take their forces back across the Indus, but added that the
generals might, if they wished, choose their own routes. On 4 July,
the Governor General despatched letters to both commanders. To
Nott, he suggested a possible withdrawal from Kandahar by way
of Ghazni, Kabul and Jalalabad. General Pollock, he added, and
one imagines with a slight touch of irony, might feel disposed to
assist the retreat of the Kandahar force by moving forward upon
Kabul. However, this should be regarded solely in the light of a
retirement from Afghanistan. Ellenborough's change of mind
raised criticism from some who accused him of Jesuitical cunning,
while his supporters argue that he was right to leave the decision
to the two commanders in the field. Ellenborough was no doubt
influenced in his decision by the Duke of Wellington, who predict-
ably stood squarely behind exacting the strongest retribution from
the Afghans to restore British prestige in Asia.

On 20 August, Pollock began to move from Jalalabad with 8,000
men, retracing the line of Elphinstone's calamitous retreat through

Gandamak, Jugdulluk and Tezeen. The sight of all those rotting corpses and skeletons at every point on the road served to fire the men's fighting spirit, so that the rage later unleashed at Kabul came as no surprise. At Tezeen alone, which was reached after three weeks of sporadic skirmishing and a few pitched battles, they came across a pile of 1,500 dead sepoys and camp followers, who had been stripped of their clothes and left to die in the snow. One officer wrote, 'In the Khoord Kabul Pass, the sight of the remains of the unfortunate Kabul force was fearfully heartrending. They lay in heaps of fifties and hundreds, our gun wheels passing over and crushing the skulls and other bones of our late comrades at almost every yard for three, four or five miles.'[12] The troops heard how these people had huddled together for warmth and upon being discovered by the Afghans, were stripped naked and abandoned to the elements. The poor wretches, women and children among them, had prayed for the Ghazis to put them to death, but there they remained for hours, until frostbite and hypothermia slowly put an end to their suffering.

On 1 September, as Pollock was resting his troops at Gandamak, he received a stark reminder of his enemy Akbar Khan's ruthlessness. Futteh Jang rode into camp, looking forlorn and quite unlike an Afghan nobleman, in tattered rags and astride a wretched pony. A couple of days before, this man had been, to some, the Amir of Afghanistan, though all the while he was treated by Akbar as a puppet, with not even a modicum of the respect the British had accorded Shah Shuja. Fearful of suffering the same fate as his father, Futteh attempted to flee to the British lines but was caught and imprisoned in the Bala Hissar. A friendly Afghan, Aga Mohammed, helped him to escape by cutting a hole in the roof of his cell, through which the young monarch fled for his life. Akbar later discovered the treachery and Aga Mohammed became a marked man. His father and brother suffered a grisly death at the hands of the sirdar, while Aga himself escaped to India, where he was given a pension of 12 rupees a month.

A week after this incident Pollock and his army stood before the entrance to the infamous Jugdulluk Pass, contemplating a horde of tribesmen clustered on the heights, waving their banners and in full battle regalia. As soon as the British troops showed their faces, the Afghans opened fire with their matchlocks, but this time nothing could intimidate, much less deter, the British soldiers from storming the hillsides, which were already being blasted by Pollock's guns. The enemy retreated higher into the hills, to what seemed an inaccessible position. Pollock was determined to give pursuit – this was his chance to humiliate a number of notorious Afghan chieftains who had appeared at the head of their tribesmen on the cliffs. The British skirmishers, mostly men of the Jalalabad garrison who had come with a score to settle, pushed on with vigour and within a short while, the day was theirs. Sale himself, who was never far off when there was likely to be hard fighting, led the way up the heights in front of his old regiment, and in the affray he received his third wound of the campaign. Sale epitomised the general who led from the front, quite often to the despair of his own men. 'Nothing could induce Sale to behave himself as a General should do,' recalls Mackenzie. 'He used to ride about two miles ahead of his troops in spite of all remonstrances, and in action he would fight like a private. During the siege [of Jalalabad] he was in the habit, like many of the officers, of taking his gun to the ramparts and firing at the enemy.'[13]

Pollock sent out orders for the entire division to march on the double and regroup at Tezeen, which the last of the rearguard reached on the night of 11 September, after having lost about a hundred transport animals and their loads, the animals being so knocked up by the forced march that they fell easy prey to the Afghan marksmen. This is where Akbar chose to make his stand against Pollock's advancing force, taking advantage of the high ground that encloses the valley to post his snipers on every available promontory. The two armies met on 13 September in what was to be the decisive battle of the British march through Afghanistan. Each of Pollock's corps – cavalry in the plain, infantry in the hills and guns everywhere – performed splendidly on that day. When the action opened, the Afghans' own irrepressible rapacity consigned great numbers of them to destruction, when a large party descended into the valley to make a grab for the baggage, which acted as bait.

The dragoons' opportunity was at hand. A cavalry charge dispersed the enemy and many were cut up in the furious pursuit. While the cavalrymen were chasing the remnants of the marauders across the plain, the infantry gallantly scrambled up the heights. The hills were swiftly taken by the 13th Light Infantry, 9th and 31st Foot. Once the top was gained, the men fixed bayonets and dispersed the Afghans, who nevertheless continued to regroup and return to the charge throughout the better part of the day. The Afghans had brought the best of their troops to a field particularly suited to their tactics, but found themselves unable to resist these soldiers, who were carried on by the energy of revenge, the sights they had seen on the road ever present in their minds. A more decisive victory was never gained. Pollock lost 160 killed and wounded, far fewer than the enemy's casualties which, as usual, were mostly dragged from the field before a body count could be carried out. Tezeen was the last hope of saving Kabul from the grasp of an avenging army. But Akbar Khan saw that the struggle was at an end. The sirdar quickly turned his horse to flee in the direction of Kohistan with one of the British hostages he had kept by his side as an eventual negotiator, or for ransom had he found himself in a tight spot. The rest of the Afghan fighting men scattered back to their villages in disordered masses. Pollock marched on, savouring the scent of victory, and two days later on 15 September, his brigade stood before the gates of Kabul.

If Pollock had expected to enhance his glory by liberating the prisoners on his arrival at the capital, he was to be disappointed. Akbar had taken precautions against losing his key bargaining piece by having the hostages sent to Bamiyan, some 100 miles west of Kabul, starting by moonlight on 25 August. More than a week before, Akbar had given his captives advance warning of his plans. If Pollock had moved from Jalalabad, he told them, the prisoners would be moved out of his reach at half an hour's notice 'to a fine climate, with plenty of ice'.[14] The party numbered in all more than forty sick and able-bodied soldiers, with women and children. It is interesting to note that when the captives pitched camp at Bamiyan nine days later, in sight of the giant Buddha cave statues that were destroyed by the Taliban in 2001, a number of the guards took to firing their matchlocks at the towering figures carved in the rock while shouting abuse at these heathen idols. To avoid provoking their fanatical captors, the ladies thought it prudent to adopt the full cover of the Afghan burkha.

The Afghan escort of nearly 400 men was under the command of one Saleh Mohammed, a man of highly flexible loyalties who had deserted Shuja's camp eighteen months before. As news of the Army of Retribution's victories filtered through to Kabul, Saleh was only too willing to shift his allegiance once more, much to the hostages' advantage. It only took Pottinger's promise of a large reward for Saleh to come completely over to the British side. Saleh was a Kazilbash Shi'a Muslim, so Pottinger cleverly played on Saleh's natural hatred for the Afghan majority of the Sunni sect, to seduce him by way of his Persian Kazilbash clansmen. Saleh at first turned down with great harshness a bribe of a lakh (100,000) of rupees to set the prisoners free. Later on, Saleh's flexible principles would take another turn.

As might be expected, Nott did not sit idly at Kandahar with the prospect of fighting before him. A fortnight before Pollock led his brigade from Jalalabad, Nott was making final preparations to put his own column in the field, to link up with the Army of Retribution's commander at Kabul, as Ellenborough had given them tacit leave to do. In July, the garrison settled down to a few weeks of restful calm, after months of uninterrupted skirmishing with Afghan raiders. The last major engagement had taken place in late May, when Nott despatched Colonel George Wymer with a large force to relieve the garrison of Khelat-i-Ghilzai, in which 200 men of Shah Shuja's own troops had for four months held out against vastly superior numbers. In doing so, Nott left his own position precariously under-manned, having sent out the Bombay European Horse Artillery with 9-pounders, three troops of the 3rd Bombay Cavalry, four detachments of Christie's Horse, 200 men of Skinner's Horse, the 2nd and 40th Foot and the 16th and 38th Native Infantry. The general also intended to order out the 42nd and 43rd regiments with 4 guns and 200 cavalrymen, as soon as carriage for supplies could be procured. This left the defence of the garrison in the hands of a skeleton force consisting of one native regiment. Fortunately for Nott, the second contingent had not yet departed when Kandahar came under attack by the warlord Aktur Khan at the head of a host of 5,000 cavalry and 4,000 infantry, in conjunction with a rebel force under Suftur Jung, Shah Shuja's fourth son. As soon as the Afghan column was spotted in the field, Nott took the offensive and sallied out with his remaining troops and soon routed the enemy completely. When Suftur Jung found himself deserted by his followers, he rode into Kandahar and surrendered to Nott. The Afghan prince was left in charge of the town when Nott put his force on the march to Kabul.

The defenders at Khelat-i-Ghilzai, meanwhile, had their hands full in repelling a last desperate enemy attack with scaling ladders in the early hours of 21 May. Three times the Afghans made a furious attempt to clamber up the walls, and three times they were driven back by the spirited little garrison that showered the attackers with grapeshot and musket balls, bayoneting the few attackers who managed to surmount the parapet. The enemy abandoned the assault after an hour, leaving at least 500 dead below the walls. When Wymer reached the fort he had nothing to do but quietly withdraw the force. The particularly dogged defence by Shah Shuja's troops caused them to be enrolled in the British forces in Bengal, thereafter as the Khelat-i-Ghilzai Regiment.

The many days and nights spent fighting at close quarters with the fanatical Ghazis had left the men hardened, one is tempted to say almost indifferent, to the brutalities of war. This is reflected in the 2 May diary entry of an anonymous officer who served with Nott from first to last: 'Three men of Her Majesty's 40th, who had wandered off some distance from their barracks, were murdered by a small party of the enemy's horse, who happened to be prowling about. The villagers brought in their headless trunks. Made a very fair racket court against the wall of our mess house, where we play every evening, using bats in place of rackets.[15]

Towards the end of July, the men were told that they were to return to India and, strangely, not all by the Quetta route. This was the extent of the information they were given and, naturally, the garrison was thrown into a turmoil of rumours and expectations. Then all was made clear in early August when orders were issued for the troops to start evacuating the city in stages along the Kabul road. By 7 August, the 42nd and 43rd Native Infantry, the last regiments remaining at Kandahar, filed out of the gates and the guards were withdrawn at sunset. General England, who was to command the Bombay and other troops proceeding via Quetta, had his camp pitched separately from Nott's massive force, which consisted of 6,630 troops and 22 guns. Khelat-i-Ghilzai, when the Army reached it ten days later, was found to be a ruin, completely destroyed by the vengeful Afghans when the garrison was evacuated. Nott's brigade encountered sporadic resistance all along the route, proof that the Afghans had plenty of fight left in them; nor had they lost their zest for the most abominable sort of battlefield mutilation.

The most serious action took place on 28 August, when the rearguard was attacked by about 700 horse and infantry. Nott's cavalry charged the enemy up a rising ground, but received so hot a fire that they were driven back in confusion and in turn charged by the Afghans. About fifty cavalrymen were killed in this action, including Captains Richard Bury and George Reeves of the 3rd Bombay Cavalry. A troop of artillery with some cavalry and a regiment of native infantry were sent out to recover the bodies of the killed. They brought back about twenty, all horribly mutilated. Of Reeves nothing was found but the trunk. Bury's head was also cut off, and the legs and arms at the knee and elbow joints. Nott was in a rage about the affair, the more so because the enemy managed to escape before the troops could overtake them.

The next day brought no relief from the horrors of desperate fighting. A wing of the 2nd Native Infantry with cavalry and guns had gone out to procure forage for the baggage animals and was attacked by a large detachment of Afghan horsemen, who were driven off by the guns. When the troops reached a fort to collect the forage, the sight inside was not pleasant, as one of the officers recalls. This spot had been held by the Afghans and was the scene of a sharp battle the day before:

There were about 100 dead bodies lying about, six or eight children were found roasted to a cinder. They had been concealed under heaps of chaff which had been burned. One woman was the only live thing in the fort. She was sitting the picture of despair with her father, brothers, husband and children lying dead around her. She had dragged all their bodies to one spot, and seated herself in the midst.[16]

By 4 September Nott's force had covered nearly three-quarters of the distance to Kabul and now found itself 4 miles from the gates of Ghazni. The men were followed a good part of the way by the unnerving sound of Afghan war drums, as the enemy marched out of sight, parallel with their advance on the other side of a low range of hills. Nott ordered his men to pitch camp on the south side of the fort, on the other side of which stood 6,000 of the enemy's cavalry. The fort itself bristled with troops, who displayed their banners from the ramparts. At sunrise the next day, the brigade moved up to a position 2 miles from the east wall. From this spot the 16th Native Infantry with the engineer officers were sent ahead to reconnoitre the north-east wall and the Kabul Gate. Later that morning Nott set in motion his battle plan: a couple of regiments and some guns were left to look after the camp, while the rest of the force advanced against the heights covered by the enemy. Hostilities commenced by Nott's light companies and guns driving the enemy from the lower slopes around the fort, and in less than an hour the British and sepoy troops all stood on top of the range. The 16th, 42nd and a couple of guns were ordered to retain possession of the heights, about 1,000yd from the fort's north face. The troops were forced to strike their tents as quickly as possible when the Afghans unexpectedly opened up on the camp with *Zubr Jung*, a monstrous brass 64-pounder cannon which was mounted on a rampart under the citadel. Miraculously, the only casualties were four camels – one shot went through four of the beasts. The British moved up their 9-pounders to replace the 6-pounders that had been in use, with which they began a relentless bombardment. A high wind came in overnight, making it impossible for the men to hear any of the enemy's movements inside Ghazni, but at daylight on 6 September all was stillness behind the walls and suspecting that the fort as well as the entire town had been evacuated, the troops cautiously advanced to find that this was exactly the case. This was the signal for the Sappers and Miners to get to work, blowing the towers of the citadel and destroying the troublesome giant cannon.

It was a momentous morning on 18 September when Pollock rode into Nott's camp to greet the late commander of the Kandahar garrison, the joyfulness of the occasion somewhat overshadowed by Nott's irritation at having reached Kabul two days after his senior officer, for whom little love was lost.

Now the two armies had converged on the capital, it was time to administer a dose of retribution. But before the punitive operations could commence, there remained the question of the British hostages lingering perilously in Akbar's grasp. Taking advice from Mohan Lal, always labouring diligently behind the scenes, Pollock ordered his military secretary Sir Richard Shakespear, with a squadron of 600 Kazilbash horsemen, off to Bamiyan to liberate the prisoners – and not a moment too soon. A week earlier, Akbar had told the hostages that preparations were under way to send them to Turkestan. The ruler of the khanate of Kulum had already sent a detachment of 2,000 men to the frontier to escort the captives to his capital, where they would most certainly be cast into prison or sold as slaves in Bokhara, or worse. Once the British colours had been firmly planted on the roof of the Bala Hissar, Pollock's thoughts returned to the hostages' safety. He instructed Nott to send a brigade after Shakespear to assist with the rescue mission. The Kandahar general naturally resented being instructed to do the obvious, and he duly sat down to write a letter of protest, alleging that his men were too tired from a 300-mile trek to immediately set off on another march. Pollock took the unprecedented step of riding into his junior officer's camp to thrash out the issue, but the commander found Nott so adamantly against having anything to do with the rescue operation, that he gave in and ordered Sale to proceed to Bamiyan in his place. Needless to say, Sale leapt at the opportunity to rescue his wife and the others from Akbar's clutches. It was imperative for Shakespear and Sale to move with all haste, for Akbar was roaming the hills of Kohistan with up to 2,000 horse under his command, while his co-conspirator Sultan Jan, with upwards of 10,000 men, was in full pursuit of the hostages. Sale assembled a brigade from the Jalalabad army and rode off in pursuit of Shakespear, only to find that the prisoners had already liberated themselves.

Just as the hostages' spirits had sunk to their lowest ebb at the dreadful prospect of being taken to Kulum, Pottinger came with the astounding news that Saleh Mohammed had acquiesced, agreeing to escort them all to British lines for a payment of 20,000 rupees in cash on their arrival in Kabul, and a lifetime pension of 1,000 rupees a month. Mohan Lal was actually the man of the hour, for it was his agents in Kabul who had offered the bribe and put together the money for the prisoners' release. On 16 September, the British began their return journey to Kabul under a heavily armed Kazilbash escort.

That night, the party was woken by a horseman bringing a note from Shakespear, saying that he was riding to meet them. 'Our joy and thankfulness at the receipt of this intelligence are not to be described,' recalls Lawrence, 'and little sleep did any of us have for the rest of that night.'[17] As they rode along the rough path towards Kabul the next day, a cloud of dust announced Shakespear's column. The hostages erupted in cheers of joy and tearful embraces at the arrival of their liberators – all that is, except for Shelton, who complained that he, as senior officer present, should have been the first to be greeted by Shakespear. On 20 September, the day before reaching Kabul, after advancing some miles the party was met by General Sale and his gallant brigade. 'It is impossible to express our feelings on Sale's approach,' writes Lady Sale after more than a year's separation from her husband. 'To my daughter and myself happiness so long delayed as to be almost unexpected was actually painful, and accompanied by a choking sensation, which could not obtain the relief of tears.'[18] For all his toughness, Sale was quick to display his tender emotions. Mackenzie trotted up alongside him on the road back and after a quarter of an hour, he found voice to say, 'General, I congratulate you.' The gallant old man turned and tried to force an answer, but his feelings were too strong. 'He made a hideous series of grimaces, dug his spurs into his horse, and galloped off as hard as he could.'[19]

The last of the captives, Captain Bulstrode Bygrave, who had been paymaster at Kabul in 1841, was brought into Kabul on 27 September. Bygrave had been in Akbar's custody in Kohistan but now, having lost the toes of one foot to frostbite, Akbar despatched him to Kabul in the vain hope of coming to some understanding with the British.

The freed hostages were barely recognisable when they entered Kabul. The men wore long beards and heavy moustaches, the women's English complexions were turned a ruddy brown after many months' exposure to the sun. All were dressed in native garb and could have been taken for a party of Afghans, had there been any in sight. The city's streets were eerily deserted and the shops' shutters drawn, seemingly in anticipation of some dreadful cataclysm to come. They did not have long to wait to see their forebodings become reality. With the British prisoners safely back, it was now time for the Army to go about the business it had been sent to do. There was some debate over whether to destroy the Bala Hissar, which was in the end spared for strategic and logistic considerations. Britain's next appointed amir would need a palace in which to install his throne. The Grand Bazaar, where Macnaghten's remains had been so wantonly displayed, did not get off so lightly. On 9 October, Pollock ordered his chief engineer to destroy the vast marketplace, after giving warning to its inhabitants to vacate their homes. Explosions continued to rock the great bazaar for two days before its destruction was complete. Though all efforts were made to save the rest of the city from wholesale devastation, little could be done to prevent the soldiers and camp followers pouring in to loot and pillage at will. Much of this work was done by the Hindu sepoys, maddened by the sight of clothes and accoutrements that had belonged to their dead comrades hanging in the market stalls. Greenwood writes:

> We continued the work of destruction until night closed upon us, and then returned to camp tired enough. Many of our men looked like just like chimney sweepers from the fire and smoke. On succeeding days other parties were sent, and the city of Kabul, with the exception of the Bala Hissar and the Kazilbash quarter, was utterly destroyed and burned to the ground. The conflagration lasted during the whole time we remained encamped in the vicinity, and we still saw it when entering the Khoord Kabul Pass, on our return.[20]

The general spared no effort to crush any suspected pockets of Afghan resistance. With the Grand Bazaar left a smouldering ruin, Pollock turned his attention to the Afghan chieftains responsible for the uprising and massacre of Elphinstone's army. Nearest at hand was Amanullah, who was known to be encamped in great force in the Kohistan hills. Before departing Kabul, he sent General McCaskill's division to destroy the stronghold of Istalif, some 40 miles north of Kabul. McCaskill stormed Istalif on 29 September after several hours' hard fighting. The defenders were dislodged with ease and sent fleeing up the mountains, not to be seen again. Unfortunately, at this time, the fugitive Amanullah also made good his escape, depriving the British of a chief tribal instigator. After this brisk little engagement, McCaskill was found sitting under a tree to the rear with a basket of Kabul plums. When an aide galloped up to announce the victory, McCaskill merely said, 'Indeed! Will you take a plum?'[21] The troops were accused in the newspapers of cruelty and lawlessness at Istalif, and there were sensationalist reports of sepoys setting fire to the Afghan wounded. These stories were vehemently denied by the sepoys' British officers, who claimed that whenever a man's loose cotton robes caught fire, it was from the fuse of his own matchlock, not an uncommon occurrence with Afghan tribesmen fighting in tight groups. All the women and children who had not fled the village, about 500 in number, were collected together on a hilltop, with guards set over them. That night they were sent with a friendly chief to join their menfolk at a place where they were known to have reassembled. The darkness of the Kohistan hills was illuminated by the blazing town.

On 2 October, the force proceeded 8 miles up the valley to Charikar, where the previous year Captain Codrington's Gurkha brigade had been cut to pieces. The troops found the town and fort deserted, so they set about torching the place as well as the surrounding villages, which were first plundered. Five days later the troops were back in Kabul, having left in the villages of Kohistan, as one officer recalled, 'such a mark as will be remembered for ages'.

On 11 October the British colours were lowered over the Bala Hissar and orders were given for the commencement of the march on the following day. Futteh Jang decided that his well-being lay with the British Army, not with the Afghan chieftains.

Consequently, he was given permission to accompany the troops to seek asylum in India. The old and now blind king, Zeman Shah, also became an exile, to end his days under British protection. The rest of Shah Shuja's unfortunate family sought and was granted leave to follow the Army back across the Indus, safely out of reach of Akbar's revenge. The Afghan chiefs friendly to the British proposed that Prince Shapur, another of Shuja's sons, should be set up in place of his brother. The prince, a high-spirited youth, accepted the Crown and a declaration to that effect was sent to Pollock's camp. As the force was leaving Kabul, the salute was heard in honour of the succession of Prince Shapur, whose reign was very brief, as he was dethroned before Pollock reached India.

The Army of Retribution's homeward march was marked by sporadic rearguard actions, some of these quite bloody and costly in numbers killed, against a still determined enemy. There may have been little left in the way of organised Afghan resistance, but this did not prevent the Ghazis swooping down on the columns whenever the occasion arose to plunder the baggage or cut up the stragglers. Nott's column sustained about sixty killed and wounded before reaching Ferozepore. The general's progress was slowed by an exceptionally cumbersome piece of baggage in his train, a mammoth wooden structure hauled by bullocks, which kept the comedy of errors going to the very end. Ellenborough had given Nott an errand to run at Ghazni: the recovery of the Gates of Somnath, also known as the Gates of Mahmud, after the first Muslim invader of India who was alleged to have carried off the great sandalwood gates from the Hindu temple of Somnath in Gujarat in the eleventh century, and who lies buried at Ghazni. Prior to the invasion of Afghanistan, Ranjit Singh had demanded the return of this holy relic as part of the price of Sikh support for Shah Shuja's restoration.

Ellenborough believed the gesture of returning the gates to their rightful place would endear him to British India's Hindu and Muslim subjects. To announce the glad tidings, the Governor General drafted yet another blustery proclamation, this one to be issued to the chiefs and princes of India. 'My Brothers and Friends,' it began, 'our victorious army bears the Gates of the Temple of Somnath in triumph from Afghanistan, and the despoiled tomb of

Sultan Mohammed looks upon the ruins of Ghazni. The insult of eight hundred years is at last avenged.' Ellenborough then goes on to commit 'this glorious trophy of successful war' to the princely rulers of India.[22] The Governor General next issued a general order instructing Nott to select an officer who was present at the capture of Ghazni, 'to accompany the Gates of the Temple to Somnath'. The soldiers escorting the trophies were to receive double rations during their special service, 'and all the native officers and soldiers will have one year's furlough granted to them on their return to their respective regiments'.[23] In composing these pieces of hyperbole, the Governor General overlooked the fact that the Muslim princes considered it an outrage, while the Hindus had no interest in receiving an object which they regarded as polluted. As for the Afghans who had been despoiled of their religious heirloom, Mohan Lal makes the point that Akbar Khan and his followers cared little whether the gates were borne away to India by the British, or burnt as firewood to warm the troops in the chilling wind of the Khoord Kabul Pass.

The first reaction in British India was that the proclamation had been the product of a humorist on Ellenborough's staff, imitating the Napoleonic style of address that Ellenborough had recently adopted. Once the proclamation's authenticity was confirmed, its author became the object of ridicule throughout India as well as England. That was not the end of the affair. Nott's Political Officer Rawlinson, a noted archaeologist who later served as president of the Royal Geographical Society, pronounced the Gates of Somnath as bogus. They were, he said, of a much later date. The gates were finally left abandoned at Agra.

Calling a halt on its journey to India, the entire force assembled at Jalalabad for a few days' rest before resuming the march to Ferozepore. As a prelude to departure, Pollock ordered Jalalabad's defences be demolished to prevent the garrison falling intact into hostile hands. Next came the fortress of Ali Masjid in the Khyber Pass, which was also destroyed. Pollock made the dangerous passage with losses kept to a minimum, having taken the precaution of posting troops on the heights to cover the retreating column.

This time it was McCaskill's turn to wage a last battle before leaving Afghan territory. The Afridi tribesmen rushed down upon the rearguard, which happened to be under the command of their old enemy Brigadier Wild. Two officers were killed and two guns had to be abandoned, though the tribesmen showed more interest in carrying off booty from the baggage animals. The Army then pushed on to Peshawar. It is indeed sad that there is no record of any encounter between the two entourages which at that time were crossing the plains in opposite directions, for it would have added yet more levity to the proceedings: as the British troops passed down the Punjab, Dost Mohammed and his attendant court were travelling westward, the Amir heading home to take his place on the throne of Kabul.

'And so ended the First Afghan War,' reflects Forbes fifty years after the conflict, 'a period of history in which no redeeming features are perceptible except the defence of Jalalabad, the dogged firmness of Nott, and Pollock's noble and successful constancy of purpose. Beyond this effulgence there spreads a sombre welter of misrepresentation and unscrupulousness, intrigue, moral deterioration, and dishonour unspeakable.'[24]

The Government of India considered the whole affair of the Army's withdrawal from Kabul an outrage and a stain upon British honour. The terms of capitulation, decries a Government report, 'were in the last degree humiliating'. The news of this convention was received in India with a feeling of indignation, and there were few who could credit the possibility of its existence, and the humiliating conditions attached to it of the delivery of British hostages for its fulfilment, without any corresponding hold upon the faith of the Afghan party. The document also greets with scepticism the claim that the surrender was dictated by a want of provisions and ammunition. 'This, however, is denied, and hitherto it has been found, from the conflicting nature of the various statements, impossible to come to any conclusion which is borne out by facts.'[25]

Epilogue

Ellenborough had come to India in February 1842 as a man of peace, intent on withdrawing all British garrisons from Afghanistan. But a rout with dishonour was out of the question. In his first message to the Commander-in-Chief, Nicolls, Ellenborough made it clear that the Government's strategy for withdrawal would rest solely upon military considerations, meaning to safeguard the garrisons at Jalalabad, Khelat-i-Ghilzai and Kandahar. Realising the British had backed the wrong horse in Kabul, Ellenborough had sanctioned what he thought would be a token expeditionary force to restore the prestige of British arms, in order to be able, in the words of his friend the Duke of Sutherland, 'to look a native in the face again with confidence'.[1] The 'butcher-and-bolt' punitive expedition that Ellenborough had envisaged mushroomed into an enterprise on a much larger scale, and the Army of Retribution's military success has already been recorded.

Honour at any price was an inherent feature of Ellenborough's character – witness his duel with a German nobleman to avenge his wife's adultery. Once satisfied that his integrity had been properly restored, Ellenborough took to celebrating in grandiose style. In the case of his country's honour, this entailed magnificent parades of elephants and bombastic proclamations to the maharajas. The redemption of British colours in Afghanistan was to be no exception. Ellenborough had dreamt of holding military rank and before leaving London he unsuccessfully asked Peel for the title of Captain General as well as that of Governor General. If Ellenborough could not wear a splendid uniform, he could still put on a display worthy of a field marshal.

The recriminations were yet to come, but this, the closing days of 1842, was made a time to joyfully receive the triumphant Army of Retribution. Ferozepore was once again to be the scene of great celebration, as it had been in December 1838 when the Army of the Indus assembled on the banks of the Sutlej for the march into Afghanistan. The several columns of the Army of Retribution marching back to India were now to converge on the same spot, where the combined force would raise the flag of victory.

Ellenborough had prepared the groundwork for the gala affair with an Orwellian piece of bombast, issued on 1 October 1842, cautiously christened the 'Simla Proclamation' to avoid the obvious association with his predecessor Auckland's notorious 'Simla Manifesto', issued four years earlier, on the same day and in the same room at Government House. Ellenborough began his declaration by neatly summing up, in the most simplistic terms, the British strategy in Afghanistan which was, in his words, to oust 'a chief believed to be hostile to British interests' and replace him with 'a sovereign represented to be friendly to those interests'. But alas, after 'events' (that is, the murder of British Government envoys and the slaughter of 16,000 people) that brought into question Shah Shuja's loyalty to the Government of India, the Amir was assassinated and Afghanistan was plunged into anarchy. The British Army was then sent in to avenge 'disasters unparalleled in their extent' and having accomplished their task, the troops 'will now be withdrawn to the Sutlej'. Ellenborough would leave it to the Afghans to create a government 'amidst the anarchy which is the consequence of their crimes'. Then with the most colossal audacity, the Governor General goes on to declare, 'To force a sovereign upon a reluctant people would be as inconsistent with the policy as it is with the principles of the British Government.'[2] End of story. One wonders if Ellenborough had ever laid eyes on Auckland's infamous correspondence with Dost Mohammed, in which he assured the Amir that 'it is not the practice of the British Government to interfere in the affairs of other independent states', or indeed, whom this proclamation was intended to deceive. One also wonders what the slain thousands, whose bones lay scattered across the high passes, would have made of this disgraceful whitewash. The pathos of their martyrdom cries out in this melancholy stanza of Edwin Arnold's 1879 epic poem *The Light of Asia*:

We are the voices of the wandering wind,
Which moan for rest, and rest can never find.
Lo! As the wind is, so is mortal life,
A moan, a sign, a storm, a strife.

One thing was certain, *The Times*, the Establishment mouth-piece of the day, was not taken in by the festive gloss with which Ellenborough endeavoured to paint the occasion. This was evident in the paper's scathing editorial comment on the Afghan misadventure: 'This nation spent £15 million on a worse than profitable effort after self-aggrandisement in Afghanistan, and spends £30,000 a year on a system of education satisfactory to nobody.'[3] Add a string of noughts to those figures and one is offered an uncomfortable picture of a Britain much closer to us in time.

One by one, the columns crossed a temporary boat bridge that had been built across the Sutlej for the occasion. The regiments then assembled on the great plain of Ferozepore where in anxious expectation, Ellenborough waited astride his charger to receive the returning victors. Sale, the hero of the day, led the procession at the head of the 13th. The regiment was greeted by a twenty-one gun salute at every principal army station that was passed, while the Lancers' band struck up *Hail, the Conquering Hero* as the troops marched across the bridge.

In England, Prime Minister Peel sang the regiment's praises in the House of Commons and Queen Victoria re-titled the corps Prince Albert's Regiment of Light Infantry. The Queen, however, was less amused by Ellenborough's initiative to issue medals, a decision that earned him a royal slap across the wrist. Victoria endorsed with enthusiasm the proposal to grant honours to Pottinger, Pollock, Nott, Sale and one or two others. Sir Hugh Gough was deemed a 'very fit' choice to succeed Nicolls as Commander-in-Chief in India. Yet as for Ellenborough's medals, the Queen 'grants with pleasure the permission to *her troops* [Victoria's italics] engaged in Afghanistan to accept and wear the four medals which the Governor General has struck for the India Army . . . ' but 'the

Queen would have thought it more becoming that she herself should have rewarded her troops with a medal than leaving it to the Governor General.'[4]

Sale, followed by Pollock and Nott, rode through a great ceremonial arch of bamboo and bunting, behind which stood 2-mile-long rows of no less than 250 gaily caparisoned elephants. It is said that Ellenborough himself took a personal hand in painting the beasts. By 23 December the entire Army of Retribution was back on British soil in India and the celebrations could now commence. There was feasting, festivities in the giant tents, after-dinner harangues and great effusion among the regiments that greeted one another after so long an absence. The year 1842 was closed with a grand military display in the presence of Ellenborough, the Commander-in-Chief, accompanied by the heir apparent of Lahore, scores of lesser British and Sikh dignitaries, with a supporting cast of 40,000 men and 100 guns. After the review, which passed before the revered General Sir Charles Napier, the conqueror of Sind, the British troops received double rations, and 30,000 *seers* (92,000lb) of native food were distributed to the sepoy regiments. Not since Waterloo had British arms cause to celebrate so remarkable a triumph. There occurred, in fact, only one incident to mar all the grandeur and magnificence. The elephants, sensing in their wisdom the sublime absurdity of the occasion, refused to trumpet on command.

The brutality and acrimony of the aftermath was rivalled only by that of the episode it sought to dissect. Mohan Lal, who was witness to the entire Afghan affair from beginning to end, condemned the Government's short-sightedness in recalling Pollock in all haste from Kabul, instead of allowing him to pursue Akbar Khan and his criminal band into the hills. 'To have punished our enemies by the stay of our army for six months at least in Jalalabad, if not in Kabul,' he writes, 'would have shown the people of Central and of all Asia, that we possessed an abundance of means . . . not only to disperse our enemies, but also to occupy their fields and their cities.'[5]

There is no doubt that Britain's prestige as an imperial power, and more so in the Muslim world, was severely damaged by the humiliation the Empire suffered in Afghanistan. The heart of the British Lion had been pierced by an Afghan rabble with matchlocks. After the rout from Afghanistan, where next would Queen Victoria's armies meet defeat at the hands of the Prophet's warriors? As early as May 1842, before the release of the hostages, *The Times* correspondent in Constantinople reported that the recent disasters in Afghanistan had already begun to affect British influence in the Muslim world. 'Since the last overland intelligence,' reads the despatch, 'it has been asserted on more than one occasion by Turkish authorities, respectable from their position, that the late reverses of England had suddenly reduced her to the place of a third-rate power.'[6] This was unsettling news, for Britain could not afford to jeopardise its security in the eastern Mediterranean which stood as the gateway to India, and even more so after 1870 with the opening of the Suez Canal.

The excesses committed by the Army of Retribution on its march across Afghanistan touched off a bitter clash between Ellenborough on the one hand, who was under pressure from London to explain the damning reports that filled the British press, and Pollock, who was determined to uphold the honourable behaviour of the troops under his command. *The Times* and other papers had latched on to stories of outrages committed against the civilian population of Afghanistan, as well as the wanton destruction of the Kabul bazaar, holy sites and the country's natural resources. 'Many detailed statements in the newspapers were entirely unfounded, and were got up with the sole object of creating a sensation,' replies Pollock to an angry letter from the Governor General. The general concedes that he may have been unaware of 'some excesses', which would only be expected among Indian troops of which two-thirds follow the Army 'for the sole purpose of plundering when a favourable opportunity offers'. Pollock insists, however, that the newspaper accounts of atrocities reflect nothing more than possible isolated incidents. The destruction of the Kabul bazaar, he explains, was fully justified in revenge for Macnaghten's murder and the mutilation of his corpse. Be that as it may, 'Those who resided at and near the bazaar had two days' previous notice to remove their property, and I am not aware of any instances of violence having occurred.'[7]

Nott was also put in the line of fire concerning the behaviour of his troops on quitting Afghanistan. As can be expected, the peppery old hero of Kandahar came out with guns blazing. Barely able to contain his anger, Nott delivers a withering blast to the Adjutant-General of the Army, in reply to a letter of enquiry about alleged excesses perpetrated in the re-capture of Ghazni:

> I will endeavour to suppress my scorn and indignation whilst I shortly reply to this charge, or suspicion, or whatever it may be called by the persons from whom it emanated. And this is the return made by the people of England, or rather, I would believe, by a few individuals, to the gallant Kandahar army, that army which was for so long a time neglected, but which nevertheless nobly upheld our national honour, and during a period of four years acted with the greatest forbearance and humanity to the people of Afghanistan.[8]

Excluding, one assumes, the people of Kandahar whom Nott had expelled *en masse* from the town. Nott then reminds his superiors that none of the residents of Ghazni could have been murdered in cold blood, as was reported in the papers, for his troops had marched into a ghost town.

Nott winds up his defence by turning the tables on 'a few people in India and in England who have sent forth gross falsehoods to the world'. The general goes on the offensive, reminding the Government that he had informed Auckland as early as December 1841 that he could have reoccupied Kabul with the force under his command. 'There was nothing to prevent it but the unaccountable panic which prevailed at the seat of Government,' he says. 'And now I am rewarded by a certain set of people in England taxing me with that which would be disgraceful to me as a religious man, as an honourable gentleman, and as a British officer.'[9]

Pollock and Nott were not the only officers to be pilloried by a Government on the prowl for scapegoats. Blame was mostly laid at the feet of Macnaghten and Elphinstone, the hand of death conveniently sparing both men the ignominy of a military inquiry. Elphinstone was up for a court martial, and the matter had come to the attention of Queen Victoria, whose diary of 12 June 1842 records an entry lamenting 'unfortunate General Elphinstone' (who was) 'to be brought before a Court Martial'[10], the Queen unaware that the gentleman in question was nearly two months in his grave.

Shelton did not get off so lightly. Ellenborough had the general placed under arrest and court-martialled at Ludhiana on 31 January 1842. Shelton was arraigned on four charges. The first and most serious was that he had 'prematurely, and without authority', given orders for the emptying of ammunition wagons to be filled with provisions for the retreat from Kabul. Elphinstone was still senior officer in Afghanistan, hence Shelton had taken matters into his own hands, ordering a retreat without instructions from the chief political or military authorities, 'such order being calculated to create alarm and despondency in the troops'. This charge alone was sufficient to bring about Shelton's personal ruin and imprisonment. The other three charges were of a lesser magnitude: using disrespectful language before the troops with reference to Elphinstone, procuring from Akbar Khan a supply of forage for his own horses, and allowing himself to be taken prisoner at Jugdulluk by want of due precaution.

It would have been inappropriate to bring disgrace on the second in command in Afghanistan, only a fortnight after the Army had gloriously returned from that land. Shelton was duly acquitted on the first charge. He was also found not guilty on the second and fourth charges. However, the general was not to get off without having his wrist slapped. The court found him guilty of clandestinely procuring forage for his own horses, but the court, 'being of the opinion that the matter was disposed of, at the time, by the censure for its impropriety by competent authority, abstain from passing any sentence against Major General Shelton'.[11]

Shelton escaped prosecution, but he was severely censured by at least one of his brother commanders, who unfortunately happened to be the British Army's hero of the hour. General Sir Charles Napier was only weeks away from achieving one of the most celebrated victories in British-Indian history. In February 1843, Napier defeated an army nearly ten times his force at Miani, in a desperate battle that brought about the conquest and annexation of the vast territory of Sind to the British Empire. Napier's loathing for Shelton knew no bounds, for in his eyes Shelton was the culprit responsible for the disaster at Kabul. The British Library holds Napier's personal copy of Lieutenant Vincent Eyre's *The Military Operations at Kabul*, which the general pencilled with scathing marginal notes, tearing apart Shelton's character and conduct as an officer. (Lady Sale, too, had disparaged Shelton as one of her habitual 'croakers'.) Where Shelton is rebuked for failing to place a guard into one of the cantonment's grain stores, Napier thunders, 'It seems to me that to Shelton may be traced the whole misfortune of this Army.' Napier comments that Shelton ought to have been shot as 'the author of all ill'. Where Eyre concludes his account of the setback at Bemaru Heights, Napier notes, 'The whole of this day's work shows that Shelton is unfit for command.'[12] Napier's opinion of the others in command at Kabul was no less scathing. After reading the diary of Lady Sale, now released from her captivity, Napier declared, 'It's enough to drive one mad – the idiots Macnaghten, Elphinstone and Shelton!'[13]

Brigadier Shelton, this impossible, fearless soldier, was a natural survivor. He survived the loss of an arm in Spain, as well as five wounds sustained in the infamous storming of Bemaru. He survived capture and imprisonment by the bloodthirsty Akbar Khan, and Ellenborough's efforts to disgrace him through a court martial, to say nothing of Napier's wrath. Shelton returned to England in late 1843 to take command of the 44th as it was being raised practically afresh. The following year he was thrown from his horse during a parade, and this mishap he did not survive. He died of his injuries three days later, in horrible agony. It is a mark of his belligerence that Shelton's own men turned out on the parade ground to give three hearty cheers upon hearing of his death.

As for the rest of the *dramatis personae*, General Sir Robert and Lady Sale, who reigned in the public's eye as the undisputed heroes of the Afghan War, stayed on in India, where the general fought bravely in the first Anglo-Sikh War in 1845. His left thigh was shattered by grapeshot at the battle of Mudki on 18 December, and he died from his wound three days later. Sale was buried in the field after the battle of Ferozeshah. George Broadfoot, considered by some the real hero of Jalalabad, also fell at Ferozeshah. Lady Florentia was granted a pension of £500 a year in recognition of her conduct as a prisoner and of her husband's services. In 1853 she visited the Cape of Good Hope for her health, and died at Cape Town on 6 July, only a few days after her arrival.

Eldred Pottinger's services received scant recognition from Ellenborough, who showed a general hostility to those who had returned intact from the Afghanistan disaster. In spite of Ellenborough's efforts to tar Pottinger with the same brush as Shelton, a court of inquiry exonerated Pottinger and praised his character and conduct. With no worthwhile employment in sight, Pottinger visited his uncle Sir Henry Pottinger in Hong Kong. There he caught typhus and died after a brief illness, on 15 November 1843, at the age of 32.

Only a month before, Nott suffered a recurrence of an illness contracted in Afghanistan, and in 1844 went on leave to the Cape of Good Hope and then to England. He was too ill even to accept an invitation to Windsor from the Queen. The directors of the East India Company awarded him an annuity of £1,000 and the city of London bestowed upon him the freedom of the city. But Nott's heart disease rapidly worsened, and he died on 1 January 1845 at Carmarthen.

Ellenborough's masterful ability to alienate his political and military contemporaries soared to new heights when in 1864 Queen Victoria expressed her outrage at his 'malignant and unmanly' criticism of her German leanings in the war that deprived Denmark of Schleswig and Holstein. On that occasion he lived up to one of his nicknames, 'the Elephant', an allusion to his uncontrollable propensity for trampling underfoot those who opposed him. Ellenborough died at his Gloucestershire seat on 22 December 1871, leaving no heir to the earldom, and was buried at nearby Oxenton Church. He left three illegitimate children from a liaison that followed his divorce.

Dr Brydon was promoted to surgeon and posted with the 40th Native Infantry, with which he served in Burma. In 1853 he was sent home on sick leave for three years. He then returned to India once more, and at the time of the Sepoy Mutiny was stationed at Lucknow, where he served with considerable gallantry. During the siege of that garrison, in July 1857, he was severely wounded when a rifle bullet injured his lower spine. Brydon was awarded medals for his service in Jalalabad, Kabul, Burma and Lucknow, and in 1858 was appointed a CB. In the following year he retired from the Indian service. He settled in the highlands of Scotland and died at his home, at the age of 62, in March 1873.

Akbar Khan, the arch-villain in Britain's Afghan tragedy, eluded capture to the end, though his own came only two years later at the age of 29, and under very dubious circumstances. It was quietly rumoured in Kabul that Dost Mohammed grew increasingly distrustful of the power and influence the sirdar had acquired during the war, and arranged to have his favourite son poisoned. Akbar Khan is today a highly revered figure in Afghanistan, who enjoys almost mythical hero status. A residential area of Kabul is named after him.

And what of the Amir Dost Mohammed Khan, Britain's ally-turned-enemy, whose alleged conspiracy with the Russians served as the pretext for waging war on Afghanistan? On his return from India, the Dost was received in triumph at Kabul, and set himself to re-establish his authority on a firm basis. It was as if the terrible days of bloodshed had never happened. The Dost sat on his throne, fearless of invasion from east or west. Mohan Lal tells us that he gave himself up to drinking and dancing parties, habits he had given up during his detention in Ludhiana. 'It is said he believes that whilst he was an enemy to wine he was always involved in difficulties,' writes Lal, 'and that since he drinks he is prosperous.'[14]

From 1846, the Amir renewed his policy of hostility to the British, allying himself with the Sikhs. However, after the defeat of the Sikh army at Gujarat in February 1849, and Britain's annexation of the Punjab, the Dost abandoned his designs and led his troops back into Afghanistan. His rule went from strength to strength: in 1850 he conquered Balkh, and in 1854 he acquired control over the southern Afghan tribes by the capture of Kandahar. Three years later, the Amir concluded a mutual defence treaty with his new-found friends, the Government of British India, through whose generosity Herat passed under Barakzai control after a successful joint Anglo-Afghan campaign against the Persians. The Dost's most singular act of solidarity with his British allies was to observe a strict neutrality during the Sepoy Mutiny. Otherwise, it is doubtful Calcutta could have held the North-West Frontier territory. In June 1863,

Dost Mohammed died suddenly, in the fullness of victory, having played a pivotal role in Central Asian history for four decades.

So it was over, but not ended. The political shock waves the Afghan war produced rumbled on long after the last detachments of the Army of Retribution had returned to India. Eight years later, Parliament was still debating where to place the blame for embarking on so disastrous a venture. In 1850, Sir John Hobhouse, President of the Board of Control, gave evidence before the House of Commons, in which he proclaimed himself responsible for the war. 'The Afghan war was done by myself, the Court of Directors had nothing to do with it,' he said. The reason alleged was 'the inveterate hostility' of Dost Mohammed to the British.[15] Hobhouse himself was the culprit who doctored Burnes's letters to make it appear that Burnes had reported this hostility and recommended going to war. When Burnes became aware of the falsification he sent home the true copies. But the fraud was not exposed to the House until 1861.

Less than forty years were to pass before another British army stood at the mouth of the Khyber, poised to invade Afghanistan for the very same reasons that had led to the calamity of 1842. It was November 1878, five months after the signing of the Treaty of Berlin which was intended to defuse tension between Britain and Russia. The Tsar was determined to ply his own course irrespective of treaty commitments, and had once more trained his sights on Central Asia. Russia had sent an uninvited diplomatic mission to Kabul, which the Amir Sher Ali, like Dost Mohammed before him, had tried to turn back in order to preserve good relations with the Government of India. Three weeks after the Russian envoys arrived in Kabul, the Viceroy Lord Lytton wrote to Sher Ali, demanding that he accept a British agent too. He refused and Lytton ordered a diplomatic mission under General Sir Neville Chamberlain to set out for Kabul in September 1878. True to his word, Sher Ali ordered his commanders to halt the party at the Khyber Pass. Britain's response was to declare war.

The more perceptive of British statesmen and military figures had watched with concern as tensions mounted between British India and the Afghan ruler. One of the Government's most outspoken critics was George Lawrence, a man highly qualified to denounce the policy of reckless intervention in Afghanistan. Nearly 70 years old, Lawrence emerged from his retirement in London, after giving forty-three years' service to India, to let loose with a broadside at those who might be contemplating another incursion into Afghanistan. Commenting on an editorial in *The Times* on the 'salutary dread' of another Afghan involvement, Lawrence sadly remarked:

> I regret to think that the lapse of years has apparently had the effect of weakening, if not entirely obliterating, these wholesome impressions, that a reaction has set in, and that a new generation has arisen which, instead of profiting by the solemn lessons of the past, is willing and eager to embroil us, in one way or another, in the affairs of that turbulent and unhappy country.

Lawrence acknowledged that the quality of British Army rifles had by then surpassed the Afghan long-barrelled muskets, and that a well-equipped army could force the passes into Afghanistan, yet 'although military disasters might be avoided, an advance now, however successful in a military point of view, would not fail to turn out politically as useless, as impolitic, and almost as expensive as the former'.[16] Doubtless, many will today subscribe to the timeliness of those words.

Victoria was no longer an unworldly girl of 20, relying on dinner-table chatter with the likes of Peel and Wellington, to keep abreast with events being played out in the far-flung reaches of the Empire. The Queen was now a mature woman of 59, with recourse to the experience of more than twenty wars fought in her name. The memory of the Kabul tragedy weighed heavily in the Queen's thoughts when shortly after hostilities with Afghanistan broke out, she recorded in her diary, 'The Cabinet had been much occupied with this alarming Afghan affair. Care should be taken that we are quite sure of success and that there should be no repetition of the misfortunes at Kabul in 1840.' Victoria had also been won over to the Russophobes, as evidenced when she asserted in the same entry that 'all depended on whether the Amir was assisted by Russia or not. That she is at the bottom of it all, there is little doubt.'[17]

A gruesome twist in this new drama, which may serve as a stark reminder of Macnaghten's fate, was the assassination by an Afghan mob in September 1879 of Major Sir Pierre Louis Napoleon Cavagnari, the British Envoy in Kabul. This time there was no question of occupation: the British forces subdued much of Afghanistan and retired to India after signing a peace agreement in the same spot where the 44th had been annihilated in 1842. The Treaty of Gandamak provided Afghanistan with an annual subsidy and vague assurances of assistance against foreign aggression. In exchange for this, the Amir's son and heir Yaqub Khan relinquished control of Afghan foreign affairs to Calcutta and received British representatives at Kabul.

The next forty-year lull ended abruptly in 1919 with the opening of the Third Afghan War. This particular conflict was provoked by the Amir Amanullah, who believed the Raj to be in a weakened state after the blood-letting of the First World War. The Amir quickly jumped on this as an opportunity to appease the anti-British elements in his army. Amanullah was suspected of having plotted his father's death, another good reason to divert attention from local problems by proclaiming a jihad against Britain, thus capitalising on existing anti-British nationalist feeling in India. The campaign was quickly wound up by Britain's fledgling Royal Air Force. The dropping of a single bomb on Amanullah's palace in Kabul sufficed to bring the Amir to the negotiating table. Britain virtually dictated the terms of the 1919 Rawalpindi Agreement, yet not without some irony, for Amanullah walked away with a key demand under his belt, the devolution to Afghanistan of autonomy in foreign affairs, thus effectively achieving full independence for the country. Small wonder that the Amir, though beaten on the battlefield, marched home proclaiming victory to his jubilant followers and distributing campaign medals to his defeated generals. Moreover, British India's worst fears were realised when Afghanistan almost immediately signed a treaty of friendship with the new Bolshevik government in Russia, and more so in 1926 when Kabul upgraded this to a neutrality and non-aggression pact.

Britain's invasion of Afghanistan 170 years ago culminated in tremendous loss of life and political prestige, and it is difficult to understand what good can come from the current military intervention in that country. The United States went in on a knee-jerk reaction to the 11 September terrorist attacks, scored a military victory over the Taliban and promptly fouled things up by failing to divert its resources to the country's social and economic needs. That military success was short-lived, as we are witnessing, with the resurgence of the Taliban and al Qaeda. What the US achieved was to force the enemy to shift its operational base from Afghanistan to the tribal belt of Pakistan with Quetta, the capital of Baluchistan, as their command centre, thereby placing General Pervez Musharraf's pro-Western government on the razor's edge. But why has Britain allowed itself to be coerced into marching up this political cul-de-sac? After three wars and 100 years of skirmishing with the tribesmen, Britain should have by now learnt the lessons of treating Afghanistan and the tribal territory as a military problem. Has the British Government capitulated to some simplistic 'with us or against us' rhetoric? Are we there to democratise Afghanistan? It is pointless to impose a one-size-fits-all Western parliamentary system on a people without a sense of nationhood. In any case, the Afghans have been exercising their own system of democracy, the *jirga*, or council of elders, since at least the first century BC, according to the earliest records. The inhabitants of Afghanistan see themselves first and foremost as part of a family unit, then Pathans, Hazaras, Uzbeks or any one of a dozen ethnic minorities, but not as citizens of an Afghan political entity. Villagers in Helmand have little awareness and even less interest in what is taking place in Bamiyan or Wakhan, and vice versa. However, people do not like having foreign troops garrisoned in their territory, least of all the Afghans, a stubborn race that has seen off conquerors from Alexander the Great to Genghis Khan,

Tamerlane, Babur, the British and, most recently, the Russians. One anecdote will serve to illustrate this tenacity of character: when the Persian ruler Nadir Shah invaded Afghanistan in the eighteenth century, the Ghilzais took refuge in the mountains amid the snow, with their families. For months the tribes fed on nothing but roots, rather than submit to a foreign invader's tyranny. They sent a handful of these roots to Nadir Shah with the message that, so long as roots could be procured, they would continue to resist.

Meddling in Afghan affairs, beyond the provision of humanitarian aid, healthcare, education and the like, to the extent that one is allowed to do so, is a losing game. The Afghans will always win. Amirs and warlords throughout history have cheerfully entered into treaties with European powers vying for supremacy in Central Asia, but they are utterly indifferent to which side emerges victorious, for that is their next ally.

There is a story of a British Political Agent who once enquired of an Afghan malik whose side his people were likely to take if it came to war between Britain and Russia. 'Do you wish me to tell you what would please you, or to tell you the truth?' the malik asked. The British officer, bracing himself for the worst, assured his host that he wished only to hear the truth. 'Then I shall tell you,' chuckled the old greybeard. 'We would just sit here in our hills watching you fight until we saw one or the other side utterly defeated. Then we would come down and loot the vanquished to the last mule! Allah be praised!'

T.S. Eliot wrote, 'A people without history is not redeemed from time, for history is a pattern of timeless moments.'[18] It would be unwise on Britain's part to regard the First Afghan War as an isolated event of nineteenth-century imperial warfare, one more episode in the Great Game, lacking in contemporary relevance. The lessons of history, as the poet said, are timeless.

Notes And Sources

EPIGRAPH

Royal Archives, RA/VIC/QUJ/1839, 7 April

CHAPTER 1

1. *Frontier and Overseas Expeditions from India*, Division of the Chief of the Staff Army Headquarters, 1910, Vol. III, p. 278, Naval & Military Press (reprint), 2006, England
2. Moon, Penderel, *The British Conquest and Dominion of India*, London, Gerald Duckworth & Co., 1989, p. 480
3. Bigham, Edward Clive, the Viscount Mersey, *The Viceroys and Governors General of India*, London, John Murray, 1949, p. 57
4. IOR/V/4/1839/40, *Correspondence Relating to Afghanistan*, p. 3
5. *Ibid.*
6. *Ibid.*, p. 4
7. Kaye, John William, *History of the War in Afghanistan*, London, W.H. Allen & Co., 1890, Vol. I, p. 218
8. Burnes, Alexander, *Cabool, Being a Personal Narrative of a Journey to, and Residence in that City*, Lahore, Research and Publication Centre (reprint), 2003, p. 142
9. *Correspondence Relating to Afghanistan*, p. 10
10. *Ibid.*, p. 24
11. *Ibid.*, pp. 20–21
12. *Ibid.*, p. 26
13. Burnes, Alexander, *Reports and Papers Submitted to Government*, Calcutta, G.H. Huttmann, 1839, p. 10
14. Kaye, op. cit., p. 213
15. *Ibid.*, p. 272

16. *Ibid.*, p. 276
17. *Correspondence Relating to Afghanistan*, p. 77
18. Kaye, op. cit., p. 193
19. *Correspondence Relating to Afghanistan*, p. 25
20. *Idem.*
21. Burnes, op. cit., p. 262
22. *Correspondence Relating to Afghanistan*, p. 26
23. *Ibid.*, p. 32
24. Kaye, op. cit., p. 308
25. *Ibid.*, p. 302
26. Durand, Henry Marion, *The First Afghan War and its Causes*, London, Longmans, Green & Co., 1879, Lahore, Vanguard Books Ltd (reprint), 1998, p. 62
27. *Ibid.*, p. 46
28. *The Times*, 6 January 1871, p. 6

CHAPTER 2

1. *Correspondence Relating to Afghanistan*, p. 3
2. Macrory, Patrick, *Signal Catastrophe*, London, Hodder & Stoughton, 1966, p. 45
3. Edwardes, Michael, *Playing the Great Game*, London, Hamish Hamilton, 1975, p. 54
4. Durand, op. cit., p. 67
5. *Correspondence Relating to Afghanistan*, p. 7
6. IOR, *Treaty between Ranjit Singh and Shah Shuja, Concluded at Lahore 26 June 1838*, printed by the House of Commons, February 1839
7. Fraser-Tytler, Kerr, *Afghanistan*, London, Oxford University Press, 1950, p. 107
8. Cecil, Gwendolen, *Life of Robert, Marquis of Salisbury*, London, Hodder & Stoughton, 1921, Vol. II, p. 159
9. *The Times*, 22 December 1838, p. 4
10. IOR, *Treaty between Ranjit Singh*, Annex *Simla Manifesto*, pp. 5–6
11. Durand, op. cit., pp. 81, 92
12. Kaye, op. cit., pp. 375–6
13. *Ibid.*, p. 387
14. Forbes, Archibald, *The Afghan Wars*, London, Seeley and Co., 1892, p. 16
15. Moon, op. cit., p. 504
16. Forbes, op. cit., p. 15
17. IOR, *Treaty between Ranjit Singh*, p. 7
18. *Ibid.*, p. 8
19. Pottinger, George, *The Afghan Connection*, Edinburgh, Scottish

Academic Press, 1983, p. 60
20. Atkinson, James, *The Expedition into Afghanistan*, Uckfield, Naval & Military Press (reprint), 2006, p. 128
21. Kaye, op. cit., p. 424
22. *Frontier and Overseas Expeditions*, p. 313
23. Durand, op. cit., pp. 165–66
24. IOR/V/4/1840/Vol. 37, pp. 11–12
25. Durand, op. cit., p. 183
26. IOR/V/4/1840/Vol. 37, p. 12
27. *Ibid.*, p. 19
29. Durand, op. cit., p. 186
30. IOR/V/4/1840/Vol. 37, p. 21
31. Durand, op. cit., p. 187
32. Kaye, op. cit., p. 477
33. IOR/V/4/1840/Vol. 37, p. 25

CHAPTER 3

1. Gleig, George, *Sale's Brigade in Afghanistan*, London, John Murray, 1879 (Naval & Military Press reprint), p. 69
2. *Ibid.*
3. *Ibid.*, p. 73
4. Atkinson, op. cit., pp. 282–3
5. Fraser-Tytler, op. cit., p. 114
6. Lunt, James, *Bokhara Burnes*, London, Faber & Faber, 1969, p. 28
7. Moon, op. cit., p. 521
8. Eyre, Vincent, *Journal of an Afghanistan Prisoner*, London, Routledge & Kegan Paul, 1976, p. 30
9. The New Testament, Matthew 24:38
10. *Frontier and Overseas Expeditions*, p. 327
11. Kaye, op. cit., Vol. II, p. 96
12. Durand, op. cit., p. 245
13. Eyre, op. cit., pp. 28–9
14. Fraser-Tytler, op. cit., p. 116
15. Kaye, op. cit., Vol. II, p. 138
16. Macmunn, *Afghanistan*, Lahore, Sang-e-Meel Publications, 2002, pp. 138–9
17. Kaye, op. cit., Vol. II, p. 140
18. IOR 9057, AA2, *The War in Afghanistan*, 1842, p. 13
19. Gleig, op. cit., p. 74
20. Forbes, op. cit., p. 62
21. Macrory, op. cit., p. 144

22. *The War in Afghanistan*, p. 14
23. Gleig, op. cit., p. 80
24. *Ibid.*, p. 89
25. Sale, Florentia, *A Journal of the First Afghan War*, London, Longman (reprint), 1969, p. 8
26. *The War in Afghanistan*, p. 18
27. Gleig, op. cit., p. 118
28. *Ibid.*, p. 122
29. Forbes, op. cit., p. 69
30. Pollock, John, *Way to Glory*, London, John Murray, 1957, p. 68
31. Durand, op. cit., pp. 360–1
32. Public Record Office, London, *Ellenborough Papers*, 21 February 1842, 30.12.89
33. IOR, Auckland to Hobhouse, 18 February 1842, Add. MS 37707, fol. 187

CHAPTER 4

1. Eyre, Vincent, *The Military Operations at Cabul*, Stroud, Nonsuch Publishing Ltd (reprint), 2006, p. 29
2. Lal, Mohan, *Life of the Amir Dost Mohammed*, Karachi, Oxford University Press (reprint), 1978, Vol. II, p. 400
3. Lunt, op. cit., p. 203
4. Eyre, *The Military Operations*, p. 34
5. Lawrence, George, *Reminiscences of Forty-three Years in India*, London, John Murray, 1874, p. 157
6. Eyre, *The Military Operations*, p. 35
7. Lal, op. cit., pp. 409–10
8. Kaye, op. cit., Vol. II, p. 180
9. Sale, op. cit., p. 18
10. Kaye, op., cit., Vol. II, p. 187
11. Moon, op. cit., p. 534
12. Kaye, op. cit., Vol. II, p. 189
13. Sale, op. cit., p. 26
14. Kaye, op. cit., Vol. II, p. 194
15. Sale, op. cit., p. 27–8
16. Kaye, op. cit., Vol. II, p. 197
17. Lal, op. cit., p. 413
18. Sale, op. cit., p. 36
19. *The Times*, 1 March 1842, p. 4
20. IOR 9057, AA2, *Papers Relating to Military Operations in Afghanistan*, p. 4
21. Forbes, op. cit., p. 78

22. Lal, op. cit., pp. 413–4
23. Durand, op. cit., p. 362
24. Kaye, op. cit., Vol. II, pp. 208–9
25. *Ibid.*, p. 209
26. *Ibid.*, p. 212
27. *Ibid.*, p. 232
28. Eyre, *Journal*, p. 96
29. *Ibid.*, pp. 98–9
30. Kaye, op. cit., Vol. II, p. 244
31. Eyre, *Journal*, p. 85
32. *Ibid.*, p. 97
33. Kaye, op. cit., Vol. II, p. 258
35. *Frontier and Overseas Expeditions*, p. 358
36. Sale, op. cit., p. 65
37. Kaye, op. cit., Vol. II, p. 281
38. Sale, op. cit., p. 75
39. IOR/V/4/1839/40, p. 92
40. Eyre, *Journal*, p. 120
41. Kaye, op. cit., Vol. II, pp. 301, 303
42. IOR/V/4/1839/40, pp. 103, 105
43. Sale, op. cit., p. 92

CHAPTER 5

1. Eyre, *The Military Operations*, p. 151
2. *Ibid.*, p. 103
3. Eyre, *Journal*, p. 160
4. Kaye, op. cit., Vol. II, pp. 371–2
5. Sale, op. cit., pp. 107–8
6. Eyre, *Journal*, p. 169
7. Kaye, op. cit., Vol. II, p. 385
8. Sale, op. cit., p. 167
9. Gleig, op. cit., p. 137
10. Sale, op. cit., p. 109
11. Lawrence, op. cit., p. 170
12. Sale, op. cit., p. 129
13. Lawrence, op. cit., p. 178
14. Sale, op. cit., pp. 132–3
15. Lawrence, op. cit., p. 180
16. *Ibid.*, p. 186
17. *Ibid.*, p. 194
18. *Ibid.*, p. 197

19. *Ibid.*, p. 207
20. Norris, J.A., *The First Afghan War*, Cambridge, Cambridge University Press, 1967, p. 409
21. Sale, op. cit., p. 210

CHAPTER 6

1. Pollock, op. cit., p. 84
2. *The War in Afghanistan*, p. 59
3. *Ibid.*
4. Pollock, op. cit., pp. 90–91
5. *The War in Afghanistan*, p. 59
6. Greenwood, John, *The Campaign in Afghanistan*, Stroud, Nonsuch Publishing Ltd (reprint), 2005, pp. 111–2
7. *The War in Afghanistan*, p. 43
8. Greenwood, op. cit., pp. 110–12
9. Kaye, op. cit., Vol. III, p. 89
10. Greenwood, op. cit., p. 120
11. Kaye, op. cit., Vol. III, p. 285
12. Macrory, op. cit., p. 258
13. Mackenzie, Colin, *Storms and Sunshine of a Soldier's Life*, Edinburgh, David Douglas, 1884, p. 299
14. Sale, op. cit., p. 150
15. MSS.Eur.9057.aaa.14, *Nott's Brigade in Afghanistan*, Bombay, Times of India Steam Press, 1880, p. 81
16. *Ibid.*, p. 94
17. Lawrence, op. cit., p. 222
18. Sale, op. cit., p. 157
19. Mackenzie, op. cit., p. 365
20. Greenwood, op. cit., pp. 164–5
21. Pollock, op. cit., p. 97
22. Royal Archives, RA/VIC/N 12/23, *Government Gazette*, 16 November 1842
23. *Ibid.*
24. Forbes, op. cit., pp. 156–7
25. *The War in Afghanistan*, pp. 33–4

EPILOGUE

1. Kaye, op. cit., Vol. III, p. 374
2. Norris, op. cit., Appendix 3, p. 451

3. *The Times*, 27 January 1843, p. 4
4. Benson and Esher, *The Letters of Queen Victoria*, John Murray, 1908, Vol. 1, p. 444
5. Lal, op. cit., pp. 488–9
6. *The Times*, 5 May 1842, p. 7
7. IOR/V/4/1843/40, pp. 5–6
8. *Ibid.*, p. 7
9. *Ibid.*, p. 8
10. Royal Archives, RA/VIC/QUJ/1842, 12 June
11. *The Times*, 7 April 1843, p. 6
12. Napier, Priscilla, *I Have Sind*, Salisbury, Michael Russell Publishing, 1990, p. 220
13. MSS.Eur.B.199, pp. 69, 75, 106, 131
14. Lal, op. cit., pp. 497–8
15. Mackenzie, op. cit., p. 302
16. *The Times*, 9 April 1873, p. 5
17. Royal Archives, RA/QVJ, 6 October 1878, p. 116
18. Eliot, T.S., *Four Quartets*, London, Faber & Faber (reprint), 1983, p. 48

BIBLIOGRAPHY

PRIMARY SOURCES

BRITISH LIBRARY ORIENTAL AND INDIA OFFICE COLLECTION (OIOC)

MSS.Eur.B.199, pp. 69, 75, 106, 131
IOR/V/4/1843/40
MSS.Eur.9057.aaa.14, *Nott's Brigade in Afghanistan*, Bombay, Times of
    India Steam Press, 1880
IOR/V/4/1839/40, *Correspondence Relating to Afghanistan*
IOR/V/4/1839/40, pp. 103, 105
IOR/V/4/1839/40, p. 92
IOR 9057, AA2, *Papers Relating to Military Operations in Afghanistan*, p. 4
IOR, Auckland to Hobhouse, 18 February 1842, Add. MS 37707, fol. 187
IOR 9057, AA2, *The War in Afghanistan*, 1842
IOR/V/4/1840/Vol. 37, p. 25
IOR/V/4/1840/Vol. 37, p. 21
IOR/V/4/1840/Vol. 37, pp. 11–12
IOR, *Treaty between Ranjit Singh and Shah Shuja, Concluded at Lahore 26 June
    1838*, printed by the House of Commons, February 1839

PUBLIC RECORD OFFICE

NI D1584A, 1 June 1842
Ellenborough Papers, 21 February 1842, 30.12.89

ROYAL ARCHIVES, WINDSOR CASTLE

RA/QVJ, 6 October 1878, p. 116
RA/VIC/A 45/61, Letter from Lord Salisbury to Queen Victoria, 26 April
    1899

RA/VIC/QUJ/1842, 12 June
RA/VIC/N 12/23, *Government Gazette*, 16 November 1842
RA/VIC/QUJ/1839, 7 April

NEWSPAPER ACCOUNTS

The Times
1 March 1842, p. 4
5 May 1842, p. 7
27 January 1843, p. 4
7 April 1843, p. 6
9 April 1843, p. 5
22 December 1838, p. 4
6 January 1871, p. 6

REPORTS AND JOURNALS

Frontier and Overseas Expeditions from India, Division of the Chief of the
    Staff Army Headquarters, 1910, Vol. III, p. 278, Naval & Military
    Press (reprint), 2006
Burnes, Alexander, *Reports and Papers Submitted to Government*, Calcutta,
    G.H. Huttmann, 1839

SECONDARY SOURCES

Atkinson, James, *The Expedition into Afghanistan*, Uckfield, Naval & Military
    Press (reprint), 2006
Barthorp, Michael, *Afghan Wars*, London, Cassell & Co., 1982
Beaumont, Roger, *Sword of the Raj*, Indianapolis, Bobbs-Merrill Co.,
    Inc., 1977
Benson and Esher, *The Letters of Queen Victoria*, John Murray, 1908
Bigham, Edward Clive, the Viscount Mersey, *The Viceroys and Governors
    General of India*, London, John Murray, 1949
Burnes, Alexander, *Cabool, Being a Personal Narrative of a Journey to, and
    Residence in that City*, Lahore, Research and Publication Centre
    (reprint), 2003
Caroe, Olaf, *The Pathans*, London, Macmillan & Co., 1958
Cecil, Gwendolen, *Life of Robert, Marquis of Salisbury*, London, Hodder &
    Stoughton, 1921, Vol. II
Durand, Henry Marion, *The First Afghan War and its Causes*, London,

Longmans, Green & Co., 1879, Lahore, Vanguard Books Ltd (reprint), 1998

Eden, Emily, *Up the Country*, London, OUP, 1930

Edwardes, Michael, *Playing the Great Game*, London, Hamish Hamilton, 1975

Eliot, T.S., *Four Quartets*, London, Faber & Faber (reprint), 1983, p. 48

Elliott, James G., *The Frontier 1839–1947*, London, Cassell, 1968

Elphinstone, Monstuart, *An Account of the Kingdom of Caubal*, Karachi, Indus Publications, (originally published in 1808)

Eyre, Vincent, *The Military Operations at Cabul*, Stroud, Nonsuch Publishing Ltd (reprint), 2006, p. 29

——, *Journal of an Afghanistan Prisoner*, London, Routledge & Kegan Paul, 1976, p. 30

Forbes, Archibald, *The Afghan Wars*, London, Seeley and Co., 1892

Fraser-Tytler, Kerr, *Afghanistan*, London, Oxford University Press, 1950

Gleig, George, *Sale's Brigade in Afghanistan*, London, John Murray, 1879 (Naval & Military Press reprint)

Greenwood, John, *The Campaign in Afghanistan*, Stroud, Nonsuch Publishing Ltd (reprint), 2005, pp. 111–12

Hensman, Howard, *The Afghan War of 1879–80*, Lahore, Sang-e-Meel Publications, 1999

Jalalzai, Musa Khan, *The Foreign Policy of Afghanistan*, Lahore, Sang-e-Meel Publications, 2003

James, Lawrence, *Raj, the Making of British India*, London, Little, Brown & Co., 1997

Kaye, John William, *History of the War in Afghanistan*, 3 vols, London, W.H. Allen & Co., 1890

Lal, Mohan, *Life of the Amir Dost Mohammed*, 2 vols, Karachi, Oxford University Press (reprint), 1978

Lawrence, George, *Reminiscences of Forty-three Years in India*, London, John Murray, 1874

Lunt, James, *Bokhara Burnes*, London, Faber & Faber, 1969

Mackenzie, Colin, *Storms and Sunshine of a Soldier's Life*, Edinburgh, David Douglas, 1884

Macmunn, George, *Afghanistan from Darius to Amanullah*, Lahore, Sang-e-Meel Publications, 2002

Macrory, Patrick, *Signal Catastrophe*, London, Hodder & Stoughton, 1966

Mason, Philip, *A Matter of Honour*, London, Jonathan Cape, 1988

Moon, Penderel, *The British Conquest and Dominion of India*, London, Gerald Duckworth & Co., 1989

Napier, Priscilla, *I Have Sind*, Salisbury, Michael Russell Publishing, 1990, p. 220

Nevill, H.L., *Campaigns on the North-West Frontier*, Lahore, Sang-e-Meel

Publications, 2003 (original edition 1910)

Norris, J.A., *The First Afghan War*, Cambridge, Cambridge University Press, 1967

O'Ballance, Edgar, *Afghan Wars*, Oxford, Oxford University Press, 2003

Oliver, Edward, *Across the Border*, London, Chapman and Hall, 1890

Pennell, Thomas, *Among the Wild Tribes of the Afghan Frontier*, London, Seeley & Co., 1909

Pollock, John, *Way to Glory*, London, John Murray, 1957

Pottinger, George, *The Afghan Connection*, Edinburgh, Scottish Academic Press, 1983

Roberts, Frederick, *Forty-one Years in India*, London, Macmillan & Co., 1914

Robson, Brian, *Crisis on the Frontier*, Kent, Spellmount, 2004

Sale, Florentia, *A Journal of the First Afghan War*, London, Longman (reprint), 1969

Skeen, General Sir Andrew, *Passing it On*, London, Gale & Polden Ltd, 1932

The New Testament, Matthew 24:38

Tanner, Stephen, *Afghanistan, a Military History from Alexander the Great to the Fall of the Taliban*, Karachi, Oxford University Press, 2002

Warburton, Robert, *Eighteen Years in the Khyber*, London, John Murray, 1900

Woodruff, Philip, *The Men Who Ruled India*, London, Jonathan Cape, 1953

INDEX